VICTORIA FEDDEN received her MFA in creative writing from Florida Atlantic University. Her blog, "Wide Lawns and Narrow Minds," was voted 2011's "Best Humor Blog" by the *South Florida Sun Sentinel*, and her personal essays have been anthologized in *I Still Just Want to Pee Alone*, *Scary Mommy's Guide to Surviving the Holidays*, *Chicken Soup for the Soul*, and *My Other Ex*. Her writing has also appeared on or is forthcoming from *Your Tango*, *Scary Mommy*, and *Babble*, among other blogs and Web sites. She lives with her family in Fort Lauderdale, and online at victoriafedden.com.

THIS IS
NOT MY
BEAUTIFUL
LIFE

A MEMOIR

THIS IS NOT MY BEAUTIFUL LIFE

PICADOR NEW YORK

VICTORIA FEDDEN

picadorusa.com • picadorbookroom.tumblr.com
twitter.com/picadorusa • facebook.com/picadorusa

Picador® is a U.S. registered trademark and is used by St. Martin's Press under license from Pan Books Limited.

For book club information, please visit facebook.com/picadorbookclub or e-mail marketing@picadorusa.com.

Designed by Anna Gorovoy

The Library of Congress Cataloging-in-Publication Data is available upon request.

ISBN 978-1-250-07528-4 (trade paperback)
ISBN 978-1-250-07529-1 (e-book)

Our books may be purchased in bulk for promotional, educational, or business use. Please contact your local bookseller or the Macmillan Corporate and Premium Sales Department at 1-800-221-7945, extension 5442, or by e-mail at MacmillanSpecial Markets@macmillan.com.

First Edition: June 2016

10 9 8 7 6 5 4 3 2 1

To my parents

Without their sacrifices, none of this would be possible

AUTHOR'S NOTE

This memoir is a true story, though most names and some details have been changed.

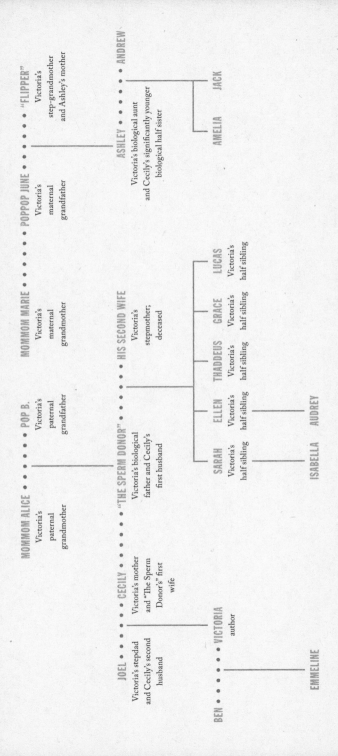

PART 1

1

When the Feds raid your house (or my parents' house, in this case), they like to take you by surprise. They'll come before sunrise and catch you in bed. Of course I didn't know that, so when the doorbell rang politely, I thought that my husband, Ben, who had just left for work, had probably forgotten something. I tossed on a T-shirt and shuffled, yawning, down the grand marble staircase to unlock the glass front doors.

I didn't know they were the Feds. I guess when I imagined DEA agents, I pictured a SWAT team with guns, but the group of men and women assembled under my parents' porte cochere looked like bouncers just off work from a nightclub. Guys with shaved heads and goatees, and a couple of butchy-looking women who wore T-shirts and cargo pants and carried no visible weapons. *Visible* being the key word.

Robbers, I thought. Thieves cased out fancy waterfront neighborhoods, and a Mediterranean-style McMansion like my parents', with a Bentley and a tricked-out Escalade in the driveway, plus a forty-two-foot cabin cruiser docked in the back, was a sure target. They were going to force their way in, tie us up, and demand the combination to the safe where my mom hid her diamonds. Or maybe they were going to kidnap me for ransom. For years my sister Ashley and I had feared that one of the shady characters my parents always seemed to have hanging around would try something like that, so I didn't open the door, and I contemplated running upstairs to my parents' room to wake them and their 130-pound Doberman. But I wasn't really thinking clearly—I'd just woken up. Also, I wasn't wearing any pants.

One of the men shook some papers, and then, all at once, they flashed their badges. I wondered how many times they'd practiced this routine, because Olympic synchronized swimmers couldn't have done it with better timing.

"POLICE!" one of them said through the glass.

"SEARCH WARRANT!"

I twisted the dead bolt open and let them in. I obviously didn't have a choice.

"I'm pregnant!" I blurted.

A couple of the guys snickered.

"Obviously," I heard one of them say.

The guy with the papers demanded to know if I was Cecily Gold.

I looked at him, confused.

"Are you her?" he asked again.

I shook my head, trying to think of what the right thing to say was, but the only thing that came to me was *anything you say can and will be used against you in a court of law.*

"No," I said, "I'm her daughter."

"Is she here?" he wanted to know.

"Honey, who is it?" my stepdad, Joel, called down from the east wing of the house. I took a deep breath.

"The police!" I called back.

"Is Cecily here?" the cop repeated.

"We'll be right down!" Joel yelled.

"I'm not wearing any pants," I mumbled.

I tugged my T-shirt down over my pregnant belly, trying to cover my thighs and my enormous maternity panties.

"Let me take you to get dressed," one of the women said. She had a mullet.

"Oh, I'm fine," I said. "I can go by myself."

"No, I'll have to accompany you," she said. She sounded pretty firm about it.

She followed me up the curving staircase, down the catwalk, and into the guest bedroom where my husband and I had been staying for the past two months while we waited for the renovations to be completed on the house we'd bought. We'd hoped they'd be done by the time the baby came, but at the rate things were going, the house might be ready by her eighth-grade graduation.

"I don't live here," I said. "I mean, my husband and I, we don't live here. We're just staying here temporarily while we're waiting for our house to be done, and all our stuff is crammed into one room."

I gestured toward a folding table we'd set up against one wall and the stacks of building permits, plans, and blueprints shuffled on top of it.

The woman nodded. "Just get dressed, honey."

I closed the door of the walk-in closet behind me. Right away she opened it, mumbling something that sounded like *policy* or *procedure* while I threw my husband's gray Miami sweatshirt over my tee and pulled on a pair of leggings.

"How far along are you?" she asked.

"Thirty-seven weeks," I said.

She made a face that I interpreted as alarmed. I figured she was worried I might go into labor at any second and totally jack up the whole raid.

"I'll need that cell phone," she said.

"Oh, um, I was just trying to text my husband to let him know what was happening."

"Sorry," she said, grabbing the iPhone from my hand and shutting it off before I could hit send.

"Look, whatever this is, I have nothing to do with it," I tried to tell her.

She kind of half-assedly apologized. No one wants to be nasty to a pregnant woman, not even the Feds.

By the time we got back downstairs, my parents had gotten out of bed and were speaking with the officers, my mom still braless in her leopard-print silk pajamas, her waist-length (thanks to extensions) ponytail wound up in a hot-pink scrunchie. The dogs were going ballistic, and Joel was yelling at them to shut up while trying to explain to the officers that the Doberman was a teddy bear and the yappy mini pin was really the one to worry about, even though he weighed less than ten pounds. At least he had actually bothered to get dressed. Joel was in his red-and-black Nike gym gear, as if he expected the raid to be over in time for his eight A.M. with his trainer at LA Fitness.

The Feds were asking about guns and drugs. Seriously? Guns and drugs? My parents didn't have any guns or drugs, but to my surprise my stepdad produced a handgun from the sideboard beside the living room fireplace and then dug out a rolled-up Ziploc of weed from a box on top of the ornate mahogany bar. I always thought that box contained mixed nuts.

"Medical marijuana. I have a prescription in California. I can show it to you. I have anxiety," he explained.

I wanted to roll my eyes. Everyone who knows Joel knows that the man has never been nervous a day in his life. Once, on the way home from one of his numerous trips to California, the plane he was on experienced serious mechanical malfunctions and had to make an emergency landing. Later, when it was over, I asked him if he had been scared at all, and what it was like to almost die? But he just shrugged it off.

"If it's my time, it's my time," he'd said.

Maybe this was because he'd already been dead. When he was nineteen, he'd been shot twice through the chest during a robbery at a nightclub in New Jersey, and had been revived at the scene.

For the next two hours, I had to sit my enormously pregnant

ass on my parents' living room sofa, without my cell phone, while these strangers stomped through the house in their boots and tight tees. Whatever it was they were searching for, it wasn't the gun or the pot. The agents had waved those aside.

"You can keep your toy gun and your dime bag. We're looking for something bigger than that."

The agents continued to ransack the house. Two of them led my mother outside onto the marble patio overlooking the swimming pool, which she'd mosaicked in pearly pink tiles. I watched through the glass doors lining the length of the house as they sat down at the patio table, and the sun rose, reflecting shades of coral on the still waters of the Intracoastal Waterway, where a fishing boat glided slowly past. Another agent followed my stepdad into the kitchen. Joel had asked them all if they'd wanted coffee—which was typical for him—and proceeded to fire up the three-thousand-dollar built-in Italian coffee system that was his pride and joy. The machine ground beans and sputtered steam, filling the house with the aroma of dark roast Kona.

I rubbed my belly as I stayed parked on the grand sofa. No one ever sat on this thing, and it was ridiculously uncomfortable, made only for show. Stiffly upholstered with scratchy gold fabric, the couch was piled with at least twenty throw pillows, all of which were adorned with abrasive sequins, rhinestones, and beads. There was no room for my wide ass and childbearing hips, so I had to throw several of them onto the floor. My mom adored this flamboyant piece of furniture—I remembered when she bought it. She had bragged that it was a Marge Carson, which meant absolutely nothing to me and sounded like someone my grandmother played Bingo with.

"Do you know how much a Marge Carson costs?" Mom had asked.

I hadn't a clue.

"Twenty-five *thousand* dollars," she'd said.

I'd take IKEA over that gaudy, useless thing any day.

The woman with the mullet milled around by the front door, lording over the row of confiscated cell phones lined up on the key table, lest I try to grab one and check my Facebook or something nefarious like that. I almost laughed, imagining what my status update might read.

Victoria Fedden is: being detained by the DEA.

I occupied myself with worrying about the baby. That had pretty much been my main pastime since March, when I'd found out I was pregnant. It was now almost mid-October, and she was due on the twenty-sixth. I'd hoped she'd be born on Halloween, my favorite holiday, but I was glad she was guaranteed to be a Scorpio like me—that was, unless the shock of the morning's events sent me into early labor, which I was convinced was going to happen. She hadn't moved in a while, so I worried she might be dead, and that if she wasn't dead, she was probably breech. I'd recently read an article that associated breech babies with high rates of autism, so I fretted about that, too.

"Whose bag is this?" called a little nebbish guy from the staircase. He'd come in behind the bigger, brawnier agents, looking a lot like Woody Allen, his pants scooted up to his ribs. He was with the IRS.

"Mine," I replied.

He dragged my schoolbag, a black leather satchel with wheels, down the steps.

"What are these papers in here?" he demanded.

"Nothing," I said. "Nothing you're interested in. It's just copies of some of my students' work."

He pulled the papers out, stacked them on the glass coffee table in front of me, and proceeded to eye each one.

"You're a teacher?" he asked.

I nodded. He looked incredulous and asked me what I taught and where.

"I mean, I'm not teaching now. I taught business writing over the s-summer at FAU," I stammered.

"College?" he asked.

"Yes."

"You don't look old enough to teach college."

"I'm thirty-six."

"I wouldn't have guessed that," the IRS agent said, pulling out my laptop.

"Please don't take that!" I begged. "There's nothing on there but my writing and my pictures. I don't have anything to do with this."

He said he had to check with the guys from the DEA and walked off with my computer in his hands, leaving my schoolbag tipped over on the floor, the essays littering the table, the comments I'd made on them glaring at me in red ink.

I sat there for three hours before they carried out cardboard box after cardboard box of "evidence." They took my parents' computers, some cell phones, and God knows what documents in green file folders. And then they took my mother.

"Don't worry about me! I'll be fine. I'm not scared!" she called over her shoulder as the agents escorted her outside and into one of their unmarked black SUVs.

Joel followed about ten minutes behind them in the Bentley.

"Don't worry, baby. I'll have her back by dinner. I've got Brad Cohen on the phone," he reassured me.

Brad Cohen was a local criminal defense lawyer, famous for having been on the second season of *The Apprentice*. But he was kicked off the show after only two weeks. I saw him around town a lot and on TV getting yelled at by Nancy Grace for disagreeing with her on cases that neither one of them had anything to do with.

The front doors slammed shut, and the glass panes rattled in their frames. Once the echo faded, the house was eerily silent. I was alone now.

I pressed the home button on my phone to check the time, and looked at the weather out of habit. A little after ten. Cloudy.

Windy. Chance of storms. I took a deep breath, knowing that he was going to freak out, and texted my husband that the house had been raided, and my mom had been arrested and taken away. I told him not to leave work, even though he wanted to, then took my keys, got into the car, and drove across A1A, the long narrow ribbon of a road that trims the coastline of South Florida.

When I got to the beach, I parked and sat, staring out at the sea, slate-colored and churning beneath rain-heavy clouds. It occurred to me that I hadn't told my sister, who was also pregnant, and due six weeks after me in December.

Mom got arrested this morning, I typed.

Her reply appeared on the screen a few seconds later.

Again?

2

A couple of hours after the raid ended, I was hovering over a toilet at my ob-gyn's office, giving a urine sample. I'm not good at a lot of things, but I've got skills when it comes to peeing in cups—perfected, of course, over nine months of pregnancy. Lately I felt like all I did was get stuck with needles and pee in cups, and that day was no different. I was going to the ob-gyn once a week now until the baby was born, but it felt strange after the morning I'd had. At first I wondered if I should cancel the appointment, but what else was I going to do besides sit around my parents' house alone, flipping back and forth between *A Baby Story* and *I'm Pregnant and . . . a Nudist*? I figured it would take hours for Joel and the "Apprentice" to bail her out, so I decided to go to the doctor anyway.

The nurse weighed me. I'd gained a little. My blood pressure was fine. She squeezed my ankles, and there was no swelling. I'd had a routine pregnancy with no complications. Clearly, the medical community didn't view my incendiary heartburn as quite the complication I did, but considering the horrific things that can go awry when you're having a baby, I supposed I was lucky. But even though things had gone smoothly, I still found myself nearly crippled with anxiety. I worried something might be wrong with the baby, and about becoming a mother, period. On top of that, there was moving to a new house; my relationship with my husband, Ben; and now the fate of my mom. I still hadn't even found out what my mom was being arrested *for*. We'd been raided by the DEA. That was drugs, and my mom was so anti-drug now that she literally wouldn't even take a Tylenol.

The doctor came in and listened to the baby's heartbeat, poked around on my belly, and then jammed his fingers up my crotch. I really hated that part, and up until now he hadn't had to do that, but we were really down to the wire, and the baby could decide to make her grand entrance at any second, so he had to check to make sure I wasn't going into labor.

I wasn't.

"You're not dilated," the doctor told me. I cringed. The word *dilate* made me recoil in the way some people do when they hear the words *panties* and *moist*. I hated when moms-to-be discussed the opening of their cervixes and things like mucus plugs. They were the same women who referred to their children's ages in weeks and months, as in *Olivia Madison is thirty-seven months, and Ava is seventeen and a half weeks*. Stuff like that drove me crazy—I just couldn't relate.

After the examination, the doctor asked me how I was, and I brought up some of my concerns.

"People have been telling me . . . ," I began before pausing to take a deep breath. "That my anxiety is affecting the baby, and I've been under a lot of stress lately and had something pretty scary happen to me. . . ."

The doctor nodded. He was an older man, tall and very thin, with a bush of gray hair on his head and a dark tan. He had a soft voice with a lovely Spanish accent that recalled his youth in Mexico City, and I found him enormously comforting. I mean, the man taught yoga classes when he wasn't delivering babies. That was how soothing he was.

"You haven't been hurt physically, have you?" he asked.

I shook my head.

"Then the baby will be fine. All indications are that she is perfect. Let me tell you something. Children are conceived in all sorts of stressful circumstances—wars, famines, violence and oppression, bombings. There is nothing so stressful as that and, yet, the vast majority of babies are born healthy and completely unaware. Your baby is shielded inside of you. She is happy and comfortable, warm and well fed. She doesn't know," the doctor told me. "Don't worry."

I wasn't sure I believed him.

"Have you ever tried Reiki?" the doctor asked, catching me a little off guard.

I told him I had heard of it but didn't really know what it was.

"My wife is a Reiki practitioner, and she specializes in working with pregnant women. Reiki is very relaxing. Take her card, and if you feel like it, give it a try. I think you'll enjoy it. She's free this afternoon."

Twenty minutes later I was pulling up in front of my doctor's house, and his wife was waving at me from the front door.

Okay, first off, it's pretty weird going to your doctor's house—kind of like how when you were a kid, it was really weird if you saw your teacher at the grocery store, because you'd suddenly realize she was an actual human being. It's difficult to imagine certain professionals having lives outside their practices. My doctor clearly had one though—and he also had an insanely hot wife.

My doctor's wife was one of those women who look like they are twenty-five when they're really in their fifties. She was supermodel tall, in perfect shape, and had long honey-blond hair she'd straightened with a flatiron. Like her husband, she taught yoga—prenatal in fact. I'd been meaning to go since I found out I was with child, because I really wanted to be one of those glowing, glorious pregnant women who ate nothing but organic vegetables and did yoga every single day, but for some reason I never quite made it to a class. I kept procrastinating the yoga and probably the organic vegetables, too, blaming it first on morning sickness, then on my teaching schedule, and finally just on my need for cake. They say children will like to eat what their mothers consumed the most during pregnancy, and I knew women who purposely ate copious amounts of greens and exotic cuisines to ensure that their offspring had sophisticated palates. If this were true, then my baby was 100 percent guaranteed to love: a) chocolate cake; b) Reese's Cups; c) pinto beans (weird craving, I know); d) guacamole (which is at least kind of healthy); and e) vanilla shakes with extra whipped cream and two cherries instead of just one, because, duh, I was eating for two, and of course we each needed a cherry. Which is a fruit. And has antioxidants.

She introduced herself as Sia and welcomed me into her home as if I were a long-lost relative, which was a bit disconcerting, but I figured that was how all those New Agey types were. The house was lovely and smelled like a Sedona crystal shop—sweet, smoky, and minty. A large blue pottery bowl filled with mangos decorated the kitchen table, and each of the Mexican-tiled rooms held a vase of fresh flowers. Stained-glass suncatchers glinted in the windows.

"My Reiki room is back here," Sia said, directing me down a dark hallway to the last door on the left.

Reiki is a Japanese spiritual healing process that involves the laying on of hands in order to expel illness, negative emotions, stress, and toxins—all of which I had plenty of. It's like a very gentle massage or a much more reserved (naturally, because it's Japanese) version of what those wacko faith healers do on televised Christian revivals, except it involves essential oils and probably some of Zamfir's magical pan flute music. In my case, there was also a French bulldog.

"I hope you don't mind dogs," Sia said.

It didn't seem like the best time for me to explain that I was more of a cat person, so I said dogs were fine. The dog that had followed us into the Reiki room was actually pretty cute—in the way that an obese white bat with really squatty legs might be considered cute.

"Rexy likes my patients," Sia said as the dog curled up under the chair where I'd set my purse before hopping up onto the massage table.

"Why are you here?" she asked, and that was all it took.

I started to sob hysterically—ugly crying—the kind that comes with snot and great gasping heaves. My face, I was sure, was a distorted grimace mottled by the attractive red spots I always got when I was upset. I wanted to tell Sia I was scared. I was scared of everything having to do with this baby—that I couldn't love her; that I'd be my usual perfectionistic, asshole self; and that I'd act this way around an innocent child. I was scared of the agony of labor and birth, scared that my body would never be the same again and that something horrendous would happen to my boobs or my vagina and that my husband would make secret jokes to his male friends about how having sex with me was like throwing a hot dog down a hallway and then he'd run off with a nineteen-year-old Brazilian, leaving me a single mom, and I wouldn't be able to make it on my own. And what about my family? How could I bring a child into a world where her grandparents' house had gotten raided by federal agents, and what was even going to happen to my mom? I needed my mother. I couldn't do this. I couldn't take care of a brand-new baby without her, and if she went to prison, what kind of life would that mean for my child? *Hey, honey, let's go see Mommom in jail for Christmas.* Her friends would find out, and their parents wouldn't want their children playing with the grandchild of criminals. I knew that shame from my own childhood, and I didn't want it for my daughter. It wasn't fair to bring a child into this mess, and *mess* didn't even begin to describe what was happening. I couldn't process it all, and the stress was unbearable, so the only words I was able to sob to Sia were: "I don't want to be a mother! I don't want to have a baby!"

"Lie down," she whispered, and I did.

Sia anointed me with dots of eucalyptus oil and had me choose an "Angel Card" from an inspirational deck of tarot. I drew "Self-Forgiveness," and that made Sia smile. She told me to close my eyes, and began to softly position her hands on my head. She whispered something about chakras and moved her fingers to my third eye and then my throat, working her way slowly down my body, and the whole thing would have been quite pleasant and relaxing if my entire life wasn't going to pieces and Sia's goddamned dog wasn't licking his balls.

In between her whispered chants over my apparently blocked energy channels, all I could hear was the *slop, slop, slop* of a wet dog tongue slapping its testicles, and if ever there were a better argument for neutering one's pets, I couldn't think of it. I tried to ignore the incessant ball-licking. I tried to focus on calming energy, goddesses, and opening my chakras, but it was impossible, because all I could hear was *slop, slop*, and I am not a mature person. I'm the kind of person who snickers if I hear the word *erect*, and I couldn't objectively look at a ball-licking bulldog and see it as one of God's creatures grooming itself. I saw it as some hysterically funny shit, especially given the context, and the force of trying not to laugh practically broke my water. But hey, at least I wasn't crying anymore.

"I want to tell you something, Victoria," Sia said, staring deeply into my eyes.

I stared back.

"Don't be afraid of this baby. She already loves you. She chose you as her mother."

I felt my eyebrows knitting together and my nose scrunching. "She did?" I asked.

Sia nodded. "Yes. We all choose our parents when we are in heaven, waiting to incarnate, and we choose them because, as souls, we love them and there are lessons we must learn from them. Your daughter is coming here joyfully to greet you, and she is here to both teach you and to learn from you, as you have taught and learned from your own mother, and she from her mother."

"So that's how it works, huh?" I said.

Sia smiled. "Yes," she said. "So welcome this baby, be open to all she has to teach you, and know that, even in your worst mistakes as a mother, you are giving her exactly what her soul needs and chose."

3

Mom was out on bond by the time I got home. Still wearing the T-shirt and leggings she'd changed into before they took her away, she sat at the round, mahogany table in the breakfast nook, shoving a turkey sandwich and Kettle chips into her mouth. Mayonnaise dripped from the crust onto the paper that the sandwich had come wrapped in, and I knew that if I were still in my first trimester, the sight of it would have sent me running for the toilet, my hand over my mouth. She barely looked up at me, and stopped gorging only to take a long sip from an iced tea in a clear, plastic cup. Extra lemons. The way she liked it.

Sometimes my mother's eating habits drove me nuts. Mom went overboard with butter. She glopped mayo and slathered spreads, poured on sauces and gravies, and took enormous bites. You could hear her chewing as her teeth, slightly buck even after the braces she'd worn at forty, scraped the tines of her fork. Never a salad-and-water woman, Mom had a man's appetite.

I didn't. Not that I'd ever been much of a salad-and-water girl myself, but I liked my dressings on the side and my sandwiches dry. I watched what I ate as best as I could, and although I wasn't skinny, even before I'd gotten pregnant, I'd never had her problems with weight. I had watched my mom yo-yo diet my whole life, never able to achieve her ideal figure, the one where she'd wear pants without elastic waistbands and go to the beach in a bathing suit in front of people. The weight she thought would make her life perfect.

People always said we looked alike, and I hated that, loathed it even, because I didn't think we looked alike at all. Yeah, maybe we had the same sloping, pointed nose, the same overbite and dark wide eyes, but the similarities ended there. Mom was olive-skinned, while I was fair. She was apple-shaped and ample, while I was as straight up-and-down as a tree trunk. My hair was chestnut-brown and staying that way until it turned gray because I would rather drop dead than dye it platinum and get a weave, especially at fifty-five, for God's sakes. Ashley couldn't stand it either, and I can't even count the number of times my sister and I had threatened to call a makeover show on Mom to give her a tasteful bob or something more age-appropriate.

"What happened?" I asked, sitting down at the table.

"Bonded out," she said, her mouth full of Panera. "I'm starving. I didn't have any breakfast."

"What were you arrested for?"

"Conspiracy to commit wire fraud," she said.

I didn't even know what that was, so I asked her.

"It's bullshit. E-mails. Wiretaps. Carmelo ratted on me." She took another bite of sandwich and pushed two more chips into her mouth.

"Carmelo?"

For a second I couldn't remember who he was. It was hard to keep track of the characters who passed in and out of my parents' front door. For my entire life they'd been surrounded by a continually fluctuating entourage of misfits and fringe-dwellers. Often they even moved in. Homeless families; paranoid schizophrenics; gigolos; porn stars; reality-show contestants; drifters of every shade, age, and persuasion; Russian mobsters (for Christmas, no less); pathological liars in knock-off Valentinos; strippers; gold-diggers; sugar daddies; flea-market peddlers; a rabbi who rode a Harley; a seventy-year-old dominatrix (my mom had given her a ride home from breast augmentation surgery); wannabe film producers . . . Hell, Michael Bolton himself had once showed up for manicotti. Over the years, I'd gotten somewhat desensitized and, to be honest, I tried to stay away from my parents as much as possible whenever they had meetings with the men and women they referred to as their "partners" and "clients."

Mom swore that Carmelo was just a friend, that they'd never worked together, and I'd run into him a few times in the past year when I'd popped in at my parents' unannounced, but he was no one I'd ever want to associate with. He was a greasy Italian stereotype—not a slick mob boss, but a goon. A five-foot-four Bluto in an Ed Hardy tee and tight black jeans, and I never saw him without the shark's tooth on a leather cord around his neck. I had a bad gut feeling about him, but I never mentioned it to Mom because I knew she'd blow me off and say I was just being judgmental.

Once, when Carmelo was down from New Jersey (of course), with his wife, Antoinette, who still sported an eighties hairdo straight out of her Paramus Park Mall days, they'd joined my mom and me for dinner, which I hadn't been happy about, but when did that ever matter? Carmelo and Antoinette were both in their late forties, and struggling with infertility. They told us about their miscarriages and failed in vitros over dinner, and that was what had sucked my mom in with these people. She and Joel had never been able to have a child together, and she knew how it felt to want a baby and not be able to have one with the person you loved.

"Yeah, Carmelo," Mom explained. "He got busted up in New York with a bunch of longshoremen bringing in cocaine, and then they used the money and invested it in penny stocks, and he made a plea bargain and ratted to get his ass out of trouble."

I nodded slowly. "So that's where you come in? The penny stocks?" I asked, still not getting it. Mom worked as a stock promoter, but as I understood it, all she did was write press releases.

She was an entrepreneur, working at home on a single computer. She didn't own a big company, rent space in a fancy office build-ing, or even have employees. Mom ran a simple operation, writing about small public companies, so what could be illegal about that?

"I'm just glad they didn't get Joel," Mom said in a near whis-per. Her comment came out of nowhere.

"Huh? Why would they arrest Joel?" I asked, even more con-fused. Joel was in the entertainment business, had been for years as far as I knew. He hadn't been a *huge* success, but he did own a production company in Vegas (they made a soft-core porn show for a cable channel), and was a partner at a record company in L.A. On top of that, he'd just produced his first feature film—a lifelong dream, finally realized. His next project was rumored to be a documentary about the reunion tour of a popular band from the sixties. What he was doing looked legit.

"Oh please, these charges are bullshit," Joel said. He'd come in from walking the dogs and was over at his beloved espresso machine, adding a new bag of beans.

I wished I could share his laissez-faire attitude. Cavalier was something I'd never been, but that was how Joel lived his life. While I didn't think I was much like my mother, we did at least share some small physical resemblances, but Joel and I had noth-ing in common at all, and my mother hated when I called him my stepfather or anything that suggested he wasn't really my dad.

"He's not your sperm donor," she'd say. "But you're damn straight he's your *real* father."

And you know what? She was right. In our family, being a parent wasn't about sharing the same genes. It was about step-ping up and being there when a kid needed you. My biological father hadn't done that. He was a stranger from Delaware, from a different life—a man who'd abandoned me when I was eleven, and Joel was the father I knew. I'd even taken his last name as a teenager to prove my loyalty. Now here we were, Mom and I—two former country girls with a Jewish last name. Joel had moved to the United States from Israel when he was fourteen, and his family was religious. His parents were Holocaust survivors and, needless to say, they hadn't been pleased when their only son married a lapsed Catholic with a kid. We did our best to make it work, though, always observing both Christian and Jewish traditions (which I thought was double the fun) out of respect for one another. Going against his family, being there for me when my own dad wasn't—Joel had earned my admiration over the years. I didn't share his starlike, gleaming charisma, his striking blue-green eyes, black hair, or aquiline nose. I feared death and airplanes and especially death *on* airplanes, but regardless, he was my dad and I was his daughter, and I really, really wanted to believe that, yeah, this arrest and these charges were a crock, nothing to fret over and easily resolved, and soon we'd all go back to our normal lives.

Joel clapped his hands and rubbed his palms together, trying to motivate us.

"What are you girls waiting around for?" he asked, but I had no idea what he was talking about.

"We've got money to spend! Come on. *Vamos.* Get in the car!" he said.

"Where are we going?" I looked at Mom, eyebrows raised. She crammed the last crust of her sandwich down her throat and wiped her mouth with a dish towel.

"Costco," she said.

4

It was almost six-thirty that night by the time we left for Costco, and by then, Ben had finally come home. After what had to have been the longest, strangest day of my life (I mean, seriously, who gets raided and Reiki on the same day?), I still hadn't eaten. I had little appetite, but figured that if it came down to it, I could make a meal out of Costco's plentiful free samples.

Mom sat in the passenger seat, chewing Nicorette gum while she tugged at the end of her nose and pushed it down over her upper lip. It was a nervous habit she'd developed early on in her marriage in an unsuccessful attempt to train her nose to look more Jewish. Joel drove with his left hand and manipulated his iPhone with his right as she hounded him about various bank accounts. Ben and I sat in the backseat.

"Is this one still open?" she asked, holding up a green debit card.

"One second, Cecily! I'm on the phone with Bank of America right now."

"How about the DL Wall Street Spectacular? Did they get that account yet? What about my Marvelous Marketing account? How about Penny Stock Power, Inc.?" she pushed.

The Feds had seized and frozen all her business accounts, and she had no access to funds, but they hadn't gotten to one of her personal accounts, which still had five thousand dollars in it. Mom and Joel knew they'd seize that one by morning, so we needed to get to Costco before they closed.

"I'm not letting those motherfuckers take my money!" Mom declared. "So we're going to spend every last cent just to stick it straight up their asses."

I looked over at Ben. The gleam from the dashboard lights reflected off my husband's glasses, and his face was illuminated by the glow of the iPhone he never put down. Ben was a frantic googler, always looking things up to make sense of the world, and what a crazy one he'd married into. He knew nothing about shady businesses or criminal dealings. My husband was the son of a firefighter and a paralegal, and had grown up in Laguna Beach. His childhood was spent surfing, and when he went to college in Colorado, he traded his surfboard for a snowboard. After that, he moved to San Francisco, chopped off his dreads, and got a respectable job in commercial banking—then met me, moved to South Florida, and ended up in the back of an Escalade typing "wire fraud" into his search engine. He always said he knew what he was getting into when he married me, but I'd never really believed him. How can anyone be prepared for in-laws who boasted John Gotti's nephew and the hooker who claimed to have screwed Mohammed Atta the week before 9/11 as their best friends?

Costco and I, on the other hand, were not friends, and that I'd actually agreed to go at all was proof of the seriousness of the situation. I dislike anything enormous and mass-produced, and if I had my way, I would shop only in artfully decorated boutiques (with, of course, the exception of Anthropologie and Whole Foods). Costco's high ceilings and exposed steel beams freaked me out, not to mention the twenty-foot-high stacks of supersize boxes of Special K. I'm sorry, but cereal should not be that big, and let's not even get into the number of people who shop there. They need some serious crowd control, because something about five-pound blocks of horseradish cheddar and megaliths of Triscuits makes people lose their ever-loving minds.

Ben loved Costco, as did my parents, though for entirely different reasons. Ben admired the company's philosophy. He liked not having to buy toilet paper for six months, even if it meant storing fifty-six rolls of it in our entryway because they wouldn't fit in the linen closet. Costco appealed to Ben's practical, frugal side, and Ben's practical side appealed to me because it was safe and sensible, but my parents liked Costco for the very reasons I did not: because it was big and over-the-top, and the apple pies there were about fifteen times the size of apple pies anywhere else. A single pie could feed an entire city block, and often it seemed like my parents *were* feeding an entire city block. They partied hard and frequently. Their parties were pretty notorious. For Joel's fifty-seventh birthday, they'd had pony rides, fireworks, and belly dancers, and when you're regularly hosting fetes like that, Costco is the only place to get the amount of plates, food, and liquor you need. And I guess it was also the best place to go when you needed to blow five grand before midnight.

Once in the store, Ben found a table in the food court where he could mess with his phone and detach from the situation. Joel hit the electronics section, but my mom and I went straight for the food, where she quickly piled the cart high with raw meat and rotisserie chickens.

"Those chickens last only a few days, Mom. Do you think we really need five?" I ventured, but she ignored me.

"Oh yeah. We'll eat them. Make sandwiches," she said.

At first I hesitated, unsure of what I should do, but there is an unmistakable appeal to heedlessly throwing items into a shopping cart—a sense of abandon and, in this case, revenge. Mom and Joel were sticking it to the Feds, pretending to get the last laugh. I soon found myself double-fisting beef tenderloins as wide as my thighs and helping Mom hoist them in on top of the chicken breasts, even though none of the items would end up in my refrigerator. I was just looking forward to enjoying them at my parents' house all winter. From the beef and poultry, Mom moved on to the real big-ticket items: king crab legs, lobster tails, and jumbo shrimp. *Hell*, I thought. We should take advantage of the situation and bring home the good shit.

And cheese. Cheese and I have enjoyed a long and passionate romance, and pregnancy had only intensified my desire. As I embraced a five-pound brick of Kerrygold, an elderly woman wearing a visor and a puffy-paint sweatshirt gave me a look she believed was knowing.

"You want to watch that appetite, honey," she said. Her cart was full of cinnamon buns and Healthy Choice Fudge Bars.

"Excuse me?" I replied, startled out of my aged-cheddar reverie.

"Your appetite. You don't want to gain too much weight. It's not good for the baby. Too much cholesterol in that cheese," she tsk-tsked.

And then, oh my god, she reached out and patted my belly.

"How far along are you? Due any second, it looks like. You shouldn't be out on your feet like this, young lady," she continued.

They say miracles happen every day, that miracles are all around us, and I am inclined to believe this because it was a miracle I didn't grab a razor-sharp Santoku knife from the Wüsthof cutlery display and try to stab this woman's eyes clean out of her skull.

The very second I had announced my pregnancy, my body ceased to be my own and became public property. Suddenly complete strangers were allowed to touch me and pat me and rub me in ways that would have otherwise been considered obscene and inappropriate and probably assault. I'm a fairly affectionate person, so I didn't mind that part as much as the unwanted advice. As soon as it became evident that I was actually with child and not just tragically bloated, people I didn't know, such as Mrs. Visor Lady, wanted to tell me exactly what I should and should not be doing, as if there weren't room in my body for both a brain and a baby.

Too much salt will give you preeclampsia.

Don't forget cocoa butter so you don't get stretch marks.
Sleep on your right side.
Sleep on your left side only.
Take folic acid so your baby doesn't get a harelip.
Stay off your feet.
You need to exercise.
Listen to classical music so the baby hears it.
Don't name your daughter that. You know, in Northern Ireland,
that's a derogatory term for a low-class factory worker.

Lovely, so I'd have to make sure that my daughter steered clear of Belfast—that is, if she lived, because I slept on the wrong side, ate too much, didn't eat enough, worried all the time, and committed a host of other offenses guaranteed to utterly ruin her life.

People are generally well meaning, though, right? In my more optimistic moments I was able to see the belly rubs and the apparent concern of strangers as evidence that I lived in a society that valued new life and that was welcoming my daughter into the world, wishing her good health and a prosperous future. This was a good thing, annoying as it might have been. What was not a good thing were the terrifying delivery stories everyone felt the need to share with me, including the woman in Costco.

"I hope you don't go through what my daughter went through." She sighed and looked up at the ceiling. "She was in labor for thirty-six straight hours, had a terrible reaction to the medication, was nearly paralyzed by a misplaced epidural, and had to have an emergency C-section. They thought the baby had cerebral palsy. He was in the NICU for three weeks. Meanwhile, my daughter couldn't stop vomiting, and got an infection from the surgery. What a nightmare. You want to see a picture of my grandbaby?"

After all that, I wasn't sure I did, but she whipped a photo of a chubby, generic-looking toddler out of her purse, and I had to drum up a compliment and force a smile.

I finally managed to excuse myself, and waddled, my block of cheese and the two wheels of full-fat brie I'd managed to pick up along the way, to a patio furniture display where I plopped down on a chaise lounge to rest my aching feet. I spotted Joel heaving cases of Jordan Cabernet into his cart, and a few minutes later I noticed Ben hunched over his phone, leaning against a fortress of boxed macaroni and cheese. We made eye contact. He gestured toward my parents, who'd met up between the wine and the fruit sections, raised his eyebrows, and shook his head, then went back to his phone. I followed his lead and was able to tap out a round of Scrabble on my own phone before it was finally time to check out.

We'd filled five carts to the point of overflowing and had become the bane of the tired Costco staff, who had to wait for us to finish our shopping spree before they could close up and go home. Costco closed at eight, and we didn't make it to the checkout until after eight thirty, and it took them nearly forty-five minutes to scan our items and box them up. Getting everything into the Escalade turned into an advanced game of Jenga. I ended up sitting on a case of canned beans, cradling a flat of eggs and a four-pack of ciabatta bread, barely able to see my poor husband. He was practically buried under several tubs of hummus and smoked fish dip.

The Escalade stopped at a red light just off our exit, and Mom spotted three homeless men panhandling between the idling cars, each holding a handwritten cardboard sign. One said he was honest and just wanted a beer, another said his wife had a better lawyer than he did, and the last simply identified himself as a stranded veteran.

"Boo-Boo, pull over," Mom told Joel.

"For what?" he asked.

"Are you okay?" I worried.

"I want to give these men a chicken," Mom told us.

Joel turned the car onto the shoulder and put it into park while

Mom hopped out and motioned for the panhandlers to come over. She handed the guy whose wife had the better lawyer a rotisserie chicken and made me undo the four-pack of ciabatta and hand him a loaf. Then she opened the hatchback and began to dig for bananas, pausing to produce a jar of peanut butter, a bag of potato chips, and a single tomato. By the time we pulled out, the three men were making chicken sandwiches on the median. Except for the drone of Fox News on the satellite radio, the car was quiet until we parked in my parents' driveway.

5

When you're dealing with the government, you can't say, *Oh sorry, those felony charges are a big inconvenience right now because my daughter's about to give birth at any second*. Out on bond, Mom was assigned a probation officer and due to appear in the federal court of Manhattan two weeks after her arrest.

"Can't you just fly up and back that same day?" I asked, already knowing the answer.

"You think I'm getting on a plane?" Mom huffed.

"What if I go into labor?" I asked.

"It's only a twenty-four-hour drive, and I'll be back long before that baby comes," she reassured me.

Mom hadn't flown since I was a child and wasn't about to start. In fact, she'd even bought a thirty-two-foot Fleetwood luxury RV to avoid flying, and she made sure Joel always drove. She'd named it "the Bus," rock-star style, and truth be told, the thing was pretty rockin'. It had a full kitchen with granite countertops and stainless-steel appliances, two bathrooms, a king-size featherbed, and a plush sofa where you could relax and watch the flat-screen TV while you rode. My parents had been across the country and back in that thing more times than I could count, but I'm sure they hadn't planned on driving it to an arraignment. Still, they planned to make the most of it, because that was how they were. The government had frozen Mom's accounts, but since Joel wasn't named in her case, he was a free man, at least for now, and his hefty bank accounts and loose cash were easily accessible. Sure, they had to be at the courthouse, but afterward they'd wine and dine at Cipriani before a shopping excursion in Soho. It was still a vacation.

As the bus pulled out of the driveway, I waved my parents a solemn bon voyage and then pressed the button on the clicker that closed the enormous wrought-iron gates surrounding their home.

I didn't want anyone coming to the door. Since the raid, the sound of the doorbell made my stomach clench and sent my heart racing. I think Mom felt the same way, because a few days after the raid she'd made Joel disconnect the doorbell, but I'd panic just the same whenever someone knocked or the dogs began to bark. I hated being in their house, even now that they were gone, and I just wanted to get the certificate of occupancy from the building inspectors so we could move into our own house and get the baby's stuff organized. We'd gone through so much hassle and red tape with the building department, trying to get the house ready to live in. It had been a nightmare, and now here I was, a bird without a nest to feather, and a baby coming in a couple of weeks. I felt so utterly fucked, and I still had no idea why my mother had been arrested. Calling it bullshit was hardly an explanation, and since I barely understood what wire fraud was, I didn't know how my mother might have conspired to commit it.

She maintained she was innocent, of course, and she may well have been. But this didn't exactly happen out of nowhere. As much as I hated to admit it, we'd been through this kind of thing before. When I was little, Mom went to jail for selling pot, and I'd had to live with my grandparents, though no one told me she was locked up, because they thought I was too young to understand. Before my mom met Joel, he'd been wrapped up in a case with his father—something to do with medallions and counterfeiting—but I never got the whole story on that one either. And I think I was in second grade, right after they got married, when he got picked up during a sting operation for selling drugs in Upstate New York. Supposedly, Mom pretended she was pregnant to win the prosecutor's sympathy, and somehow Joel got off. He'd been arrested and jailed again for a few weeks when I was in the tenth grade—traffic violations, bad check charges—and when I was in my twenties, they'd both been arrested for operating an illegal telemarketing room in Florida. They fled to Georgia and opened back up, but a couple of years later the FTC raided their offices and shut the place down. That had been a civil case, and it had resulted in a multimillion-dollar judgment that, as far as I knew, went unpaid.

Each time, my mother maintained she was the victim. To the Feds, my mother was a career criminal, but in her mind she was an enterprising businesswoman who worked hard and took risks. Every time she made money, the government would swoop in and grab it from her.

"I was careful. I never crossed the line. Never broke the law. I always had my disclaimers, and I didn't work with shady companies," she explained right after the raid. "There were dogs in my industry, lowdown, dirty dogs, but I knew who they were and I steered clear."

The "industry" she was referring to was stock promotion. Companies paid her to let potential investors know about their stocks. She wrote press releases, which the prosecution would later allege were fraudulent, about upcoming developments that might make people think a company's stock was going to skyrocket, and that they should get in before it did. She talked up the stocks in newsletters and all over social media. It didn't seem that bad to me, but I'd later realize that what Mom was accused of doing was a lot more complicated.

We got the CO on our house about ten days before the baby was born, and a troop of generous friends and neighbors chipped in to help Ben and me move in and unpack. It was nice to finally have a house of our own. We were within walking distance of the beach, on a long, wide avenue of one-story homes with grassy front yards lined with hibiscus trees and plumeria. Each morning I'd watch a brigade of retirees speed-walk back and forth around the block, followed by a troop of stroller mommies and dog walkers. The dog walkers would parade down the street again at sunset, and they'd all stop by to chat. One neighbor, Barbara, who lived across the street from my parents with her husband, Arlo, even brought us a chocolate cake. I didn't think that existed in Florida, but here it was: a beautiful life.

There were moments when I regretted our decision to move during my pregnancy, but a family of three plus a cat just wouldn't fit in the small condo I'd bought back when I was still single. Plus, we'd fallen in love with our cottage by the beach and, at the time, we liked the idea of being steps away from my parents. When we bought the house, it was in foreclosure, and the previous owners had used it as a rental. We underestimated the extent of the repairs it would need. The house had toxic mold and required a full gutting to be safe for anyone, much less a baby, and by the time we found out how much work had to be done, we'd already found someone to live in the condo and had to move in with my parents. That was when the stress really set in and, on top of that, Ben had just started a new job, so he'd work all day and come home and bust his ass on the house, painting, cleaning, and hammering until the wee hours of the morning. I didn't know when he ever slept, but he knew how important it was for me to move before the baby was born, so he sacrificed for us.

It seemed like the house would never be ready. As soon as we'd get one part of it fixed, we'd find something else that needed to be done: new drywall, new plumbing, rotten cabinets that needed to be replaced, a leak under the tiles. It was like that movie *The Money Pit*. We dealt with unreliable contractors, an uppity architect, cranky building inspectors, and even a family of rats before it was finally over, and when we got the go-ahead to move in, I couldn't have been happier or more relieved.

The day we moved, I was excused from everything. I set up camp on a fold-out lawn chair in the middle of my newly tiled living room—which still smelled vaguely of paint and whatever other toxic chemicals they'd used to make the house safe to live in—and directed everyone else, using an outstretched hand. Every so often I'd complain about being hot or that my feet were aching, and several people would rush over to me, bringing me iced Snapples and, once, even a meatball sub. It was magnificent, I tell you. I felt like a queen. One neighbor even organized my entire kitchen in the span of two hours—a job that would have taken me weeks, and I still wouldn't have been able to find the Microplane zester. But look! There it was, right beside the stove!

My parents arrived the next day. They'd gotten my mother to her arraignment and then somehow managed to make it to southern Delaware in time for my uncle's third wedding, a backyard barbecue where everyone except Mom and Joel had worn Hawaiian prints. My mother told him they had to leave early in case I went into labor, but truth be told, I think she just wanted to hit every Marshalls, Ross, and T.J.Maxx off I-95 between Dover and Pompano Beach. Some people travel across the country in RVs with the romantic dream of visiting every baseball stadium in the United States. My mom, well, she used her RV to travel cross-country and hit up discount clothing stores, and she spoke of the Beverly Hills T.J.Maxx in the same reverent tone that a Red Sox fan would use to describe Fenway Park.

"And you should see that Ross they have just outside of Vegas." She'd sigh. "I'll never forget buying a Calvin Klein T-shirt with Swarovski crystals on it for three ninety-nine. You know what that would've cost me full price? A goddamned fortune, that's what!"

After my parents had parked in front of our house, they unloaded bag after oversize plastic bag from the RV. It honestly looked like they were the ones moving instead of Ben and me, and my mom still wasn't done shopping. They barely had the stuff in the house before she told me we needed a few more things for the baby.

"And you need pajamas for the hospital," she added.

"I do?"

"Have you packed yet?"

"Packed what?" I asked. I had to pack? Oh Lord. What else was I going to have to do? Keep an entire human being alive? Off to the mall we went. We bought nursing bras and pajamas and planned on hitting the Carter's outlet and then HomeGoods to find some decorations for my new place. My mother loved the attention I was getting, and she escorted me through the stores, one hand around my shoulders and the other on my belly, just beaming. In each store, she'd strike up conversations with the cashiers and salespeople about how excited she was, how my last ultrasound had gone, and how my baby had the best possible scores on both of her genetic tests and some kind of fetal movement test they'd recently conducted—which obviously meant she was going to be the valedictorian of her class and would get accepted at Harvard when she was fourteen.

By the time we got to Carter's, I was getting pretty fed up. Strangers who confronted me to discuss my pregnancy annoyed me to no end, but I always bit my tongue with Mom. I knew why she did things like this. There hadn't been much joy in her own pregnancy, and I think she always wished she could have had a do-over. My baby and Ashley's would be her second chance.

Our experiences were worlds apart from my mom's, and the glaring, most obvious difference was our ages. For a long time, I'd played a sort of game with myself where I compared what my mother had done at a certain age to what I was doing. We both grew up in the same small town in the country, and lost our virginities to bad boys who played drums in garage bands when we were fifteen. At sixteen we became high school dropouts, but at seventeen—that was the age where we started to diverge. I got my GED and applied for college. My mother got engaged. My drummer pierced his nose, enrolled in art school, and promptly dumped me for a tattooed painting major. Her bad boy got a job working the graveyard shift at a frozen foods warehouse, and when he asked her to marry him, what else was there to do but say yes? It was '73. She was poor, and she thought she was dumb. Only the smart, rich kids went to college, so my young parents bought a trailer on the woodsy outskirts of town, married in January, and I came along the following November.

I'd like to say I was conceived by parents who were madly in love with each other after a romantic Valentine's Day, a night filled with red roses, candlelight, and a heart-shaped box of Russell Stover, but I think it was just a coincidence that sperm and egg met around February 14 and resulted in me. People thought they got married because Mom was pregnant, but I was born a full ten months after their wedding, and she'd always told me I was planned, though I never believed it. My life had always felt like an accident, or if not an accident, then an outright mistake. They were barely even married a year before my mom left him. That was why I'd done things so differently. I knew better than to ruin my life by having a baby as a teenager. I wanted to travel. I got an education, eventually went to grad school even, and bought my first house in Atlanta when I was twenty-four and single, the same age Mom was when she married Joel.

When Ben and I married, I was thirty-two. I played the age game with that, too. When Mom was thirty-two, I was fourteen and a freshman in high school. I went to two different schools that year and saw little of my mother and Joel, because they spent every waking hour running a discount junk store in Newark, Delaware, called Crazy Closeouts. They'd had big dreams of a nationwide chain, blowout promotions, and some kind of movie tie-in (don't even ask), and they were going to be millionaires, closeout tycoons sitting on top of a fortune made from selling irregulars, discontinued products, and impossibly priced items that had "fallen off trucks." I had to give Mom credit though. The whole thing had been her idea, being an avid discount shopper herself, and she had made that dream a reality through a lot of hard work and sacrifice. I remember spending late nights with her after the store had closed, sorting inventory and pricing palettes of chipped Capodimonte figurines and Home Shopping Network rejects we'd then superglue and touch up with nail polish until they looked new. Looking back, it was hard to believe my mother had been only thirty-two when she started the company. That seemed so young. After a year, Mom and Joel gave up their store and moved on to their next venture without explanation.

Thirty-two was when I finally got my bachelor's in English, since I'd dropped out of college my first try. I owned a condo in the artsy part of Fort Lauderdale and planned my wedding while I worked in the homeowner's association of a glitzy Boca Raton country club. It was a solid job, and I liked the stability of working for an established organization. Having health insurance made me proud. My parents, neither of whom had ever held down a nine-to-five or "worked for the Man," had never had health insurance and still didn't, so it felt like a huge accomplishment, even if it wasn't as big as owning my own store.

I'd waited until thirty-two to marry, and I'd planned to wait even longer to have a child. I had more places to go, more things to learn, and a teaching career to establish. I wanted our lives to be in order before we even considered adding a child to the mix, and by thirty-six, I still wasn't sure I'd done everything right to ensure that my daughter would have a beautiful life, that her childhood would be the opposite of mine. When Mom was thirty-six—and this never fails to blow my mind—I was already eighteen, the age she was when she'd had me.

As I stood in Carter's, holding a tiny white sweater, I thought about this. When I was eighteen, I was already dropping out of college. My parents had bought a small pink house on the beach in Florida with some money they won in a lawsuit and, as usual, were working on whatever deals they were able to bring in. Joel was traveling back and forth to Europe a lot, Germany especially, and there was some talk about importing shoes and maybe opening a pizza restaurant in the suburbs. We fought a lot, that year I was eighteen. I didn't speak to my parents for six months because I was so mad at them. Rumor had it that Joel had been having an affair in Germany, and I hated him for it, and my mother for defending him. I didn't understand how she could just let her husband supposedly run off for weeks at a time with a girl my age, the niece of a friend no less, but my mother said she loved Joel and he was a good father to me, that it was ungrateful of me to criticize his actions. Instead of getting mad at him, it was like she turned her anger toward me—I needed to get back in school, figure out a career already, move out of her house. She hated my boyfriend and wanted me to date this older Jewish guy she knew who wasn't even my type, and her fault-finding just seemed so hypocritical. I couldn't take it, so one night, after a terrible fight, I took off to Atlanta with my boyfriend and some friends. I wanted to make my own life, but that only lasted about a year before I gave up and came home.

I took one last look at the sweater and put it down. Mom was at the checkout with a mountain of baby clothes. She loved baby clothes. I already had enough to stock my own store if I'd wanted to open one up, but she never got tired of buying them. I still wanted the small, white sweater though, but I knew better than to bring it up to the register. You'd think that adding one more item to the heap of onesies wouldn't have mattered, but it did because Mom hadn't picked it out. She only bought things she chose. If she didn't like it, I wasn't getting it, no matter how much I wanted it, and that was why running off to Atlanta and getting a job had been so freeing. I'll never forget shopping for myself for the first time, buying an outfit—a striped tee and bright purple jeans (it was '92)—and thinking that Mom would have hated it, and how that made me like it even more.

I'd buy the little cardigan later, I decided. I'd come back without Mom and get it with my own money.

I should've done that with the curtains, too.

6

We left Carter's and then took a brief jaunt to HomeGoods, where we didn't find anything but a giant pearlescent sea horse that Mom thought worked in my master bath and that I didn't enjoy lugging through the mall. That sucker had to have weighed at least twenty pounds and my feet were swelling and I'd already peed at least fifteen times, so I was starting to get crabby. I wanted to go back home and sit in my lawn chair while everyone else did all the work, but Mom insisted we go to Target to buy curtains.

"You need white sheers to go over those French doors that open out onto your back porch," she said.

I didn't think a back door needed window treatments, but the last thing I wanted was to argue with my mother over curtains because, seriously, who really cared?

I didn't think the curtains were such a big deal, but once we got home with them, I realized Ben and my mother each held very firm opinions about the way they should be hung.

"That looks terrible," Mom told him.

"No, you hang curtains outside of the doorframe!" he argued. "Why would you want to cover up the view? That's ridiculous!"

"I never heard tell of anyone hanging curtains outside of a doorframe. Do you know how many curtains I've hung in my life? How many houses have you had, Ben? How many curtains have you hung? Hang the curtains inside the doorframe!" Mom yelled.

I was sitting on the floor, in my lawn chair, and was supposed to be supervising. I hated when my mother and husband
fought. It had been happening more and more lately, and it was
always about the house. They argued over which contractors to
use, and clashed over paint colors. Don't even get me started
on the blowout over whether we should have used matte or
semigloss. The biggest battle, though, was the screamfest that
ensued when Ben decided to pull permits for the renovations.
My parents weren't permit people. They believed that the
building department was nothing but a scam to get money out
of people, but Ben and I valued integrity. We wanted to follow
the rules, something my parents saw as a sign of weakness and
conformity.

Ben slammed the cordless drill onto the floor. He threw up
his hands and looked at the ceiling, his face red and his hands
shaking. He took a few deep breaths, and then he spoke.

"It's my house, and if I want my curtains on the outside of the
doorframes, that's where I'm hanging them," he said. Ben spoke
slowly, as if he were trying not to completely lose it.

"Who bought those fucking curtains, Ben? Who bought every
fucking thing in this house? When you buy the fucking curtains,
you get a say," my mother said, glaring at him.

He glared back, and then they both turned and glared at me.

"How do you want them?" my mother asked, and I knew it was
a challenge. Which side was I on: his or hers? Where did my loyalty lie?

"I-I-I don't know. Does it matter?" I stammered.

Again, I didn't really think it was that big of a deal, and come
to think of it, why were we hanging curtains over doors in the first
place? They both continued to stare at me, and I'm pretty sure I
felt a contraction from the stress of being caught between the
two most important people in my life—who could never seem to
agree on anything.

"I think, I think we don't need curtains over doors because

when we go in and out, they will get in the way," I said, which was a diplomatic answer and also the truth.

"Then why the hell am I up here, trying to hang fucking curtains over a door?" Ben asked, shaking his head in disgusted disbelief.

"If you didn't want curtains, why the fuck did you let me buy curtains? You think I don't have better shit to do with my day?" my mother yelled. "You know what? Put your own fucking house together. Trying to do anything with him around is a waste of my time."

She shot Ben a nasty look, grabbed her purse, and stormed out. Ben went to the kitchen, grabbed a beer from the fridge, cracked it open, and disappeared into the bedroom with his phone.

A few minutes later he said he needed to get away to cool down, and he left me alone on the lawn chair in the middle of my house, surrounded by boxes, crumpled newspapers, and a used-up roll of packing tape, all the detritus of our new lives. I imagined giving birth completely alone while my mother and husband stewed over curtains, and I sat in my lawn chair and cried.

Ben came home at two in the morning. I hadn't gone into labor, but I'd spent the entire night in the grips of severe anxiety—the kind that tightens your chest, makes your heart race, and clamps down on your intestines like a vise. It's the kind of anxiety you can't see a way out of, a blend of hopelessness and fear, and I kept asking myself over and over what had I done in getting pregnant, and how had this become my life.

Having a baby made me helpless. I was counting on Ben and my parents to help me get through this emotionally, physically, and financially. In every way, my life now depended on them, whereas before, I'd had a job and my own money and could easily have taken care of myself. I didn't believe I could do that with a baby, and I had absolutely no idea how to raise a child. Even the basics escaped me. I'd barely ever held a baby before, much less changed diapers—and God, breastfeeding. I was petrified of that, and the Internet hadn't helped assuage my fears one bit. According to every website, message board, or blog I came across, if you didn't nurse your baby, you were basically unfit to be a mother. You don't want to breastfeed? Why don't you just give your baby a bottle of rat poison then? Mix it with some Mountain Dew while you're at it. But poring over the Internet kept me from thinking about the bigger issues, namely that the people who supported me couldn't stand each other and that my mom might be going to prison.

Ben apologized to me the next day. He was stressed and scared, probably as much as I was, and he just wanted the house to be perfect for me and the baby. He promised to make it up to me. "I'm going to create an outdoor paradise for our little girl."

Though the inside of our house was furnished and decorated, the outside was still a catastrophe. Our new yard made the jungles of Vietnam look like wide-open prairies. I mean, technically, there was a yard, as in the house was on some property, but it was overgrown with ficus, weeds, and horrifying tropical vegetation that could've easily concealed a large band of silverback gorillas. The day we moved in, I took one look at the yard and wanted to weep. *Agent Orange*, I thought. That was the only thing that could possibly make a dent in this hopelessly tangled knot of runners, vines, and leaves. Even in October, the tropical heat and humidity of South Florida made me feel like I was living in the middle of a rain forest.

Our backyard didn't intimidate or deter my husband in the slightest. With a hacksaw and a machete, he'd spend hours after work each night, trying to cut out a clear space. He had a vision that one day it would be a beautiful place for our daughter to play in, but I thought he was nuts. It seemed like the more he chopped away back there, the worse it got. Ben reminded me of the prince forging through a hundred years' worth of briars to rescue Sleeping Beauty, except I could hardly compare myself to a fairy-tale princess, and I wasn't sleeping, because at this point my heart-burn was positively volcanic.

Then one day my husband went truly, certifiably insane. The weekend after the curtain debacle, our last weekend before my due date, he went out to run some errands—to get some "gardening" supplies. The fool came home with a tree. Like we needed another one, for God's sakes.

"Look," he said. "It's a strawberry tree. I had to get it."

A strawberry tree does not produce strawberries. Its real name is *muntingia calabura*, which sounds like a disease, but its flowers look like strawberry blossoms, and Ben and I had seen one a few years earlier on a carefree date at a botanical garden. The strawberry tree produces these lovely, pearly pink berries that, I swear to God, taste exactly like cotton candy. Obviously, I became enamored of them.

"I have *got* to get one of these," I'd said after our tour guide handed out berries to sample.

The tour guide had told us that they were extremely rare, though I couldn't imagine why, because they were fantastic! Why wouldn't everyone in Florida want one of these trees in their yard? It was tall and leafy and covered in flowers that smelled like dessert.

That had been a long time ago, and I'd kind of forgotten about the strawberry tree, but Ben had remembered for me. He'd researched and hunted, made phone calls to nurseries that dealt in exotic specimens, and now here it was, my own strawberry tree, but where on Earth were we going to put the damned thing? We settled on the side yard off the dining room because that part was mostly cleared. The tree was barely more than a stick, and a sickly looking stick at that, so we figured it would have more than enough room there, if it even made it. I didn't think it would.

We planted the tree ceremoniously. It was for the baby. It would be her special tree, and it would grow up with her.

7

The night of my labor induction, Mom made me a pot of chicken and dumplings. My doctor had instructed me not to eat anything past seven, so we had an early dinner, like my grandparents always had, at five, which was totally unlike us. I can't even tell you how many nights Ben and I, along with my parents and the usual mooching members of their entourage, would start dinner after eight with several cocktails, at least three bottles of wine, and twice that many splits of champagne. We'd finally get around to ordering our entrees at ten, maybe. Bone-in aged rib eyes, spears of asparagus as thick as my thumbs and smothered in hollandaise, baked potatoes the size of footballs, and lobsters so big, they could have starred in a World's Largest Lobster sideshow—it was no wonder we all had acid reflux. After the servers had cleared our table, we'd start on another course and finish after midnight, everyone laughing drunkenly about how our meals were so huge, they took two days to finish. Except me. I'd sigh and plunder the dessert tray anyway, removing every last bit of graham cracker crust from a slab of cheesecake and leaving the gooey middle just because I could. But I was sick of that lifestyle, and when Mom asked me where I wanted to go for my last meal before baby, I told her I wanted to stay home.

Chicken and dumplings represented our roots. In Sussex County, Delaware, slippery dumplings were a way of life for generations. Everybody's mommom made them best, they'd claim, but Mom and I had proof that our family recipe could beat them all, hands down.

Mom grew up working in her grandmother's restaurant. As a kid, she bused tables, took orders, wiped the counters, and polished the pie case. She got paid in dumplings and ice cream, which her grandmother, Mommom Beryl, would let her dip out for herself into frosted, fluted sundae bowls. The Ellendale Restaurant was no ordinary roadside diner. The place was famous, and though it had been closed since the sixties, it was still a great source of pride for our remaining family members.

The meal was everything I wanted—chicken and dumplings and cubes of potato stewed in rich yellow gravy, green peas, a tangle of sweetly tart coleslaw, and cranberry sauce right out of the can and sliced on the lines, and a simple chocolate pie for dessert. It was just cook-and-serve pudding poured into a crisp pie shell, but nothing could have been more delicious.

I needed food that felt like home to give me strength. In a few hours I'd be hooked up to every machine imaginable, and a capsule of Cytotec would be jammed up my crotch to start my contractions. My baby girl was being evicted per the perinatologist's orders. Because of my age and blood-type incompatibility (I was Rh negative, and the baby was not), the perinatologist said there was a chance that my placenta could begin to break down if I went past my due date. Out of an abundance of caution, he believed the best option was a labor induction, and my ob-gyn agreed.

After dinner, Ben and I went home and took a few final pictures of me looking enormous. One day I wanted my daughter to look back at these photos and know that her mother wanted her. I wished I had a picture like that of my own mother, so I smiled even though I was terrified of the pain I was inevitably about to experience.

I freaked out on the way to the hospital because in the melee of the past few weeks, we'd forgotten to write up a birth plan.

"That's what you're *supposed* to do," I told Ben. "All good parents make a birth plan."

"I've never heard of one. Why don't you get a piece of paper and write something now if it'll make you feel better?" he replied, steering the car through the evening traffic.

"No, it's supposed to be typed up, multiple copies made, and it has to be predistributed! I can't just scribble something at the last minute! How would that look? Besides, I don't even know what I'd want it to say," I confessed.

Ben parked our car at the hospital and put a reassuring hand on my shoulder before we went in.

"Calm down," he said. "You're going to be an amazing mother, whether or not you made a birth plan."

It was a quiet night on the maternity ward when we got to the hospital. Someone had decorated the walls with cardboard cutouts of cats and jack-o'-lanterns for Halloween. The hall lights were dimmed, and the nurse who checked us in had been doodling idly on a notepad when we showed up. They'd been expecting me, so the process was quick: hospital gown, bed, IV, and then a capsule was administered to start my labor.

Ben and I waited for something to happen. He dozed off in a chair during *The Tonight Show*, but I couldn't sleep. I felt some cramps. Was this it? I couldn't tell.

By eight o'clock the next morning, I knew something was definitely happening. I had asked at least a dozen women about what childbirth actually felt like, and had received only vague answers about how I would forget the pain because it was all about the baby. But fuck all that starry-eyed, whimsical bullshit. I was in pain and it was real and I would certainly remember it.

You want to know what labor feels like? Remember your worst case of food poisoning and then multiply it by a hundred. Combine that with an excruciating charley horse—the kind you get in the arch of your foot where the pain is so intense, you thank God it lasts only a few seconds. Now multiply that, too, and imagine, instead of just your foot, the pain encompasses your entire body—yes, all of it, and by the way, it lasts for much longer than a few seconds. Then picture that while you are experiencing all this and simultaneously barfing and trying not to crap yourself, several random strangers descend on you all at once with the sole purpose of digging around in your vagina. This is labor. And you'll want to kick every single one of those assholes in the head repeatedly.

A nurse arrived to tell me I was getting an epidural and that I was also getting an immediate emergency C-section. My joy at hearing this was testament to my suffering. If I was actually happy to be strapped to an operating table, pumped full of narcotics, and cut completely open, you know things had to have been pretty bad.

The nurse informed me that the baby was in distress, but at that point I wasn't particularly concerned. This was perhaps my first failure at actual motherhood, and I felt guilty about it later, like I should have panicked, wept, and I don't know, *cared* about my baby's well-being in some obvious fashion—but at the time I mostly wanted her out as quickly as possible, so in my head, I thanked the baby. Her distress had gotten me off the hook big-time, and the only emotion I could identify was a detached sort of relief.

Plus, Mom wouldn't be allowed in the delivery room now, and I could blame it on hospital policy. Only birth partners were allowed in the OR—C-sections are too gory and too risky for an audience, whereas routine vaginal births . . . well, you can have whomever you want in there. Shoot, you could set up bleachers if you wanted and have the damned thing catered.

Oh, look, the baby's crowning. How about a cocktail and some Lit'l Smokies?

Umm, no thanks. That communal birth stuff was so not my style, but Mom, predictably, was all about it. Look, I loved her enthusiasm, and I understood every single reason why she wanted to be present, but at least half of them had to do with reclaiming her own birth story, and dammit, this was *my* birth story, and I only wanted to share it with my husband. My C-section made this a moot point, thank God. I could have my privacy (and my morphine) without hurting anyone's feelings.

My assured, yoga-practicing, Reiki-believing-in ob-gyn pulled my daughter safely from me at 11:41 in the morning. As he unwound the cord from her neck and her body, Ben played Bob Marley's "Ride Natty Ride" on his iPhone, which he tucked beside my right ear. I could barely hear it, but the song wasn't for me anyway. We'd wanted music to be the first thing our child heard.

Have no fear, have no sorrow, the song went, and I wanted that to be the theme of our daughter's life.

I was still strapped to the table and delirious when a nurse showed me my daughter for the first time. The baby had been tightly swaddled in hospital blankets, and she blinked quietly in the nurse's arms, looking around the room with what appeared to be at least a sort of awareness of things. She had a perfectly round, lightbulb of a head with a thin layer of sandy-brown hair, pink cheeks, and large almond-shaped dark eyes. They looked exactly the same as mine.

"She's very alert, this one," the nurse said.

"Is she okay?" I asked. "Like, *normal*?"

"Oh God, yes. She's perfectly fine. Healthiest baby I've seen in a while. What's her name?"

"Emmeline Alice," I said.

The nurse nodded in approval. "An old-fashioned name. Nice. Her classroom's going to be filled with Sophias and Olivias, so she'll stand out."

"We named her after both of our paternal grandmothers," I explained. "We're going to call her Em for short."

I never knew my husband's grandmother. She was a mother of five, had lost a baby when she was a newlywed, and had seen her little brother killed by a car on the streets of New York City. She'd grown up to be a telephone operator, and then moved across the country to California with a husband who didn't deserve her. After their divorce, she was known as the sweet lady who lived in the pink house on Flower Street in Santa Ana. Her children and grandchildren worshiped her, and even though she died before I could meet her, I could tell she was a woman who should have a little girl named after her.

Alice was my biological father's mother, the one who'd raised me as if I were her own. My Mommom Alice had given me a strong, stable foundation during my early childhood, when my own parents weren't able to. Though her son abandoned me when I was eleven, she didn't. She did the right thing in a tough situation, was steadfast, and loved me unconditionally, and I wanted my child to share her great-grandmother's name in hopes she would also share her virtues.

My parents had waited outside of the OR door during my C-section, listening for clues or cries or any hint of what was happening inside. Then they'd paced in front of the nursery windows, waiting as I was sewn back together, for the first glimpse of their new grandchild. I thought Mom would be the first to hold Em and that she would be all about the baby, but I was wrong. Once she saw that the baby was fine and got a good look at her, she came to sit with me instead as I shivered alone in the recovery room, having been instructed not to speak for an hour so I wouldn't make myself nauseous or out of breath.

"I know you're not supposed to talk," Mom said, "but I wanted you to know how proud I am of you. You did it. You gave birth to a beautiful, healthy baby. You should see her in there, looking all around at everything. I've never seen anything like it."

Mom laughed and I smiled. She went on.

"I am so proud of you, Vic. You took such good care of yourself when you were pregnant. You sacrificed so much to make sure you had a healthy baby, and you went through so much shit most women don't have to deal with, and you did it." Then my mother sat there in silence with me, holding my hand and beaming her slightly bucktoothed smile until the nurses came to wheel me into my room.

Ben and I had a few hours alone with the baby while my parents went to lunch. They came back later that afternoon, when the autumn sun angled through the window in my room. A few visitors had already appeared, and every available surface was already covered with pink bouquets, "It's a Girl!" balloons, and stuffed bears. Many of them came from people I didn't even know: partners and clients seeking to impress my parents.

Em, still tightly swaddled in several layers of blankets, slept in the crook of my arm while I watched *Ellen*.

"Do you want to hold her?" I offered.

Mom seemed almost tentative, but I gathered the baby and held Em out to her.

Jabbing at his phone, Ben mumbled something about a Starbucks run and made a quick getaway to avoid any tension with my mother and give the new grandparents some time alone with the baby.

They sat on the empty bed across from mine. I'd gotten lucky— it was a slow week for baby-having, apparently, and I had a room to myself, and as Mom rested the bundle of baby on her knees, she stared into Em's sleeping face, which was still pink and crinkled from birth. Joel reached out and touched Em's fuzzy hair, and for a long time we sat in complete silence, the light streaming in from the window, backlighting my parents so they became a haloed silhouette: two dark figures huddled close and surrounded by brightness.

8

My first twenty-four hours of motherhood hadn't been too bad. I had an IV drip of morphine, so that may explain my contented bliss, and since the morphine made me itch, I'd also been given Benadryl. The strange thing was that, apparently, I could function perfectly well on opiates (this being my first experience with hardcore painkillers), but add some harmless over-the-counter antihistamine to the mix, and all of a sudden I was zonked. By the time my sister and her husband, Andrew, arrived to meet Em—there'd been a little mix-up, and the front desk had mistaken Ashley for a patient—I was a loopy, giggling, partially slurring hot mess, but at least I wasn't sobbing. Yet.

I called and had the baby delivered from the nursery, where she'd been hanging out with the nurses, chugging formula while I recovered from surgery. Emmeline arrived, perfectly clean, tightly swaddled, and wearing an eeny-weeny hand-knit hat with a pom-pom on top. I held her for a few minutes, had a good, long sniff of her sweet baby head, and handed her over to meet her aunt and uncle.

Ashley and I weren't actually siblings, but when your family tree more closely resembles a briar patch, it's a lot easier to call your half aunt, who's almost nine years your junior, your sister. We both left Delaware to live with my parents in New York at the same time, when she was three and I was eleven. It was the summer of 1985, and my mom was obsessed with Paul Young's "Every

Time You Go Away," and we lived in a house, one nearly devoid of furniture, on the edge of a reservoir. We rented it from a wealthy Indian man named Mr. Patel, and I have no idea how my parents were managing the bills, as I have no recollection of either one of them working that summer. It should have been strange for me to be suddenly uprooted and to instantly find myself with a sister, but kids are unusually resilient, and I never questioned my reality much until I got older. At the time it didn't seem peculiar that my mother's father would take up with a girl younger than all four of his adult children after twenty-five years of marriage to my grandmother, that he would have two more children—a girl and a boy a year apart—and that his young wife would up and leave for Ohio one day, divorcing him and mysteriously taking the boy but leaving the girl, and that the girl would then come to live with me as my little sister. Or if it did, it didn't seem worth it to fish for the details until I was older and had a better grasp on the complexities of adult relationships, alcoholism, and general white trash dysfunction.

None of that mattered to me, though. I was just really happy for my sister (because that's what she feels like to me) to come visit us. She and Andrew were naturals with babies, but I definitely wouldn't have thought that a year earlier. Ashley and I both spent our twenties recovering from our childhoods. We dropped out of college early, chased boys, ended up in relationships that were legendary disasters, and having absolutely zero positive role models for money management, we both obliterated our credit. The one thing I can say is that Ashley probably had a better time ruining her life than I did, because at least she drank. Wallowing in depression and regret, I watched indie films, while Ashley partied away her first decade of adulthood with shocking abandon. She had years she couldn't remember, and I had years I'd much rather forget.

But those days were behind us. Ashley and I had managed to get ourselves together, finishing degrees and getting married, and now we were having babies less than two months apart. As Mom told us one afternoon while we gorged on spinach dip at a waterfront table at Houston's, "You girls did good. You both got men who didn't beat the shit out of you."

Mom hadn't been joking. Serious as a heart attack, she was truly relieved, because where she came from, scoring a man who didn't slap you around was a pretty big deal. She had a different set of standards, but Ashley and I had set the bar a little higher. When Ashley and Andrew, a union sheet metal worker and a veteran of the war in Afghanistan, got engaged, I'd been so thankful. Her last few boyfriends had included a manic-depressive cocaine addict, a guy with *Fuck the World* inked across his pecs, and a pathological liar who'd stolen her bank card and drained her checking account. Andrew was pretty awesome, and not just in comparison to her loser exes. And because he was the second of eight siblings, he probably knew babies better than any of us.

"I think she might be pooping," he said as he held Em.

"Really?" I said. "How do you tell?"

Ashley looked horrified. "Umm, she's . . . *gurgling*," she said with a grimace.

Andrew handed the baby back to me.

"I don't smell anything," I said, but then I, too, heard the sound emanating from her diaper. "What *is* that?" I asked.

I felt the panic beginning to rise in me and looked at Ben. He shrugged.

"What do we do?"

"Change her!" Andrew said.

Wait? We had to change the baby? Oh my god. We had to change the baby. How exactly did that work?

"Call the nurse!" Ben suggested, and I pressed the call button on the side of the bed repeatedly, sort of like how you press an elevator button over and over, hoping that will actually make it get there faster.

The nurse's voice sounded static-y over the intercom.

"Ye-es?"

She was obviously annoyed. She'd probably been enjoying her break in the empty nursery, watching TV or doing her nails.

"The baby, um, the baby—the baby *pooped*," I said.

"Okay, so change her," the nurse said.

"Uh, well, uh, I don't know how," I confessed.

"There are diapers and wipes beside the bed. Use those. You'll figure it out," Nurse Nasty instructed. She was definitely judging. I could hear it in her tone, and I imagined her telling her coworkers about those asshole yuppies having a baby for the first time and how the mother couldn't even change a goddamned diaper.

Ben fumbled for the diapers and wipes while I unraveled the baby from her impossibly complicated swaddle. She was covered in some kind of horrible black goo that looked like something out of the movies—you know, the black stuff that seeps from the walls of demon-possessed houses. What was coming out of my child? And where was my mother? She could have fixed this, but she was out to dinner at a swank hotel on the beach—something to do with the next movie deal Joel was working on.

With shaking hands, I opened Em's diaper. There was no getting around this. I had to clean her off myself.

"Oh my god, oh my god, what *is* this stuff? Is she sick or something? It's black! I thought baby poop was supposed to be yellow? And there's so much of it!" I cried.

Worse yet, it—whatever it was—was still coming out. This brought to mind the time I accidentally broke the handle off the soft-serve machine at Morrison's Cafeteria when I was eleven years old, and the chocolate ice cream would not stop pouring out of the dispenser.

By that point Ashley was laughing so hard at my incompetence, she was in danger of breaking *her* water. Andrew was shaking his head and looking at the ceiling, and Ben was frantically trying to google something.

"Okay, I got it!" Ben shouted. "It's meconium."

"Is that fatal? Should we call, like, a Code Blue to the nurses or something?" I asked.

Ashley hooted with laughter and suggested that it was more like a Code Brown, which was so not funny to me at the time. I wanted to throw the box of wipes at her head.

"Okay, relax. Sounds like it's totally normal. Meconium is a baby's first stool. The baby sheds the lining of its intestines, which contain everything that it ingested in utero," Ben explained, never once looking up from the screen of his phone. He then showed me a couple of truly disgusting images, and I quickly became satisfied that whatever was oozing out of my newborn's bottom was totally normal. When the drama was over and Emmeline had been rediapered for the third time (we put the first one on backward, and after we managed to get the second one on straight, she pooped again), Ashley and Andrew decided it was time to go. I could only imagine the conversation they were going to have on the way home. Even Em seemed to look at me suspiciously.

Are you kidding me? I imagined the baby thinking. *I got a mom who's never even changed a diaper? What was she doing for nine months? She must be the only mother who's never read* What to Expect When You're Expecting. *Jeez.*

We were hopeless, and by the time I was discharged, our parenting skills hadn't improved a bit.

Since I'd recovered well from surgery, we were allowed to go home at the end of the week. When it was time to check out, Ben and I got another chance to show off our utter incompetence. We had forgotten to install the car seat. I had to sit in the waiting room for nearly an hour while Ben ran home to get the car seat I received at my shower and brought it back to the hospital, where he then attempted to install it without really reading the directions, because how hard could it be anyway? Turns out that car seats are extremely difficult to install, but even more difficult was actually strapping a teeny seven-pound newborn into one of them.

"Didn't you play with dolls when you were little?" Ben asked.

Being female, I clearly should've learned the art of infant care by the time I was six, I guess.

In a way he was right to think that. All the other little girls on my street were definitely wrapping dollies in blankies and changing Baby Alive's diaper, but I thought Baby Alive was gross. I wanted to be Princess Leia instead, so I could get my own X-wing fighter and blast the shit out of some Imperial Stormtroopers. I always aspired to be more of a badass warrior princess than a mom, but here I was, the furthest thing from a badass anything, having a breakdown because I was scared to put a baby in a car.

The ride home was harrowing, mostly because I made it that way, but I felt like, instead of strapping our daughter in a safety-regulated car seat, we'd actually tossed her into the rattly cart of an old, Coney Island roller coaster and sent her careening down a hundred-foot vertical drop. The world was going to be scary and dangerous, and I was destined to fail at protecting her from it, just like my parents hadn't been able to protect me, though in their own way they'd truly tried. On the way home from the hospital, all I could think about were the ways in which my child might suffer in life: playground bullies, heartbreak, poverty, exclusion, head lice, stomach bugs, car accidents, learning disabilities. . . . The list was as long as I was powerless.

By the time we pulled into the driveway, Em had fallen asleep. Still sore, I stepped gingerly out of the backseat, gathered the baby, and shuffled to my front step. Ben was with me, but I still felt alone. My old life was about to disappear forever. There would be no convenient hospital nursery to call when I needed to sleep, no nurses to bathe and swaddle this baby. I'd be on my own as a mother, just me and this little person I'd created, and I would have to keep her alive. *Me.*

A large white gift basket had been delivered to our door. It was wrapped in cellophane and tied with a big yellow bow. A teddy smiled out from the plastic. He was nestled in among some baby bottles, washcloths, a onesie, and a couple of bibs.

"Aww, what a beautiful basket," Ben remarked. "Let's see who it's from."

He bent down and turned over the tag.

"'Love Sarah, Ellen, Thaddeus, Grace, and Lucas,'" he read. "Who are all those people?"

"They're . . . They're my . . . my brothers and sisters?" I said, but it came out sounding like a question.

"Oh yeah," Ben said. "Well, that was nice of them. How did they know?"

I shrugged. "Facebook?"

"Do you talk to them?" he asked, confused.

"Only Sarah and Ellen, and pretty much only online," I explained.

Sarah and Ellen were the oldest of the five kids my biological father had had with my stepmother, who he'd married when I was nine and who had died a few years earlier. They were grown up and married, but the three younger siblings still lived at home with their father—our father, really—although it sounded weird to me to say that, and they didn't have Facebook accounts, so I didn't communicate with them. Sarah was the rebel of the five, the self-proclaimed black sheep and an atheist who'd escaped from Bob Jones University, and was now an exile. My father wouldn't speak to me because he believed I'd chosen my mother over him, and he had little to do with Sarah because she'd turned her back on their fundamentalist Baptist church and questioned the way she was raised. Sarah's ultimate act of rebellion, though, had been to reach out to me when her mother died. She felt a kinship with me and wanted to hear my side of the story.

Sarah lived in Philadelphia and had married a couple of months earlier. She invited me to her wedding, but being in the throes of first-trimester nausea, I had to turn her down because, at the time, I couldn't walk from my bedroom to the kitchen without puking. When I felt better and was up for traveling, my cousins in Delaware threw me a shower, and Sarah drove several hours to attend. Afterward, she and I had dinner together, crab soup in a coastal resort town. I wanted to like her, but I didn't know what kind of relationship I wanted to have, and I was worried about complicating my life and betraying my mother, who I knew was sure to have strong opinions about me being in touch with my siblings.

The restaurant was one of those tourist traps decorated with old buoys and plastic lobsters, but it was known for its fresh seafood dishes. We sat across from each other, under a large fishing net that had caught some fake crustaceans and dusty starfish, and as Sarah read the menu, I scanned her downcast face.

We looked nothing alike. I tried to find some common feature between us, but I came up short. She had a round face, thick auburn hair that fell almost to her waist, and the fair, faintly freckled complexion of a natural redhead. If we went out in the sun together, Sarah would blister in about two minutes while I could stay outside all day and come home with little more than a rosy glow on my nose. Unlike my eyes, hers were blue. All of my siblings' eyes were blue. I knew this because once, on Facebook, Sarah had posted something about how all five of them had blue eyes. She hadn't meant to hurt my feelings, but she'd been raised to exclude me, so it hadn't occurred to her to say *except Victoria*, or that there were actually six of us instead of five (and, honestly, that might have made me feel worse anyway).

Lots of full siblings look nothing alike, though, and after all, we were only half sisters so why did I even care? We probably had other similarities—look, we both liked crab soup! Then she went and ordered salmon. I would rather eat a can of cat food than let a piece of pink fish anywhere near my tongue, so clearly we didn't even have some sort of genetic predisposition toward liking the same foods.

I questioned her about my father, probably a bit too relent-lessly, but there were so many things I needed answers to, and I thought this was my only chance to get them. How could he have abandoned me? Was there something wrong with me? Did he drink coffee in the mornings? Were there pictures of me in their house? What did he say about my mother and stepfather?

"He told me that your mom and Joel were drug dealers," Sarah said.

I nodded. Sarah took a bite of her arugula salad (I didn't like arugula, either) and told me that our father said my mom was wanted in several states.

"She was like this imaginary Disney villain, the way my parents described her," she explained. "Dad told me that one time, when you were really little, you were living with him at Mommom and Poppop's house. You were supposed to be visiting her, but for some reason you didn't go and then shots were fired at her house or something."

I laughed. I thought I knew the story she was referring to—my mom told me about it when I was a teenager. I had always loved it when she told me tales from her drug-dealing days, because those stories were edgy and crazy. To a sixteen-year-old who'd just tried pot in the backseat of her boyfriend's car in the grocery store parking lot, having a former, drug-dealing mom was cool as shit.

As I remembered the story (there were several versions), Mom found an old abandoned farmhouse in the middle of a cornfield out in the sticks, and that was where she hid the weed she was trafficking up and down the East Coast. This was a couple of years before she met Joel, and she always made a point to tell me that the only reason she ever sold drugs was because it was the only way she could make enough money to hire a lawyer to help her regain custody of me from my father and his parents. Mom and her crew would bring the weed in from somewhere, Jamaica maybe, hide the stash at this farmhouse, and then distribute it accordingly from there. Well, as I recalled hearing, one night, she and some of the guys who worked for her were at the farmhouse when a rival clan of drug dealers tried to bust in and steal their shit. Armed with shotguns, Mom and her boys fought back and blasted the living hell out of those sonsabitches.

"I don't know what happened. All I know is, I let the buckshot off into the sky to scare 'em and took off fast as I could into the cornfield. Hid there all night till it got quiet. Then I left and never came back. One of my boys got hurt, but nobody ever knew I'd been there. Cops never knew it was my stuff at that farmhouse," Mom told me.

That had to be what Sarah was talking about. I think it had been in the news back when it happened, but like Mom said, no one else knew for sure she was there, except, I suppose, my biological father, although I don't know how he found out. There were always so many holes in our family stories, and the answers only prompted more questions. I often thought that if I had been there to witness some of these events, I'd tell them a lot differently.

"Dad explicitly said he believed you were unsafe with your mom and Joel. He felt like you would have been better off if you had stayed with him and my mom," Sarah said.

"I felt unsafe with your parents too, though, the fire-and-brimstone stuff they preached," I said. "I never felt like they really loved me. I never felt like theirs was the family where I truly belonged."

Sarah reached across the table and touched my hand.

"I'm sorry you had to grow up feeling like that. That must have sucked," she said.

I slid my hand back. "Let's order dessert," I replied. "The pregnant woman needs cake."

I hadn't met my half sister Ellen yet. She married the summer before and had not invited me to her wedding, but I hadn't expected an invitation. I didn't know her, after all, but she had apologized to me, via Facebook, saying she didn't want her big day to be awkward and she didn't want to upset our father, whom she felt, probably correctly, wouldn't have wanted me there. Ellen had moved to Ohio with her husband and, a few months later, became pregnant with her first child. That was when we kind of bonded—or bonded as much as two half sisters who were practically strangers and communicated only through comment threads and like buttons could. We were pregnant at the same time, a coincidence that brought us a little closer. We compared notes and ideas, and since she was a few months further along than I was, she'd been able to keep me informed of the upcoming milestones. I was terrified of the glucose tolerance test, but Ellen had been through it and reassured me that I would be fine. I was grateful to have her, plus she always posted really good recipes in her status updates.

But that was the extent of it. After having dinner with Sarah in Delaware, I came home and hadn't called her since. Sometimes my half sisters would message me and I wouldn't respond for days, but I couldn't explain why. I was too busy, I told myself, and now with the baby, I'd be even busier. There was no room in my life for new people, and for now I needed to focus on learning how to care for Emmeline and managing my anxiety, so I texted Sarah a quick thank-you for the gift basket, but it would be months before I spoke to her, or any of my half siblings, again.

Ben wrapped his arm around my shoulders. I looked down at Em's sleeping face, and then at my husband.

"Oh my God, we're really parents now. I don't know if we can do this," I said.

"Little late for that," he said, and laughed, unlocking the front door. "We'll be fine."

But I wasn't so sure.

9

Each Thanksgiving I try to make a list of the things for which I'm grateful. I think I saw this on *Oprah* at some point and thought it sounded like something enlightened people did. Usually my lists were pretty unoriginal. I was thankful for my family, my friends, and my cat, blah, blah, blah, but after a month with a newborn, my list that year was different. I was grateful for any brief moment of sleep I could possibly get, the fleeting moments when my boobs didn't hurt, and the rare times when there was someone else around to hold the baby. Most of all, I was thankful when I could find five minutes to actually take a shower, which usually happened twice a week (in fact, if someone would have told me that instead of celebrating the upcoming holiday, I could take the entire day and spend it alone in the shower, I would have accepted their offer enthusiastically).

Thanksgiving was my mom's big deal. She loved the holiday so much that when she'd built her dream house, she'd specifically had the downstairs walls of her mansion painted the color of pumpkin pie. Behind her Viking range stove, a glass mosaic of an overflowing cornucopia gleamed, and her office ceiling was adorned with an Italianate mural of plump cherubs fluttering around a gaudy wreath of autumn fruits and vegetables.

I wasn't sure I could handle a holiday, and there was no way in hell I'd be able to cook my usual volume of pies and sides with the baby. Some people got babies who napped serenely in their ruffled bassinets, but I'd received one who seemingly never slept. Emmeline was clingy, demanding, and very vocal about her grievances—in short, she was exactly like me, except redder and smaller and with a cry that sounded like a crow's. From the day we brought her home, she'd made it abundantly clear that we were not to put her down under any circumstances, and that if we did happen to rest her on her back, there would be dire consequences for everyone involved. Nursing wasn't meant to be done according to the schedules experts discussed in parenting books, but twenty-four hours a day, so screw turkey, I had enough on my plate already. Besides, my in-laws were visiting.

"I'm not doing a big dinner this year," Mom promised. She'd come over, like she did every day, to help me give Em a bath because I was so petrified of the terrible things that could happen when one combined an infant with soap and water, I refused to bathe her alone. I thought she would be so slippery, I might accidentally drop her on the bathroom floor.

"You say that every year," I replied.

"No, I mean it this year. Just family," Mom insisted.

We'd been through this before, though. Every year Mom swore she was toning down her usual holiday celebration, but it never happened. To her, not doing a big dinner meant that, instead of sixty people, we'd probably just have a modest forty, meaning we'd need only three turkeys and two hams instead of, like, sixteen. On Thanksgiving, South Florida's homeless had soup kitchens, but Fort Lauderdale's losers and douchebags? Well, they had my parents. Mom believed they *were* our family, but honestly, I'd rather not claim as kin a bunch of sex workers and ex–personal trainers turned penny-stock promoters.

Another reason I hoped for a more low-key Thanksgiving that year was that Ben's parents were visiting from California. They'd given us a month to acclimate to parenthood, but they were understandably excited to meet their new (and only) grandchild, so they decided to fly out at the end of November. I was happy for them to visit, but I didn't want them finding out about Mom's arrest. Ben and I agreed not to tell them about it, at least not until we had to. The last thing I wanted to do was answer a bunch of their questions about details I'd prefer to keep private. I was embarrassed. I always sensed that Ben's parents thought he could've done better than me. Ben and I had been married for five years, so it wasn't like they hadn't figured out what my family was like, and it was easy to understand why I might not be the girl they'd envisioned for their only son. Why couldn't he have stuck with someone normal? A blonde from the Midwest who went to community college for something practical (and generic) like communications? She'd work in a bank, be a wiz with spreadsheets, and score bonus points for enjoying conservative talk radio.

When my in-laws first got to my parents' house Thanksgiving afternoon, they looked a little shell-shocked, and I was pretty sure it wasn't jet lag. They were shy, unassuming types who were out of place among my parents' flamboyant entourage, and they quickly planted themselves on the plush brown velvet sofa in the den, where they could avoid making small talk with Mom and Joel's friends. I breathed a sigh of relief that they chose *this* sofa, instead of the Marge Carson where I'd been detained six weeks earlier. *That* was the sofa where a triple-X porno had been filmed. A few years ago one of my parents' associates, Nort, had convinced them to rent out their home to a film crew that made flicks with dignified titles like *Hungarian Titty Explosion*. The living room couch had apparently been the perfect location for Fernando and Natasha's on-camera romp. When the porno wrapped, my parents seemed proud, starstruck even, by the fact that their house had appeared in a dirty movie, something that never ceased to perplex me. I mean, it wasn't like it was the set for *Schindler's List* or something. My in-laws would've died if they knew some of the things that had gone on in this house.

With Ben's mom and dad safe in the den in front of the big-screen TV, I plopped down nearby in the recliner, Em permanently attached to my chest. She never took a break from nursing. The baby books called this "cluster feeding." *Clusterfuck was more like it,* I thought, but at least incessant breastfeeding gave me an excuse to interact as little as possible with the other guests who were quickly packing the house. As predicted, that year's Thanksgiving was smaller than usual, but only by about ten people.

"They have nowhere else to go," Mom reasoned, but Ashley and I were less sympathetic. All we ever wanted was a small gathering with just us.

Growing up, Ashley and I had always imagined what a normal holiday might be like. Only relatives in attendance, real china instead of Chinet, everyone seated at a long dining room table (kids arguing about who's getting the last crescent roll), Harry Connick Jr. crooning from a stereo, and no one wearing anything close to leopard print or pleather.

I couldn't help but groan when Ruffina arrived, bearing gifts for everyone and a large tray of lasagna. The neighborhood busybody, Ruffina was from Italy, short, top-heavy, and overly tanned. Her hair was styled in a shaggy bob she'd dyed the color of cheap Lambrusco, and a slight underbite made her look like a Muppet bulldog. Ruffina had tarted up for the occasion in a skintight black shift and a pair of her signature sky-high, red-soled Louboutins she got for a discount because she worked in the shoe department at Neiman Marcus.

"She's got her eye on Baron," Mom observed incorrectly. I'd long suspected it was Joel she was really after.

Mom was referring to Baron Von Bod (obviously not his real name), a former male model and recovering drug addict who'd recently started a male escort service called Nites 4 Princesses. I'd first met him a couple of years earlier when he was still Skip Johnson and lived one street over from Mom and Joel in a big Key West–style mansion on the water as the kept man of the notorious local madam, Velva Haux (and God only knows what *her* real name actually was). Skip and Joel knew each other from walking dogs in the neighborhood, and somehow that morphed into them becoming workout partners at LA Fitness.

One cannot expect a relationship between a madam and her much younger, recovering-addict eye candy to end in wholesome marital bliss. Pretty soon Skip and Velva broke up, and Skip ran to my parents for advice, solace, and eventually a place to live. And this was where my parents' behavior split dramatically from that of normal healthy people. You see, sane people would find out that a madam and her boy toy were living a street away and keep a crazy mess like that at a distance. Wave, say hi, and then go make fun of them with the other normal neighbors. My parents, on the other hand, find out this shit is going on and decide to become their best friends.

Skip Johnson began his transformation into Baron Von Bod as soon as he moved into the downstairs guest room of Casa dei Sogni—the name of my parents' house—which was Italian for "House of Dreams." His broken heart mended quickly as he forgot Velva and dated at least six or seven other girls, possibly more, but it was kind of hard to keep track because they all looked alike. A few modeling jobs here and there weren't cutting it, so Skip resolved to follow in Velva's footsteps and start an escort service. With my parents' support, he gained the confidence he needed to start his own "business" doing what he loved—dating mentally unstable rich women—and helping other enterprising young men to do the same while giving him a cut. Somehow this led to appearances on *Dr. Phil* and *The Tyra Banks Show* and now, at Thanksgiving, Baron Von Bod—clad in his usual ripped jeans, white, V-neck tee, and unbuttoned suit vest—was bragging to everyone within earshot that he was about to get his own reality show on cable.

"Yeah, right. I'll believe it when I see it," I grumbled under my breath.

Handing Em off to Ben's mother, I joined my mom in the kitchen, where she was aggressively plunging an electric hand mixer into a vat of boiled potatoes and melted butter. Joel cranked up the music. Pitbull. *How freaking festive,* I thought.

I tried to whisper in Mom's ear. "Look, I don't want you to say anything about your arrest around Ben's parents," I told her.

Mom jerked her head back and glared at me.

"What is *wrong* with you? This is Thanksgiving and this is my house and I can talk about whatever I want."

A few feet away Joel stepped in time to the music, a glass of Cab in his hand, while Ruffina and my mom's best friend, Allegra, twerked for him in front of the buffet table. Baron joined in on the action, adding some cheesy disco moves.

"I just don't feel like explaining it to Ben's parents." I sighed.

Mom put her hand on her hip. "Oh really? You don't want to explain it to Ben's parents? Do you think I care about that? What Ben's parents think is the last thing on my mind, and here they are sitting in *my* house, eating *my* food that *I* cooked, and you think I give a shit what they think about me? Because, no, I do *not* care. Put these mashed potatoes in a bowl."

I should have known better than to say anything. Now Mom would probably find a way to mention it on purpose just to piss me off.

I almost said something back, but the doorbell rang and saved me from starting an argument I would've regretted.

Joel danced to the door, and I followed closely behind, desperate to see who it could possibly be. Please not the process server or the cops or anything, and please not another guest. *Please.* Please just let me have an uneventful first Thanksgiving with my baby, I prayed. But this was not to be. I recognized the guy's face immediately. It was Ian Greenberg, and he was listed as a coconspirator on Mom's indictment. She was not to have contact with any of the men named in her case.

"What the hell is Ian Greenberg doing here?" I asked, perhaps a bit louder and more shrilly than I'd intended.

"Baby, stop. Just relax. I've got this," Joel said, and placed his hand firmly on my shoulder.

"You can't let him in!" I protested.

Mom appeared, wiping her hands on a dish towel embroidered with pumpkins, and I repeated myself, but this time it was a demand.

"Don't let him in here!"

Mom furrowed her brow, which was difficult because she'd recently had Botox, and pointed toward the kitchen.

"Get out of here," she told me, but I stayed.

I couldn't believe Joel opened the door and let that sonofabitch in. What was he thinking?

Ian Greenberg resembled a rat in every possible sense of the word: a rat in a trilby hat and a necklace that looked like a bike chain. He was pale and sweaty and looked like he'd recently eaten a bad plate of mussels marinara. The dude was clearly scared shitless to be here—something was definitely up.

Joel high-fived him, but Ian looked like he was about to crap himself out of fear, so Joel offered him a long slow hug. Ian tried to pull away.

"You look hot, man. Let me take your jacket," Joel said.

Ian clung to his lapel. "Naw, naw, dude. It's all g-good," he stammered.

"No, seriously, take off your jacket. Stay awhile," Joel said, only now it sounded more like an order.

"Let me get him a plate," Mom suggested, but she didn't.

Ian shifted his weight a few times and squeezed his chin with his hand.

"So, uh, can I, like, talk to you guys a minute?" Ian asked.

"Victoria, go fix him a plate," Mom said.

I couldn't fucking believe my mother just asked me to make this guy a plate. Dinner hadn't even been served yet.

"You have some nerve coming over here!" I yelled at Ian. "This is our family's holiday, and you were not invited!"

Mom grabbed me by the arm and dragged me into the butler's pantry behind the kitchen.

"I do not need you causing a fucking scene at my house on Thanksgiving!"

"Why are you letting him in?" I argued.

"You don't worry about my business! Go take care of your baby and stay out of it!"

Mom stamped her rhinestone-studded heels into the kitchen, where, with a clenched jaw and pursed lips, she slapped a plate together for Ian.

I slid down the pumpkin-pie-colored wall behind me and rested my forehead on my knees, unable to contain my sobs. Ben called for me, the baby was cawing, but I didn't respond. Someone else could comfort her for the time being.

Andrew and Ashley walked past me on their way out. They were already leaving. Ashley paused and asked me what I was doing on the floor, and I quickly explained the situation.

"Screw this," she said. "I'm nine months pregnant and starving, and I'm not waiting for them to figure out whatever bullshit is going on, so I'm going home and ordering Thai."

"But he was arrested with her! He works with Carmelo! And they fucking let him in here!" I cried.

"Not my problem," Ashley said.

"He's probably wearing a wire!"

"Good, if they're stupid enough to trust him, they deserve to get caught," Ashley said.

But I couldn't detach the way she could. I wanted to save my family.

I got up and wiped my face, went out to the living room, and made a joke about how my hormones must have made me a little emotional. Joel told everyone that dinner would be just a little while longer because he had some unexpected business to attend to, then hooted something about turning the music up a little louder because it was time to really get the party started.

I went into the den, sat back down in the recliner, and gathered the baby in my arms again. It was calming to hold her.

"What kind of business is your dad doing on Thanksgiving?" my mother-in-law asked.

I shrugged.

"Is it something with the movie?" she pressed.

"Yeah, probably," I said.

I watched Joel, Baron, and my parents lead Ian back to the hallway by my mother's office, the music reverberating through the house at a deafening pitch. Joel kept his hand on Ian, who was an awkward mess of nervous gestures. Baron stood, his arms crossed over his chest and his head cocked to one side, while my mother pointed a lot and in countless directions. The plate of food sat untouched on the glass coffee table in the living room, and as my parents ushered Ian outside a few minutes later, he glanced toward it.

"Take it," my mom told him.

He looked at her, unsure, but ultimately refused the food. He said he had somewhere important to get to, so he hurried out.

When Ian's car pulled out of the driveway, Joel locked the front door behind him, laughing as he brushed his palms together a few times like he was dusting them off. Mom picked the plate of food up and took it to the table, where she began to inhale the stuffing, mashed potatoes, and turkey.

"Let's eat!" Joel announced, and within seconds the buffet line was mobbed. Dinner started, guests made their plates, and everyone found a place to eat anywhere they could (even the floor), because at our house there was no such thing as a formal, sit-down meal. It was the usual holiday pandemonium at Casa dei Sogni, and in a few minutes everyone except me seemed to have forgotten Ian's interruption.

I don't remember eating a thing that year, but I remember

cleaning the kitchen and I remember Mom bitching about how there were no leftovers again and that all she ever wanted was just enough to make a good turkey sandwich the next day. But there was nothing except three ragged turkey carcasses, picked as clean as if they'd been attacked by vultures.

10

I'd started off on foot in the dark without shoes. But in February even Florida gets cold sometimes, so I turned around. I wasn't going back in there though. I was getting the car. I wouldn't *run* away from home. I'd *drive* away and just keep driving.

It was four thirty in the morning, and I was alone. The chill in the air stiffened my feet, but I ran anyway. Wet grass soaked my pajama bottoms. I barely felt it. Everything was dark except for the motion sensor light on the corner of a neighbor's house that I'd accidentally set off. It was quiet, all crickets and stars. Only the insane went outside in the wee small hours.

I leaned against the trunk of a palm tree to catch my breath. My fingers dried tears from my face, and I used the back of my hand to wipe my runny nose. I bent over at the waist, my hands on my knees, because I hoped it might help me breathe better. I'd seen runners doing this, but when I tried it, my boobs, which were sore and heavy and hurt in ways I'd never imagined that boobs could hurt, splattered milk onto my bare feet and soaked through my pajama top. It was disgusting. For three months now I'd spent my days glazed in saliva, breast milk, and spit-up. I smelled like rotten fettuccine Alfredo, and I vowed I would never eat it again once this was over.

Focus. Get the car, I reminded myself. I would get a hotel room with blackout shades and a rumbling AC that puffed out air so cold, it looked like frosted breath, and I wouldn't care—I would sleep on smooth, clean, cool sheets under a thick comforter in a nest of pillows. Then I would take a hot shower and sleep some more. I would sleep for days until they found me.

As I drove to my parents' house, I wept. Even they were asleep. Every light in their house of dreams was off and the gates were closed, so I spun around in their cul-de-sac and drove in the opposite direction, circling the block and passing the Catholic church a street over from my house.

Behind me, a car suddenly shined its brights, and the glare on the windshield temporarily blinded me. I sped up and so did the car. I was being followed.

My cell phone rang in the console. Ben. My husband was following me. I knew there was no car seat in his car because we only had one, and it was in my backseat. He had left Em alone in the house to come find me. The baby was in some sort of terrible danger, and it was all my fault.

An alternative future flashed through my head. Something was happening to Emmeline because I'd run away in the middle of the night. I'd soon end up on *Nancy Grace,* where she'd call me a "tot mom" and hiss and snarl about what an abomination I was. Brad Cohen would come on and talk about my mother, and Nancy Grace would sniff and make a haughty remark about how evil must run in our genes.

Defeated, I stopped the car on the side of the road. Ben pulled up behind me like a cop, got out, and walked up to my driver's-side window. I'd wanted a tender word of reassurance, but I got a "What in the fuck are you doing?" instead.

He was in his pajamas, his hair a mess, his glasses askew on his face.

I couldn't answer. He sounded near hysterical.

"Don't give me that deer-in-headlights bullshit, Victoria. I have to get up for work in less than two hours! You have a baby to take care of! What are you doing outside in the middle of the night? Are you crazy?"

I nodded. "Where's Em?" I asked.

"She's home in her crib, sleeping," Ben said.

"You left the baby alone in the house!?" I shrieked.

"I had no choice! Barbara called me and said she saw you running barefoot through the neighborhood!"

"Barbara? What was she doing outside?"

"Walking her dogs. What does it matter?" Ben said. "Where were you going?"

"I don't know."

"Come on. Let's go home," Ben said, and we both got back into our cars.

I pulled the car out into the street and rushed home, half expecting to find the baby dead, but when we got inside, she was still sleeping soundly, unaware that her mother had completely lost her mind.

11

It was no wonder motherhood was wearing on me. Taking care of a baby all day every day can be monotonous and isolating. It was everything my pre-baby life wasn't. I missed coffee shops and poetry readings, uninterrupted meals, and things like having free use of my arms.

Whoever invented the BabyBjörn, though, should be awarded a Nobel Peace Prize. I could almost use my arms all the way when I was wearing it, and Em loved it because she could hang out and see things other than carpet. A few times I even managed to muster enough courage to take her to Target with me in the Björn, and I found myself wandering the aisles almost nostalgically, touching the items and wondering what I might have purchased if I had disposable income and actual places to go.

I took walks though, short ones usually. They weren't enough to make a dent in the baby weight, but Em could at least temporarily deal with the stroller without completely losing her shit, so we'd take the SnugRider hot-rodding around the block once or twice a day.

For the past twenty years, every place I'd lived was literally a block or less away from a church, and my new house was no different. The Catholic church I'd passed when I tried to run away in the middle of that dark winter night was pretty much in my backyard. I could see its roof through my screened-in porch.

The church was an orange eyesore, a monument to everything

that was hideous about 1960s architecture. It was so ugly, it was near offensive, but since it was close, I passed it on my daily walks. Built onto the church's back wall, facing the parking lot, was a small grotto with a fountain. Made from white rocks and landscaped with rangy-looking poinsettias, the grotto was decidedly tacky, but I was into it because of the waterfall. I was a sucker for any kind of water feature, and there was a small stone bench where I could take a load off in front of the chlorine-scented pond. At the top of the waterfall, there was a pile of shiny ivory-colored stones, and on top of that stood a statue of the Virgin Mary. She was painted in vivid colors, and at her feet kneeled a statue of a little girl (Saint Bernadette of Lourdes, I guessed), and both of them were strung with real rosaries and bestowed with wilting plastic-wrapped bouquets of carnations from Winn-Dixie. The whole thing was sort of obnoxious to behold, but it was cool in an almost John Waters kind of way—I could appreciate its kitschiness. It made me feel better, and Lord knows not much else could have made me feel worse.

Heartache is a real thing. It's not a metaphor or a term saved for shitty poetry, but I never knew that until I felt it in my body. I'd been sad before: lonely, scared . . . depressed, too. I'd known plenty of regrets and failures, but I had never felt anything this dark and heavy pressing into my chest. Every cliché about sorrow is true. You really do feel like you're drowning.

Once, when I was a scrawny twelve-year-old, I'd been sucked into the undertow of an enormous wave while enjoying a day at the beach in Ocean City, Maryland. I'd been utterly powerless against its force, and as the wave dragged me, turned me inside out, and held me down, I'd thought, *Okay, this is it. I'm going to die before I even get my period.*

But someone saved me. I don't know who. It was a stranger who yanked me out by the strap of my bathing suit and flung me onto the muddy shore, where some kids were digging sand crabs and building a drip castle. I crouched on my hands and knees, gasping like a castaway, looking around for my mother, my grandfather—any familiar face—but no one had noticed I was missing or that I'd almost died. They were eating fried chicken, sitting in their beach chairs, oblivious.

Twenty-four years later, I was being dragged out again and held under. I was suffocating while, all around me, no one paid attention or really cared. They were all busy, their hands buried in buckets of gristle and grease.

Sure, I'd tried to talk about it and ask for help, but no one understood, not even my OB or my daughter's pediatrician. Both doctors had me fill out questionnaires about my state of mind. I'd been brutally honest, asked for assistance, but neither doctor followed up or mentioned my answers. Filling them out had been pointless. Did I need to be hallucinating, to see satanic glow-in-the-dark wolverines barking at me from the crisper drawer of my refrigerator before someone recognized I needed help or what?

My family told me to get over myself. They rehashed the same old examples, citing people in third-world countries and how they had it worse. If I tried to vent to Mom, she'd bring up her own pregnancy and say that at least I wasn't eighteen and living in a trailer with an abusive husband. Each cry for help was met with a guilt trip, because new mothers aren't *supposed* to be depressed. Motherhood is bliss and something women should delight in and be thankful for. Women were *made* to do this, after all, so the ones who struggle with it must be defective or selfish or spoiled.

I heard that because I was depressed I was a bad person. Because I pined for an hour alone in a Starbucks, just so I could savor a cinnamon dolce latte in a big soft chair without being puked on, people treated me as if I may as well have been Jeffrey Dahmer. If I wanted to see a movie, take a hot bath, and sleep all night without interruption, I was a narcissist, and my inability to snap out of it was going to destroy Em's life. Everyone I knew believed depression was a choice, and if I really wanted to, I could "choose" to be happy—that I *would*, in fact, "choose" to be happy if I really loved my baby.

So I shut up, even though this was bullshit, which was why I liked the Blessed Virgin: I could pour my heart out to her, and she couldn't respond.

It was late afternoon, probably the end of April, maybe the first week of May. I'd lost track because I didn't have a calendar or need one anymore, since every day felt exactly the same. I'd walked Em to my parents' house so I could snag some leftover lasagna, and both Mom and Joel were home, which was odd because Joel had been traveling a lot to L.A. and London and Panama, and God only knows what for. When he wasn't away on business, he usually spent most of his days out and about.

Ashley was there that day too. She and Andrew and their four-month-old daughter, Amelia, had recently moved in with my parents. The first week they were there, Ashley had told me she didn't know if she was going to survive living under their roof as an adult with a family. Her new house, right next door to mine, was being renovated and, unfortunately, the lease on her apartment had run out before the remodel was complete. Since her landlord wouldn't renew on a month-to-month basis, she, Andrew, and the baby were temporary residents at Casa dei Sogni, just like Ben and I had been.

"It's worth it, and then we'll be neighbors!" I squealed when Ashley told me.

Ashley nodded. I thought her smile looked a little forced, but I hoped she was just as excited as I was.

The house beside mine had been vacant for months. Prior to that, an old lady named Reba had lived there for almost fifty years, but Reba's family had stepped in that fall and moved her to a nursing home, and before they could even list the place, Joel had finagled a deal that allowed Ashley and Andrew to buy it. Their beachfront studio apartment had been too cramped for the baby, and now, to Mom's delight, the entire family would be in the same neighborhood and within walking distance of one an-other's homes.

Living with our parents had gone more smoothly than Ashley initially thought it would, and she was in good spirits the day I went over there for lasagna. Her house was almost ready, and she genuinely seemed to love taking care of her baby. Though I was happy for her, her apparent ease at transitioning from bartender to mommy made everything harder for me. There's nothing like some sibling rivalry to really kick up your postpartum depression.

From the moment she went into labor, Ashley had taken moth-erhood in stride. I'll never forget the day my niece was born. Ashley had been induced in the evening, just like I'd been. Since I was up every two hours nursing Em, who was six weeks old at the time, Ashley and I texted all night long as her labor progressed easily. It went so well, she was able to have Mom and Joel at the hospital in time for the birth. Mom even got her lifelong wish to be present for the moment the baby slipped into the world. That was when things got complicated, though.

Ashley had sailed through labor and delivery like an athlete. She had no complications—it was like she was born to have kids or something. But her baby, Amelia, tested positive for a danger-ous strep infection and was rushed to the NICU, where she stayed for the next two weeks. Everyone was worried. Amelia was hooked up to IVs and monitors, stuck with needles, and heavily dosed with antibiotics, yet Ashley seemed unfazed. It had to have been heartbreaking for her to leave the hospital empty-handed, and even worse to see her daughter struggling in an incubator—Amelia stopped breathing twice—but Ashley remained stoic throughout the ordeal. Dutifully, she spent her first two weeks postpartum traveling back and forth between her apartment and the hospital, pumping breast milk and following the doctor's orders to the letter. She never cracked once, whereas, if I had been in the same situation, I would have been a mental case.

It wasn't just our birth stories that differed dramatically. As a mom, Ashley was a total overachiever, while I felt like I'd failed a remedial parenting class. For instance, I'd buy a jar of Earth's Best, and be all proud of myself for feeding Em healthy baby food, and the next day Ashley would show me up by hand-milling organic butternut squash she'd roasted herself. If I asked Joel to install Em's car seat in his Bentley, I'd soon see Ashley outside making car seat installation—which I'm positive requires an advanced engineering degree to master—look simple. She could break down strollers with the flick of a wrist, fold laundry while effortlessly pumping breast milk, and had a baby who slept all night. Em, on the other hand, seemed to be competing for the world record for the longest hours a baby has ever stayed awake.

While I didn't even know what month it was, Ashley adhered to a schedule. She took Amelia everywhere, without experiencing crippling anxiety, and she proudly breastfed in public. But me? I had fuzz balls all over my floors, I forgot to pack diapers and wipes on the rare occasions I left the house, and I avoided going anywhere in part because breastfeeding in public skeezed me out. Breastfeeding was natural and beautiful, just not when I did it.

Ashley's triumphs highlighted my failures. At the root of it all was the sad realization that I was trying to compete with my sister. Parenting wasn't supposed to be a contest, but I was jealous that becoming a mother had given Ashley a purpose and an identity. For me, it felt more like motherhood had robbed me of who I was and the work I loved.

During lunch, Mom and Joel praised Ashley and ignored me, or at least it seemed that way. After we finished eating, I handed Em over to Joel so I could go to the bathroom, and Mom disappeared into her office to play video games. She'd been doing this a lot lately. Before her arrest, she'd spent hours glued to her desk chair, obsessively watching Alphatrade and cheering when the prices of the stocks she promoted soared. She reminded me of a football fan, sometimes even jumping out of her seat to cheer when her "team" scored, but she couldn't do that anymore. One of the conditions of her bond was that she couldn't work, so instead she played online word games with strangers.

From the bathroom I heard Em scream. It was a real scream, high-pitched and urgent. I'd heard her make this noise once before, when an ant had bitten her, and I knew immediately it was a sound she only made when she was hurt. There is no worse sound than a baby in pain. I couldn't get to her fast enough—all I wanted was to save my child from whatever was hurting her.

Em's foot was caught in the bouncy seat. I thought she was too little for the stupid thing—she was barely six months old—but my parents insisted it was adorable and that babies loved them. I'd relented, because it gave me something to put Em in while I choked down a meal faster than Takeru Kobayashi.

Joel was trying to untangle her, and had twisted her ankle at an unnatural angle, causing her screams to escalate. For me, the sound was unbearable.

"Stop it!" I yelled. "Get your hands off her!"

I pushed him out of the way, which pissed him off. Mom heard the ruckus and, by the time she came running in, I was near hysterics, trying to get Em out of the seat.

"Calm down," Ashley scolded.

"Victoria, what the hell is your problem?" Joel said.

"Did you just push your father?" Mom asked. Now she was pissed too.

"He was hurting her!" I protested.

"He would never hurt that baby! Are you crazy? Is this more of your drama?" Mom argued.

"She's being ridiculous," Ashley said. "And stop yelling around my child, please."

I turned on Ashley then. "You know what? Go fuck yourself. You think you're so perfect? How would you feel if *your* baby were screaming in pain?"

"More drama. Just ignore her. She does this for attention," Joel said, rolling his eyes at Ashley and dismissing me.

I swept Em out of the bouncer and hastily strapped her into the Bjorn, completely forgetting I had the stroller with me, and stormed out of the house. I didn't know where to go, so I walked to the church, which wasn't exactly easy. It was ninety degrees and humid, and I was crying hysterically, my baby strapped to me like we were about to hurl ourselves out of a puddle jumper at ten thousand feet.

I hadn't gone there to pray or to have a religious experience or anything of the sort. I went to the grotto to sit in a quiet spot near the water so I could calm down, but something came over me when I looked up at the statue of poor, orange-faced Mary in her electric-blue gown.

Sometimes, when we've lost our faith entirely, we just need a little visual to remind us that something greater is still out there in the universe, rooting for our team. That was what the Mary statue was to me—a stand-in for the spirit of all the struggling moms throughout time, and dammit, she *got* me. Somehow I knew she had my back.

I sobbed so hard to that statue, I almost threw up. Not that that was unusual lately. I cried constantly: when nursing, when not nursing, in the shower, on the toilet, with the baby. I even learned to cry silently so I wouldn't scare her.

I cried because I had disappointed everyone I loved, and I cried because I felt defective as a woman. Because I would rather be sitting alone on the floor of a bookstore, flipping through essay anthologies, than singing "The Wheels on the Bus" at tummy time. I cried some more. The night before, I'd attempted to make homemade macaroni and cheese and had a meltdown when I spilled olive oil all over the kitchen floor, and although I had already cried about that, I decided to cry about it again because it had been so aggravating and upsetting to clean and because, at the end of it all, Ben had asked me why I didn't use the truffle oil when I knew how much he loved it. And then I cried because I had thrown the remote in anger and it had hit him in the head, and although I sincerely swear to God I hadn't meant to hit him, I was secretly sort of glad I had, and took this as further proof that I was a shit person.

The Virgin Mary didn't judge me or bitch me out or tell me to quit whining. She listened silently and waited patiently until I was done. I tried to genuflect, but since I wasn't Catholic, I think I may have done it backward. Plus I still had a baby harnessed to my chest.

"Thank you," I whispered to the statue as I turned to walk back home.

"Wait."

I looked around, startled.

The voice was coming from inside my head. It was calm and gentle and reminded me of my two greatest gifts—Em and writing—and that I was not alone. I realized somehow that my daughter had come to me *not* at the worst possible time, but at the exact *right* time, when I most needed her, and she had come to help me. What Sia said had been true after all. Things were hard and scary for the time being, and they would be that way for a while longer, but not forever. I'd felt trapped and had wanted someone to give me the key to get out, but I already had it.

By the time we got home, Em had miraculously fallen asleep. I went on the Internet, something that seemed utterly indulgent at the time, and the first thing I saw was a Mother's Day essay contest in our local paper. It definitely wasn't the National Book Award—write 250 words about your special memories of mom and win a hundred-dollar gift card to Red Lobster—but I entered it, and decided to win.

12

Take Mom to Dinner! Share Your Favorite Mom Story! the contest ad read. Except for the Cheddar Bay Biscuits, channeling my competitive urges toward a group of local writers who all wanted a hundred-dollar gift certificate to Red Lobster seemed healthier than directing them at my sister.

Lord knows, I had plenty of favorite stories about my mom. Most of them weren't fit to print, but I also had stories of her amazing generosity and kindness. They were stories that needed to be shared, especially now, when the papers were writing about how she supposedly illegally manipulated stock prices. And I wanted to be able to take *her* out for once, to tell her, *This one's on me, Mom. Order whatever you like.*

Deciding on the perfect story had been easy. When my parents married, they were so in love, it didn't matter that Joel couldn't afford an engagement ring, but he promised her anyway: one day he'd make it big and get her the rock she dreamed of. We weren't rich when I was a kid—not usually, anyway—and when we had money, my mother always spent it on me and Ashley. She made sure we had the most important thing to her—the education she never got. We went to private schools and made fun of my mother's home perms, ugly sneakers, and sweat suits, never realizing she went without so we could learn from the best.

Joel finally got her the real diamond ring she'd always wanted when I was seventeen, and Mom flashed it proudly. That was right when I got into my dream college, and when I got the news we couldn't afford the tuition, I was devastated.

We tried everything to figure out how to pay. A few days later Mom came to me.

"You're going to that school," she told me.

I didn't understand how we'd found the money until I saw her bare ring finger.

"Your education is more important than a piece of jewelry," she said.

Since the entries had to be short, mine didn't tell the whole story. For Mother's Day, I focused on the nice part of what happened—what my mother was willing to do so I could have the education she didn't get. I left out the part about how I squandered her sacrifice and royally messed up, setting off a chain of screw-ups that took me more than a decade to break.

As a high school dropout, I'd gotten my GED with a bunch of people from jail when I should have been starting twelfth grade with my friends. I did a semester of community college, took only the classes I liked, and then ran off to New York to live with my boyfriend. Yes, I was barely seventeen when I did that and, yes, for some reason Mom let me. I tried community college up there, taking art classes and withdrawing from math after only a couple of weeks. My boyfriend was an artist, and I wanted to be just like him. I was always good at drawing. I'd won a fire prevention poster contest in elementary school, after all. Things were fine until my boyfriend applied to an art school and was accepted. He was leaving for Boston, and I couldn't go along, while at the same time, all my friends who hadn't dropped out of high school were getting ready for college too. Most of them were headed to the Ivies, and I didn't want to be left behind like a loser. I wanted to be an artist and I wanted to have more than my GED, so I'd applied to Bennington College, an extremely small and extraordinarily expensive liberal arts college set in the idyllic Vermont countryside.

Bennington worked for me because it was beautiful and quirky. They didn't require SAT scores, barely wanted a transcript, and were more tolerant of things like GEDs and patchy high school records. They seemed to overlook the fact that I'd failed the tenth grade and had to attend summer school at an academy for disturbed teens.

Getting into Bennington was a huge deal for me. I was shocked they accepted me and saw it as my chance to redeem myself for all the things I'd messed up in high school. This time I'd study and do my work. I'd stay organized and not let my personal life interfere with academics. Better yet, I'd be only a three-hour bus ride from my boyfriend in Boston and all my friends in the Ivy Leagues. I felt like I was one of them again, not some trailer park, white trash dropout who'd shacked up with her boyfriend when she was a teenager.

Bennington, at the time, was the most expensive college in the country, and my mom had sold her ring so I could go there—and I went there for all of three and a half months.

The reasons why I dropped out were complicated, but the story of how I got there won the essay contest. Readers went wild and voted for my story so much, I crushed the competition. When I got the call from the paper, I packed Em up and raced over to my parents' to tell my mom the good news. We were going to Red Lobster!

But when I got there, Mom shushed me as soon as she opened the front door and then she gently pulled me into the house.

"What's going on?" I asked her.

"I need to talk to you about something," she whispered.

"What?" I asked. "You never said anything was going on when you called this morning!"

She said she couldn't talk about it over the phone. She'd been paranoid for years, and had always believed her phones were tapped. Ashley and I had discussed it countless times, and neither of us could decide if Mom was right or crazy. It could have easily gone both ways, but I guess she figured her backyard wasn't bugged, because she told me we had to talk about it on the dock. Whenever Mom wanted to talk about something important, she did it outside of the house.

"But wait, I have good news!" I interrupted.

"Just hold on a minute," Mom said.

She lit a cigarette right in front of me, since she'd given up trying to pretend she'd quit. She blamed it on stress.

"I think Allegra's working for the Feds," Mom said.

"What? Allegra?"

"I think she's an informant. I think they planted her here to watch me. Think about it."

"I *am* thinking about it," I said. "And I think it's pretty far-fetched, and I have no idea why you felt the need to drag me outside to tell me this."

"She was in some kind of trouble," Mom explained.

Allegra "Allie" Alonzo, one of Mom's best friends, was a tall blonde who drove an old Jag and never went anywhere without her fox terrier. She was thirty-nine, never married, had no children, and told us she was from Delaware, just like us, but I often said that if we'd told her we were from Nebraska, she probably would have said she was born in Omaha. I never knew her to date anyone, or if she did, it wasn't discussed, but her flamboyantly sexy (and expensive) dresses certainly advertised that she was available. And while Allie looked like your standard implanted, bedazzled South Florida gold digger, she really didn't fit the stereotype. Allie was one of the most creative people I'd ever met. She decorated and sewed, and her cooking was seriously unrivaled. Truth be told, I liked the girl a lot. I just didn't trust her and, apparently, neither did my mother.

Like Mom said, it was true that Allie had been in trouble, though we never knew exactly what had happened. Shortly after we'd met her, she'd disappeared for nearly a year. She'd returned with amazing tales about Dubai, where she'd supposedly been designing glitzy shopping malls and housing complexes for wealthy Europeans, but Ben heard about a group of scammers who were operating in the Middle East out of South Florida, and he put two and two together. We didn't have proof that Allie was involved, and our suspicions could just as easily have been a symptom of the paranoia that ran rampant in our household, but there was enough circumstantial evidence that even Mom thought it made sense.

According to news reports, the group set up fake corporations and made false claims that these companies had been the victims of other stock schemes. They'd file bogus class-action lawsuits, and they'd funnel the settlement money through accounts in places like Dubai, the UAE, and Qatar when they won. But they needed shills to set up the foreign accounts, and an attractive American in a low-cut Cavalli would have been the perfect plant. The ringleader of the group—who'd turned out to be as good at being an informant as he'd been at being a con—had been one of my parents' associates. They'd invited him to my wedding, though he'd politely declined and sent us a pricy Tiffany vase.

Allie had actually introduced my parents to several of the main players in this racket. Her motive could have been to lure them into another con job she could profit from, or she could have been working for the "good guys," setting up a sting operation to save her own ass—hell, maybe she had no motive at all and just thought they'd enjoy one another's company.

"I think she put bugs in the house," Mom continued. "Don't you think she spends an awful lot of time over here?"

"Well, might that be because you invite her? Or if you don't, you also don't tell her *not* to come. Your house is like Grand Central Crazy. You have people coming in and out all the time, and you never put a stop to it!"

"Look, just watch out. Don't say a word around her about anything. I don't care what it is. And I need to tell you something else," Mom added.

I waited. This had better be good, because I still hadn't gotten around to telling her about the essay contest.

"I got some inside scoop on Carmelo," Mom said.

"From where? Don't tell me it was from Ian Greenberg. You aren't supposed to be talking to anyone connected to your arrest, and you yourself told me just a couple of months ago that Ian was broke and working out a plea deal because he couldn't afford to defend himself! You can't trust him."

"It doesn't matter where I heard it from," she said.

We already knew that Carmelo had set Mom up via e-mails and a recorded phone conversation. That was where her conspiracy to commit wire fraud charges allegedly originated, but according to Mom's mysterious source, Carmelo, while wearing a wire, had intended to visit her in person the month before she was arrested.

But the sting hadn't happened. In the summer of 2010, right before Em was born, my parents had driven cross-country with Baron Von Bod in their RV. After years of pursuing his dream of becoming a real Hollywood producer, Joel had finally secured enough financing to make a movie. They had Ed Asner! Kelly Osborne! The girl from *Napoleon Dynamite*! Joel was in the big leagues now, at least in Mom's mind, and his indie romcom was going to be the next big thing. Hell, they'd probably win an Academy Award, so Mom was already picking out her gown.

Filming wrapped the week of Ashley's baby shower, which was to be held at Casa dei Sogni. Mom had planned to fly home for the party, but at the last minute she'd changed her plans. She claimed she couldn't abandon Joel on his big night. The cast would be toasting him at the wrap party; it would be a once-in-a-lifetime event, and his moment to finally shine. Ashley had been really upset because she felt that the baby shower was *her* once-in-a-lifetime event, so I'd called Mom in L.A. and begged for her to reconsider, but she wouldn't change her mind.

"I'm paying for it! Why do I need to be at the baby shower?" Mom had said.

She *had* paid for it, and Allegra and I had pulled together quite the fete, but Mom's absence had been palpable. People asked about it. We smiled and covered for her and talked about how proud we were of Joel's movie because that was what we knew we were supposed to do, but when the guests left and the cake was trashed and Mom wasn't there, Ashley's resentment lingered.

"She's only my mom when it's convenient for her or when it makes her look good," Ashley had said.

At the time I'd tried to convince Ashley that wasn't true, but now Mom was trying to make me believe divine intervention was responsible for her absence.

"So, I have some really great news!" I said, desperately hoping to change the subject.

"What?" Mom seemed disinterested, but I was sure when I told her she'd be delighted.

"I won!"

"Won what?" Mom's voice was dull.

"You know, the Mother's Day essay contest in the paper. I won! As in *me*. I won! Remember the story I wrote? About your ring?"

"Good! Congratulations! I knew you'd do it."

"And they're sending a reporter out to do a photo shoot with us, and we're going to be on the front page of the lifestyle section on Mother's Day! Plus we get a hundred-dollar gift card to Red Lobster!"

I couldn't conceal my excitement. This was going to be the best Mother's Day ever. Every year I agonized over what to get my mother because she truly had everything, and the things she valued, I couldn't afford anyway. I usually made her brunch, but this was going to be way better.

"Excuse me?" Mom said. She crossed her arms protectively over her chest and chewed her bottom lip.

"What?" I asked.

"No. No way. Absolutely not. You are *not* having reporters come to this house and put me in the newspaper."

"Why? What's the big deal?"

"What's the big deal? Are you crazy?" Mom was yelling now, and her hands shook as she fumbled to light another cigarette. Her thumb flicked and flicked at the lighter, but she couldn't get a flame.

"I can't be in a newspaper. *No way*," she said.

"But this is beautiful," I argued. "This is exactly the kind of press you need. It's positive. It shows what a good person you are. That you have a family who loves you. It'll be good for your case!"

"You can be in the damn paper if you want, but I can't. I know you're disappointed, and, Vic, I'm sorry, but I just can't do this for you right now."

Mom turned her back on me and walked inside.

I walked home and called the reporter back. Explaining that your mom is facing federal charges and flat out refuses to be featured in a fluffy personal interest story is never not awkward, but in the end, the paper agreed to run the story without my mother's name. They used an old black-and-white photo a friend had taken of her in which my mom was unrecognizable.

After I hung up the phone, I broke three dessert plates into my kitchen sink. I would have smashed all of them, but a shred of my sanity remained, and that tiny bit of good sense told me that dragging Em out to IKEA to buy a new set of plates would be a hassle, so I broke and rebroke the same pieces of glass until I cut my finger. As I bandaged my pinkie, I sighed. Breaking the plates seemed satisfying in the moment, but now I had a mess to clean up, not to mention an injury, and my disappointment and frustration remained.

13

On Em's first birthday, Ben and I took her outside to see her straw-berry tree. Neither the tree nor the baby was recognizable com-pared with the year before. Em had come into the world yellow and scrunched, a lazy nurser who'd lost an alarming amount of weight in her first two weeks of life, and I spent the first year of her life terrified of falling asleep. I thought if I took my eyes off her for a second, she would stop breathing.

But Em had proven to be a lot more resilient than I'd realized. Now she could walk. And climb and run and get herself stuck under her crib. She'd developed opinions on things. She liked to explore and to see, to pull the cat's tail and grab chunks of its fur, which were apparently delicious. She'd dance to any kind of music. Em was a sturdy girl now. She was still pretty much bald, but with huge brown eyes and rosy round cheeks, squishy legs, and a scrumptious little butt the size of a hamburger bun. We hadn't quite come to an agreement about sleeping through the night, but we'd called something of a truce over naps. Not that it even mattered anymore. I loved her to absolute pieces.

Our tree, which had started out as an unpromising twig, was now as tall as our one-story roof. The tree had accomplished in twelve short months what I had assumed would take years, and perhaps we should have done our research better, because the strawberry tree is one of the world's fastest growing. A lot of times that first year, when things had been so hard and felt so bleak and it seemed like nothing could grow, I would look at that tree and my child, both of them thriving beyond measure, and wonder, *How in the hell?* And seeing them both keeping on gave me the strength to keep on too, because if a helpless infant and a pitiful stick could make it in this world, then dammit, so could I.

We'd had a small party in our backyard the weekend before Em's birthday. Ashley and Andrew had moved in next door at the beginning of the summer, so now we had a huge, shared back-yard with plenty of room to spread out on the fresh sod. We had gotten Em a banana cake to smash and a red wagon we could pull her around in. The weather had cooperated, and we'd been blessed with a rare mild and dry day. I'd been gifted with an equally rare sense of wholeness.

I sat in the perfect grass of my finished and finally manicured backyard, laughing so hard as Mom and Joel pulled Em and her (now fully recovered and also thriving) cousin Amelia in the wagon, I spilled Diet Coke on my gray sundress. Joel looked pre-dictably dapper that day in pastel linen and suede Louis loafers, and Mom was elegant in a chic black ensemble from Chico's. Joel carried a glass of California Pinot Noir in one hand while Mom enjoyed a bottle of Corona, and when Joel splashed wine on his Bermudas, Mom was ready with the Wine Out she'd unearthed from her enormous fake Chanel bag. They looked so . . . normal. Okay, maybe not *normal*, maybe a little fancier than your tradi-tional grandparents, with their blinged-out watches and sunglasses and Mom's Marilyn Monroe makeup, but still. They looked happy and right and in love—not just with each other, but with life—and for a second I felt like that too.

I love these people, I thought to myself. In spite of everything, I love these crazy-assed fools and for once, for this short, sweet evening, I have the peace of not having to question that.

The tranquility and mild weather had lasted all week, so on Em's actual birthday, when we took her outside, we were able to enjoy yet another blissful evening. She toddled around in the grass behind us, while Ben and I led her to the side yard to see the strawberry tree. As she explored the landscaping, stooping to examine rocks and reaching for white cabbage moths that fluttered past, she sang and mumbled to herself in her own little language.

"Look at your tree, baby girl!" I said.

Ben lifted Em so she could smell the sweet blossoms that laced the strawberry tree. She shook the branches and white petals flurried down around us. She thought that was hilarious, and oh my God, the laugh of this little one almost brought me to my knees with gratitude. We'd kept her alive for a year, and she was happy, strong, well, and overflowing with life. She even had a sense of humor.

"Bia!" she yelled.

That was her word for *berry*.

"Bia!" Em insisted, until I picked handfuls of the tree's pink pearly berries, which we proceeded to stuff into our mouths. They really did taste like cotton candy.

Out of everyone in my family, I was the only one who listened to the weather reports, so I knew we were in for a storm. Downpours, thunder and wind, days of lightning, and even floods were expected straight up until Halloween. Trick or treat might be canceled, but that was fine because Em was too little anyway, although Allegra had sewed her the perfect monkey costume just for fun. I could see the dark clouds advancing from the west out past the Intracoastal, and over the tin roofs of the Key West–style mansions that edged the waterway. The dark days were coming.

"We better get inside. Getting ready to storm," I told Ben.

"It's beautiful out," he protested.

"Not for long," I said.

I wondered why it seemed like I was the only one who could hear the thunder.

14

The Eyebrow People showed up around Thanksgiving. That was what Ashley and I called them, among ourselves, of course. If we'd called them the Eyebrow People to their faces, they probably would've kicked our butts—Mom would have anyway, because she loved them like family.

The first time my parents rolled up in their RV with them, I almost passed out. It had been a couple of years earlier, and Joel and Mom had been gone for several months. They'd been traversing the country in the bus—visiting friends, relatives, partners, and clients, and when they returned, it seemed they'd picked up some unusual passengers.

The Eyebrow People were comprised of two couples—Darryl and Jasmine and Kenny and Lena. They were in their mid-twenties, basically just kids. Why were my middle-aged parents suddenly hanging out with kids younger than Ashley and I were? I wondered. And, even weirder, how could they call them their best friends?

Darryl and Jasmine had been married a year earlier at a lavish wedding in the Bahamas. Joel had attended, but my mother, having just been arrested, had to surrender her passport and couldn't leave the country. Mom was pretty bummed about it: the event had been organized by a famous wedding planner with a fairly popular reality show and was rumored to have had a three-hundred-thousand-dollar budget. One might wonder how two kids in their twenties could afford such a shindig. Did they come from wealthy families? Anything but. Darryl had made millions promoting penny stocks. He was the mastermind, while Kenny seemed like more of a lackey—the fat, doofy sidekick.

Mom had raved that Darryl was a genius when I dared to ask why she decided to bring them home with her.

"At what?" I'd asked. "Looking like a fucking moron?"

"Making money. The kid is brilliant. I've never seen anything like him. The focus he has. The dedication and organization. He's absolutely mind-blowing. You should see him work," Mom gushed.

"I have a bad gut feeling about him," I told her.

"You don't like the way he looks, is all. But you have to understand how he was raised. He didn't have it good like you and Ashley did. His parents had nothing. He had to scrape his way to the top. How many times have I told you, Vic? Don't judge people by how they look or where they come from."

But how could I not judge them for how they looked? Darryl and Kenny were obsessed with shaving designs into their body hair. They'd cut elaborate pointed swirls and flames, stars and lines, and sometimes lightning bolts into their scalps until their heads looked like geometry textbooks. They styled their eyebrows and beards the same way, which was appalling, and I often wondered what they did with their pubic regions, but I didn't think I could handle the truth. Apparently, this style—at least according to Mom—was popular where Darryl and Kenny came from in Upstate New York. I'd seen pictures from the wedding, and every single guy in attendance subscribed to this trend, so maybe she was right.

For the past few years, the Eyebrow People had been making mysterious appearances at Casa dei Sogni with little warning and often in the middle of the night. When they came, they would stay for days or weeks at a time and then leave as quickly and mysteriously as they'd arrived, and it was these people who first cemented my distrust for Baron Von Bod.

It had happened when Baron was still Skip, back when he was a golden retriever of a guy—nice, happy-go-lucky, a little goofy, and very enthusiastic about his recovery from addiction. I liked Skip for his cheerful, generous nature. I liked that at my parents' lavish parties, he was the only person besides me who stayed sober, and I was grateful to him when, one time, he stepped in and tried to intervene in a family emergency. That was why I wanted to do him a favor.

We were packing the RV for another one of my parents' trips across the country. Skip was going with—partly because my parents had recently set him up with a beautiful heiress they knew in Beverly Hills—but also because this trip was about business, and Skip was learning the ropes of stock promotion. The Eyebrow People had left a couple of days earlier after an extended stay at my parents' house, and like a puppy dog, Skip had latched on to Darryl. He couldn't stop talking about him, and his adoration made my mom's admiration for Darryl look mild.

Skip and I were alone in the RV. I was stocking groceries in the RV's fridge while Skip carried in racks of my mother's clothes. Mom and Joel were still in the house, so I took the opportunity to warn Skip.

"Skip, I'm so thankful for what you did for our family that time . . . ," I began. "But I need to warn you. Stay away from Darryl. This guy is big-time bad news. I have a terrible feeling about him. I never liked him, and I think he's a criminal. You're a good person, and I don't want to see you get in trouble."

It was dim inside. The window shades were drawn, and my eyes hadn't adjusted from being outside in the sun. Skip turned around and leaned toward me. He was enormous, but he'd always carried himself in a way that made him seem sort of unassuming. But now his intimidating posture made him seem huge and looming. His chiseled jaw was clenched, and his eyes narrowed. Shadows flickered across his strong features. He brushed one of his long curls off his face and squinted at me silently, nodding slowly, staring at me for an uncomfortably long time.

"Oh yeah?" Skip finally said. "Well, I never liked *you*."

"What?" I said. I was actually startled by this revelation.

"You're a stuck-up little know-it-all. Miss College. You think you're better than Darryl? Let me ask you something," Skip said.

"Fine, ask away," I challenged him.

"How much money do you make? What about your husband? How much does *he* make?" Skip asked.

"None of your business, but I make enough to live on and so does Ben and we're happy," I answered.

"Well, Darryl? This kid who came from nothing? He's a fucking millionaire. So who do you think is smarter now? Someone who came from nothing and managed to make millions overnight, or some spoiled, ungrateful brat who relies on Mommy and Daddy to pay all her bills so she can play around in school and write stories? By the way"—he laughed—"what have you had published?"

"I can't even believe you just said that. You, a person who's been living in my parents' house for free for the past year? Look, I was trying to be nice. I told you I liked you and I was looking out for you and you want to fucking insult me? I know what you do back there in your bedroom," I yelled, even though I didn't know for sure. "All of a sudden you're set up with three computers. I saw the Alphatrade screen. See how far this gets you," I told him. I was so mad, I was shaking.

"You have no clue what I'm doing. No proof whatsoever. Cute shoes, by the way. Who bought those for you? Dinner at the Capital Grille last night? Who paid for that? I never saw you or Ben reach for your wallets. You say you have a problem with Darryl, but you don't seem to have a problem accepting the money your parents make from him, do you? How about this? You can criticize Darryl when you give up your Coach bags and the Tory Burch shoes your mom buys you."

"Like I said, Skip. See where you end up one day," I said.

But now, a few years later with another hectic holiday season before us, it was Skip who was having the last laugh, at least for the time being. Skip was sitting in high cotton. He was Baron Von Bod now. He really *did* score his own reality show: *Stud Muffins*. It had premiered last spring. My parents had hosted a party in his honor, which I hadn't attended, not being all that interested in watching male prostitutes bang porn stars pretending to be lonely housewives. He bought a Range Rover and gloated about how he'd managed to go from homeless houseboy to D-list celebrity pimp in such a short time, so who was the smart one now?

Sorry, it was still me.

Still, a lot had changed in the past year, and this November people were asking for Baron's autograph at Thanksgiving dinner. We also now had Darryl, his eyebrows shaved into twin lightning bolts, carving our turkey.

Darryl and Jasmine didn't stick around long, though. They needed to skip town. You know, like *really* skip town, fugitive style—someplace where they could lie low from the Feds. Not that they'd been arrested or anything, yet, because they hadn't, of course, but just somewhere where they could stay safely under the radar. Another country.

Like Panama, at least until the Feds caught up with Darryl and extradited him to Buffalo a couple years later.

Casa dei Sogni was simply a pit stop on their convoluted journey to Central American freedom. They'd devised an elaborate plan to journey from Fort Lauderdale to Panama, where I guessed they meant to stay permanently. I wondered about this elaborate plan. It seemed unnecessary and pointless. Masquerading as ordinary tourists, Darryl and Jasmine—sans Kenny and Lena, who were staying in the United States because of Lena's kids—left on a cruise. Once the ship sailed to Panama, it would continue on through the Panama Canal, but it would do so without Jasmine and Darryl. They'd take a shore excursion, claim Jasmine was pregnant and ill (she was not), and tell the ship's directors that they needed to fly back to the United States. Except they weren't going anywhere, because Panama City would be their new home. Joel would fly down to meet them as soon as they got there, because apparently, he had some unrelated business to attend to anyway, and he'd help them get set up in a cushy apartment building, which they were excited about because they'd heard Trump had a tower there too. Why they didn't simply book a one-way flight, I'd never know.

"This seems far-fetched," I mentioned to my mother.

"It's brilliant. It's a foolproof plan," she said.

What is it that they say about the best-laid plans? Oh right. *They often go awry.*

15

If you looked in the windows of my parents' house a few days before Christmas 2011, you would have encountered a scene of near Christmas card perfection—a sort of Currier and Ives meets Donatella Versace, awash with glitter and leopard print, but glorious nonetheless. A magnificent twelve-foot Christmas tree twinkled; its branches laden with hundreds of ornaments until it gleamed like a Miss Universe contestant. Prelit pine boughs wove through every ornate wrought-iron railing. There were wreaths on every door (all twenty of them) and a three-foot velvet-clad Santa greeted guests in the entry. Em, now an adorable, fourteen-month-old toddler in red plaid, sat in a high chair, gnawing with glee on a lemon shortbread cookie. Yet, in the midst of all this pimped-out Christmas swag, we were totally freaking out.

My mom and I leaned against the kitchen island for support. Allie sat on the counter by the espresso machine, wearing a micromini and thigh-high patent leather boots. None of us had any idea what the fuck we were going to do.

"I don't know," Mom said. "Maybe we should cancel Christmas?"

"You can't cancel Christmas!" Allie shouted.

"I don't want all these damn people coming. I can't do it this year. Not now," Mom lamented. She rubbed her forehead, pushed her nose toward her chin, and asked Allie to make her a vodka cranberry.

Joel was in jail. No one had seen it coming. A yearlong investigation, which had begun after my mother's arrest, had resulted in a superseding indictment, wherein Joel had been added to my mother's case as a codefendant. His tally of charges was as long as Santa's naughty list, and the Feds had picked him up at Fort Lauderdale–Hollywood International Airport on his way home from Panama. We were waiting for him to be booked and hopefully bonded out of the Broward County Jail in time for Christmas.

"We still have a few days. You were in and out in an afternoon," I reminded her.

"He's got to get in front of a federal judge," Mom said. "I got lucky. This is the holidays. People at the courthouse are on vacation. Plus he was coming in from another country, and his charges are worse than mine. Money laundering! It's a shit show."

She turned to me and asked if I had called Ashley.

"She's packing," I said.

Ashley wouldn't be home for Christmas that year. She was spending the holidays in the Carolinas with her in-laws, and Mom had been pissed about it.

"Your father's in jail, and she's still going on vacation?" Mom said.

I shrugged. "It was planned for weeks."

"Focus!" Allie yelled from the bar, but we ignored her. Her heels clicked across the travertine as she delivered my mother's cocktail.

"Call everyone and tell them I'm canceling," Mom said. She took a long swig of her drink and asked for more vodka.

"Stop it! That's from Pottery Barn!" Allie said, swatting my hand away from a bunch of artificial grapes. I'd been absently picking the purple glitter off them.

"I can't get in the Christmas spirit. I can't do it," Mom cried.

"That's insane, Cecily, of course you can. Joel's going to be out any minute. This isn't a big deal," Allie said.

"We can make cookies?" I suggested. I immediately ran to the fridge and took out a carton of eggs and two sticks of butter. "Put on some Christmas music too!" I added.

"I have a better idea," Allie said. "I know what your mom really needs."

"What?" my mother said.

"We're going to the mall, then we'll go to that new bar Olive Juice and have martinis! Victoria, you stay here and hold down the fort since it's too late for Em to be out."

When the going gets tough, the tough go shopping.

In seconds they were slinging oversize purses over their shoulders, swinging the car keys from their red manicured nails, and heading out the door.

I was alone again, just me and Em with Burl Ives demanding that I "have a holly jolly Christmas." Whatever, Burl. Ben had worked late that night and proceeded to get stuck in holiday traffic, so I stayed at my parents' house long past Em's bedtime. I had nothing to do, and a Christmas to save, so I made batch after batch of cookies—chocolate chip, oatmeal, peanut butter, jam thumbprint—to keep myself busy, and my mind off Joel's arrest. By the time I stopped, it was almost eleven, Em was fast asleep in her play yard, and Mom and Allie still weren't back.

Joel got out the next day. Mom and Baron picked him up. Later my mom would brag on Facebook about the marvelous Italian lunch she shared with her husband. She'd update her status, saying how her day had *started out shitty but ended fabulously*, which it had. After lunch Mom, Baron, and Joel did some more shopping, and Joel insisted on stopping at the butcher to pick up a prime rib of beef so enormous it had cost him nearly five hundred dollars. From there they headed over to the seafood market for a bounty of lobsters, jumbo shrimp, calamari, mussels, clams, and scallops.

By the time they got back that evening, the house was already filled with people awaiting Joel's return. Ben and I were there, along with an assortment of friends and neighbors and a few family members who were in from out of town. It was the usual chaos—the dogs were going nuts, and Em was trying to pull all the low ornaments off the tree. The stereo was blaring, and when Joel walked in the door, "I Love Rock 'n' Roll" started playing. It was like we were in a movie, and Joan Jett was providing the soundtrack. Joel barely looked tired. His face was red with excitement, and his grin widened when he heard the music. Right away he unloaded the parcel of prime rib onto the entryway sideboard and started clapping in time to the beat. Em ran up to him, and he swooped her into his arms and danced with her all the way into the kitchen, where he was met with a round of applause and a standing ovation.

A neighbor asked if he was okay, and pretty soon everyone rushed to hug him.

"I'm fine! Magnificent. I have never been better!" Joel reassured us. "This is all bullshit. They're just grappling for something to intimidate us, to get Cecily to take a plea deal because they have no case against her, and they know if they go to trial, they're going to fucking lose and look like the idiots they are. This is nothing! What are you waiting for? Let's get this party started!"

Someone whisked Em away from the mob and took her over to look at the Christmas decorations, while several arms stretched toward the wineglasses hanging over the bar. We lit candles, popped champagne corks, and Joel cranked the tunes up so loud, the windows quaked. He was in his element, reveling in all the attention, while Mom stared at him with doe eyes and an adoring smirk. She kept her arm hooked in his, never leaving his side, like she was posing for an awkward prom photo, the wallflower who'd miraculously managed to score the varsity captain as her date.

Tom Petty started to play, and Joel sang along to me. "'Oh my, my, oh hell yes. Honey, put on that party dress.' Look at you in jeans and a T-shirt during a celebration like this! Leave the baby here with me while you go home and get dressed. Put some lipstick on! Wear the Chanel shoes I bought you," he said.

He gave me a playful smack on the ass, and I feigned annoyance and stuffed a cookie into his mouth.

And then I heard the old familiar guitar riff that always made me smile involuntarily. When Joe Walsh started singing his wry, funny lyrics about the rock-star lifestyle, that was our cue to join in. We'd jammed to this song many a time: Joel, Mom, Ashley, and I. It was our family anthem: *Life's been good to me so far.* We all knew the words. We stood in the kitchen around the massive island, arms around one another's shoulders, and the group swayed and shuffled and became a freaky glee club, brought together by wine, song, Christmas cheer, and charges of stock fraud and money laundering. Joel belted out the lead vocals while everyone else sang along.

"'They say I'm crazy but I have a good time!'" he shouted.

"'I'm just looking for clues at the scene of the crime,'" I replied. My pitch was perfect.

PART 2

16

They were watching us. They had been for a long time, of course, but now they made it obvious, sitting for hours across the street from my parents' house, in unmarked cars with heavily tinted windows. They'd called Mom and Joel's business associates too, demanding answers, and one beautiful Sunday morning in the early spring of 2012, they even showed up in a helicopter.

My parents, Ashley, and I had been relaxing, sitting with big cups of Italian coffee on the back porch, while Em and Amelia played on the marble terrace at our feet. We were enjoying the warm dry weather before the muggy misery of the rainy season set in, when our peaceful reverie was interrupted. Helicopters were common in the area. When you live on the beach, you see them zipping up and down the coast several times a day, but this one was closer, louder, and more threatening.

"What *is* that?" I asked. I sat straight up in the soft love seat where I'd been lounging, and Em ran to me, calling, "Mama! Mama!" her little brow furrowed in concern. I covered her ears because, like me, she was sensitive to loud noises.

"Joyride," Joel mumbled, not even looking up from his phone. He was texting someone, like always.

Mom slid her reading glasses down her nose and looked out over their frames. Tentatively, she got up and walked across the patio and onto the dock. The dogs followed her, jumping and yapping. She looked around, confused, and then with a sudden realization, she looked up. When she saw the copter directly above, beginning a careful descent over the canal, she booked it, heading right for the house. She nearly slipped on the marble patio, but recovered and kept running, leaving one bedazzled flip-flop behind like Cinderella.

"Grab the babies and get inside!" she yelled.

My heart seized. I couldn't breathe or think or move. Were they coming for us again? What did they want?

The black helicopter circled the house. It was so close, the rotors whipped up the grass, swirled tornadoes of leaves into the pool, and blew the powdered sugar off a plate of French pastries that sat on the patio table. They remained untouched.

Those motherfuckers, I thought. They were taking pictures of us, and I wish I'd had the balls to flip them off. Some agent was leaning out of the chopper, and I imagined him laughing his ass off at us while he snapped away with his long-range lens at my parents' obvious life of luxury. Later these photos would be used during the trial to appeal to the jury's sense of envy, to make them say, *Look at these greedy pieces of shit. Of course they're guilty, living like that.*

Finally, with a whoosh and a roar, the chopper ascended again. It rose above the palms, whipping their fronds into a frenzy, and then hung a sharp right and swung out of sight like an enormous mechanical dragonfly. As quickly as it came, it was gone.

We were all shaken, Mom especially. Joel just laughed at us as usual.

"Don't you see? This is intimidation, nothing more. Cecily! They have *no case.* This is what they do to scare you into making a plea deal when they know they can't win. They're shitting their pants because I have Shargel," he said.

He was referring to his new lawyer. Brad Cohen had been convenient and efficient in the beginning, but for whatever reason, he was now off the case, and Joel had secured Gerald Shargel, who had made his name for having once gotten John Gotti acquitted of murder. Joel's logic was that if this hotshot attorney could beat a mafia murder charge, then piddly nonsense like manipulating stock prices and money laundering would be a sure win. But even Mike Tyson lost a match once in a while, didn't he?

Mom apparently had her own celebrity lawyer, or at least he was close to it. I remembered Joel's excitement a year earlier when he told me. I'd been having one of my usual meltdowns, and in the middle of it I'd cried that I couldn't manage taking care of Em if Mom went to jail. Joel told me not to worry.

"Don't you know the news?" he said. "The Apprentice is off the case, and now we have Roy Black. *Black Magic.* Do you know who this man is? Have you seen him on TV? He got that Kennedy kid off. Rush Limbaugh. O. J. Freaking Simpson—"

"No," I interrupted. "O. J. had Dershowitz and Kardashian."

Joel ignored me. "Let me ask you one question."

"What?"

"Did your mother stab two people in cold blood?"

"What? No. What are you talking about?"

"Exactly." Joel clapped his hands. "Boom. No one is going to jail," he said.

To Joel, winning a case was as simple as star power, but the funny thing was, I'd later learn that Mom hadn't retained Roy Black after all. He was too expensive. Besides, I doubted the government was all that intimidated by Joel and Cecily Gold. Compared to a lot of federal cases, they were small fry, and even John Gotti had died in prison. He may have gone free once, but the good guys got him in the end.

When we were sure the helicopter was gone for good and that the cops weren't coming back for us, we scattered. Ashley took Amelia and went home immediately, and Mom sought the shelter of her office so she could chain-smoke and rock back and forth in her desk chair while she perused anti–Tea Party message boards, looking for people to argue politics with—somehow that seemed to take her mind off things. Joel took off on his bicycle and didn't return until dinnertime, when, after a rushed shower, he called and said I needed to get dressed up nicely because we were going out for stone crabs (which often went for more than fifty dollars per claw). His call was exactly what I'd needed, though. I didn't have much of an appetite for shellfish, but it would be good for me to get out of my house, for me to be distracted.

All day I'd cried. I'd wandered around the house for hours, softly whimpering. I felt ghostlike and detached, like I'd gotten so scared, my brain had temporarily called it quits and disassociated itself from the day's events. I'd begin a chore, like sorting laundry or putting clean dishes away, then space out and forget what I was doing right in the middle of it. I was so shaken up by the helicopter, I found it hard to tend to Em, so I placed her in front of the television out of desperation. Ben was in New York that weekend for work, so I was alone and had no one to relieve me of parenting for even an hour, and God, what I would've given for some time alone—a matinee, a pedicure, a quiet moment to sip tea and thumb through a copy of *Real Simple*, a hot bath . . . anything to help me calm down. Instead I found myself sitting blankly in front of my laptop, scrolling through old Facebook posts, searching for some bit of life before motherhood and before the raid, but that life had long since evaporated—it almost felt like my body had disappeared along with my mind. (After birth and breastfeeding, I hardly recognized it anyway.) I wondered if I even showed up in photographs anymore.

17

Ashley called me one morning shortly after the helicopter incident. This wasn't unusual, by any means; she called me every morning.

Ben had been traveling a lot for work lately. I knew nothing about finance, so Ben's job was largely a mystery to me. It seemed to involve a lot of complicated spreadsheets, intricate record keeping, and knowledge of compliance laws. His company had an office in New York City, and he'd been up there, working on a series of new projects. When I first found out he'd be spending so much time away, I'd been panicked. How was I going to handle Em all alone? What if something happened to me? My biggest fear was that I would die, and no one would know it, and Em would be trapped alone with no one to take care of her.

To my anxiety-addled mind, the possibilities were endless: I could have a heart attack or an aneurysm, choke to death on a Goldfish cracker, or slip on spilled baby shampoo in the shower and end up with a traumatic brain injury. On some level I realized this was crazy talk, but things like this could and did happen. I'd read the stories and didn't want to become some tragic headline: *Mom Dies and Baby Cries Alone in House for Six Days. Survives on Cat Crunchies.*

Ashley had rolled her eyes when I asked her to check in with me every day to make sure this never happened, but she did it anyway. She'd been doing so much for me, and I was grateful to have her living next door.

I'd been reading a lot of New Age self-help books lately because they made me feel better, like somewhere out there, there really were people who got up and watched the sunrise barefoot while drinking herbal tea and meditating about—I don't know, whatever people meditate about. World peace or being nice to animals or something. I liked the idea that there were actual human beings who lived their lives according to inspirational quotes, and that these people were happy and could somehow magically "manifest" all kinds of good things. In these books, people always talked about how certain souls come into our lives for different reasons at different times, and how on a spiritual level we all love the hell out of one another, and that even though things often seem like an absolute shit storm here on Earth, the shit storm happens for some very good, important reason. For, like, our spiritual growth or . . . whatever. I didn't fully understand it, but I clung hard to the idea anyway, given that my life was, well, a shit storm, and I needed something to give meaning to the calamity.

Though I couldn't yet see why all this was happening, I could easily see how Ashley's soul was helping my soul and all that. She had had a baby at the same time as me, which was proof right there of a higher power. I was almost two months pregnant when I'd finally taken the test, and when I called Ashley, I'd begged her to get pregnant too, because I couldn't do it alone. She'd laughed and said she and Andrew might start trying soon, but she was already pregnant and didn't even know it. It was like the universe had looked down at me freaking out, thinking I would never be able to take care of a baby, and said, *Oh jeez, we're going to have to send her some backup.* Ashley and Amelia were my reinforcements. Because I had someone close who I loved and trusted to share the experience with—someone who I could call up at any time to openly discuss leaky boobs and the consistency of baby poop—I could get through the toughest days.

Em was officially a toddler now: a walking, sort-of-talking, getting-into-everything, real-live kid who was sometimes quite indignant. She needed stimulation and entertainment, and she needed to explore, which meant she was absolutely exhausting, especially since she still kept me up most of the night. But right next door she had a playmate. Ashley and I could relax on beach chairs in the thick grass of our combined backyard while the little ones dug in the sandbox and splashed in small pails of water and did their thing. We did this almost every afternoon, and it was the best part of my day. I could even enjoy a cup of coffee in peace for the first time in a while, which was a small, yet important victory.

But when Ashley called me that morning, she wasn't calling to see if I had died in my sleep, and she wasn't calling to make a playdate. She had dirt.

"I can't wait to tell you this one," she said.

I switched the TV to Nick Jr., hoping Em would become mesmerized by cartoon pigs so I could focus.

"What happened?" I asked.

"I caught Joel with his girlfriend," she said.

"What?" I was flabbergasted, though not exactly surprised. "Was it Ruffina? I always thought she was after him," I said.

"Eww, no. Not her—somebody else," Ashley said.

Last Sunday, the same day the helicopter swooped in on our morning coffee, Ashley had decided to take Amelia and run some errands to get her mind off things. On her way home from Whole Foods, she'd decided to take the scenic way home, along the beach. That was when something had caught her eye.

"I was almost at our turn when I saw this couple, like, totally making out on the sidewalk," she said.

Ashley recognized Joel by his bright red tennis shoes, and decided to pull up and stop the car next to them. *Note to self,* I thought, *if you're ever going to cheat, wear something understated when out in public with your lover.*

"What did you do?" I asked.

"Oh, you should've seen him. He looked like he was going to s-h-i-t his pants," she said. Now that the babies were learning to talk, we had to watch our language around them, so we'd resorted to the age-old method of spelling out cuss words. I'd gotten good at it too. I could rip someone a new *a-s-s*-hole using nothing but a string of letters.

"Who was the girl?" I asked.

"No one we know," Ashley said. "She was skinny with long dark hair. I didn't get a good look at her because she took off when I stopped."

"Which means she is well aware of the fact that she is messing with a married man and knows she has to hide it," I deduced.

Joel didn't have a lot to say apparently. Ashley said she glared at him for an awkward minute while he fidgeted and fumbled and tried to play Mr. Cool.

"So," he finally said to her. "You coming over to the house later? I'm taking everyone out for your favorite dinner. Stone crabs!"

So that explained the fancy meal. I'd thought he'd wanted to take us out because of the helicopter, but all he'd really wanted was to curry favor with Ashley because she'd caught him red-handed—or in this case, red-shoed.

"And that's not even the best part," Ashley told me. "About a half hour later he shows up in my driveway, acting like nothing ever happened. All of a sudden he says he was thinking he'd like to make half of my car payment for me."

"Half?" I laughed. "Are you serious? Why not all of it? Your silence is worth only *half* a monthly car payment? Cheap bastard. According to his indictment, he's worth a *s-h-i-t*-load more than that. How much is your whole payment anyway?"

"It's only two hundred bucks!"

"Are you effing kidding? He's only willing to pay you off with a hundred bucks a month?" I asked.

"Whatever. I'll take what I can get," Ashley said.

I asked her if she was going to tell Mom anyway, and she said no.

"But believe me, it's not because of the money," she answered.

"Why then?" I asked, but I already knew her answer: it wasn't worth it.

"She shoots the messenger," Ashley said. "And besides, I don't want to deal with her rocking in her chair, pulling on her nose, and chain-smoking, acting like the world is going to end during Easter and Passover and making everyone miserable. And you know that a week later everything's going to be perfect again, and she'll say she and Joel are on a honeymoon. It makes me sick."

"Then she'll still find some other reason to stay pissed at you," I added.

"Exactly."

Joel had a knack for showing up exactly when people were talking about him, and today was no exception. He knocked on my door right as Ashley and I were hanging up. He said he'd come over for a hug, to see Em and bring me a brisket sandwich from my favorite deli, and I couldn't help but wonder if his kindness was genuine. I knew he loved Em to pieces, but did he really want to see *me* that badly? Was he bringing me my favorite sandwich for the same reason he wanted to take Ashley out for stone crabs, because he knew she would probably tell me she'd seen him with Madame X (as we'd decided to call the mystery mistress) and he wanted to buy my sympathy and silence? Perhaps he felt guilty, and the gifts were not so much a bribe but a conciliatory gesture. But see, that was the thing in our family: you just never knew anyone's real motives. I trusted no one, but I still took the sandwich. What can I say? It had horseradish, and he'd even remembered to get me seedless rye.

"I'm on my way to the gym, baby," Joel said. "I gotta run, but come over to the house later. We'll go out to dinner. You want sushi? You tell your papa, and we'll get whatever you want."

I gave him a sideways look. He had to know I knew.

"Okay, sounds good," I said.

But I wasn't interested in ginger and wasabi. I wanted information. I wanted to catch him in the act too, so when he pulled his Hummer out of the driveway, I decided to follow him. I waited until I saw the hulking SUV round the traffic circle at the end of the block, and then I gathered Em up as fast as I could, somehow got her buckled into her car seat, and then I took off after my cheating father.

I don't know what I thought I was going to accomplish. More than anything, I think I wanted him to know I wasn't a sucker. I wanted to call him out on his bullshit—Mom never would—and I wanted to get a look at whomever he was prancing around with on A1A.

It was a perfect sunny day. People were out, going to the beach, enjoying afternoon Pinot Grigios in sidewalk cafés. A biplane sputtered over the beach, dragging a banner that advertised two-for-one shots and a hot bod contest at some tourist dive on the strip, and I got stuck at an intersection because about twenty spring breakers wanted to cross. But I still had the Hummer in my sights. Joel was about four or five cars in front of me, and I could see him on his cell phone, windows down, arm hanging out the window, the blinding diamonds on his Rolex glinting in my eyes.

I followed him west over the drawbridge. He turned north onto US 1, and for a hot second I was sure he was going to turn into the parking lot of the most popular strip club in town, but no, he was just changing lanes. Maybe he saw me on his ass. The Hummer finally made a quick left and wove its way through a line of traffic into the parking lot of LA Fitness. I hung back and watched from a distance while, still on the phone, Joel got out, locked the doors, and walked inside. A bald goateed gym rat waved to him and he waved back—and that was it. Joel had beat me. I hadn't caught him doing a damn thing except telling the truth, and for some reason I was livid.

Later, while Em was napping, I turned to the Internet. I didn't know what I was looking for, but I began Googling anything I could about adultery, cheating, affairs, and sex addiction. I wanted to know why and how these things happened and what made me feel so bitterly betrayed, as if I were the one who'd been cheated on instead of my mother. Nothing I found made me feel any better, but I did see a number of those dumb quizzes I remembered from back in the day when I read women's magazines like *Cosmo*. *Is Your Man Cheating? Take This Quick Test to Find Out . . .* On a lark, I decided to take one.

Does he shower as soon as he comes home? Yes.

Has he all of a sudden gotten into great shape? Started dressing sharper? Yes.

Does he sometimes "fall off the map"? Yes.

Do you feel like your man isn't paying attention to you the way he once did? Yes.

Is his cell phone password protected? Yes.

Does he take the phone into the bathroom with him? Yes.

Does your man make plans without you? Yes.

Has he shown less interest in having sex with you? Yes.

I answered yes to every single one of them.

This wasn't about Joel anymore. When I took the test, I was answering questions about Ben.

18

On my wedding night, once the ceremony was over and I'd managed to escape from my corset and the hundred or so pounds of tulle that had me trapped in my gown, I sank back into my king-size hotel bed in total bliss. I had a man, and getting married seemed like the prize I'd finally won at the end of a very long and tiresome game I'd never wanted to play in the first place. I would no longer have to contend with the Mars-Venus bullshit of dating. Never again would I have to worry about playing hard to get, seeming too clingy, or impressing a man. Finally I could be myself, happily ever after.

Jesus Christ, was I naïve.

Six years in, and I was still trying to keep my man's interest, still trying to impress him, and still hoping for his phone calls and compliments. I'd never stopped playing the game, and time hadn't improved my skills. If anything, I'd gotten worse after the birth of our daughter, because having a child had changed the dynamic of my relationship with Ben. He'd fallen in love with me when I was independent. My life had had direction back then, when I was a student. I'd had goals to graduate, to win this fellowship and that award, to be published, to get a cushy teaching job at a college, and being an overachiever, I hadn't missed a single mark. My ambition must have been attractive.

The raid and the baby broke me, though. All of a sudden, I was scared of everything. Plans to go back to work lapsed as I let offers slip away, because I couldn't imagine handling the stress of a commute, grading papers, lesson planning, keeping house, dealing with day care, and being stalked by federal investigators. The needy, sniffling girl, who required both a constant stream of validation and grocery money, was not the fierce woman my husband had married, and by not being able to rise up and be strong instead of succumbing to my fears and emotions in the face of adversity, I felt like I had failed my family.

Before the baby had come, in our life before the raid, Ben and I had showered together in the mornings. At night sometimes we'd even take long hot baths, where we'd relax in a cloud of suds and talk about things that now seemed superficial: an interview on NPR, the books we were reading, a sketch from *The Daily Show*. Now Ben showered before I even got up. He came home late from work and his evening yoga class, and showered again while I sat on the toilet lid and tried to extract some drip of meaningful conversation out of him. I only wanted a couple of words to remind me that I still had a brain, and that there was still a world of current events and pop culture out there, but mostly we'd end up arguing.

He needed to decompress when he came home. He worked fourteen-hour days to support us, and thought I was being negative. *I complained too much,* he'd say, while he lathered up and the bathroom filled with the clean, peppery scent of lavender.

"But all I wanted was a hug! I haven't washed my hair in three days. I wanted to take a shower too," I'd whine.

First I'd get mad, and then I'd second-guess my anger and feel guilty. I *got* to be a stay-at-home mom. Em didn't have to go to day care. I could head on over to the grocery store anytime I wanted and load my fridge up with food. *I was lucky.* Then the self-loathing would set in. I was a terrible wife; a horrible, miserable mother; a drama queen; and the cherry on top of the sack-of-shit sundae I'd become was that I was also a spoiled brat who was no longer contributing to the family bank account. I was a hard worker who'd once had dreams of becoming a famous writer. I'd won awards and fellowships, and now I had nothing to show for any of it except a gift card to Red Lobster that hadn't been used. Now I sat in the house all day, worrying about things like diaper rash remedies and which homeopathic teething tablets worked best. On top of that, I was getting fat, because the one thing I *could* still do was go to the goddamn grocery store.

While Ben enjoyed his showers, I sat and stewed and imagined an elaborate fantasy life where my husband got home at six every evening, carrying flowers and a card, and immediately took the baby so I could have a break. After that we'd eat dinner together at the dining room table instead of on the couch, and then we'd get in the shower together, because in my fantasy life, we'd have a child who went to bed before ten P.M. Ben would shampoo my hair and admire my body, which would be skinny and smooth and devoid of any stretch marks, cellulite, zits, or wiry black hairs in strange places. We might even get to actually have sex. Why was this too much to ask?

Insecurity stepped in with the answers. *Because he doesn't love you*, it said. *Because you are flabby and out of shape and, look, you have no chin, either. Eww. You don't have the life you dream about, the life your friends have on Facebook, because you don't fucking deserve it.*

I lived in the Amityville Horror house of emotions with Insecurity as the resident demon in chief. Instead of scrawling *Get Out* on the walls in blood, it wrote, *You Aren't Good Enough*. I wanted my husband to save me from the monster under my bed that whispered these insults to me, but every time I fished for compliments from Ben, I reeled in a slime-covered boot.

"Do you think I still look pregnant?" I asked him.

"You should try yoga," he told me.

To me, this translated as: *You need to move your fat ass, you cow*.

Ben had recently dropped twenty-five pounds and had begun to wear V-necked T-shirts. He also had a snazzy new haircut, a tan, and six-pack abs. It was like someone had come in the middle of the night, swapped out my sweet and delightfully nerdy husband, and replaced him with some edgy, hip hot guy, and I didn't really want a hot guy because hot guys had never been attracted to me. Plus, hot guys demanded hot girls, and I was impossibly far from babeness. Worse still, Ben's weight loss seemed to have required very little effort. Basically, all he did was start eating a lot of hummus and going to yoga. Fucking men. I swear, my husband could lose five pounds by walking from the front door to the driveway. But me? I could exercise an hour a day, eat nothing but a freaking Activia, and then gain the five pounds Ben lost just by driving past the Dairy Queen. It wasn't fair, and being a frump married to a hottie intensified my Insecurity hurricane up to a category 5.

My husband had to have been cheating on me. There was simply no other explanation. I mean, my God, even the Internet agreed with me on this one. So one night I decided to follow him, too, just like I had with Joel. He said he was going to yoga again. *Yeah, right,* I thought. *He's going to his girlfriend's house and I'm going to find out who she is and . . .* Okay, so I didn't really know what I was going to do if I caught Ben with another woman, but I imagined I would kick both of their asses (although the reality was that I would probably just cry really hard and apologize to him for being so fat and nosy).

Sure enough, Ben had been telling the truth, just like Joel. His car was parked in front of the yoga studio, exactly where he said it would be. Except . . . what if he was going to yoga *with* his girlfriend? That was it. He was going to yoga all the time because he was in love with some lithe and limber yogini who was really into tantra. They probably fucked like Trudie and Sting. Simply imagining this chia-seed-eating bitch had me worked into a rage before I even got out of the parking lot, and I'd had enough. I was taking control of this situation once and for all. I would become the woman I believed my husband wanted, and then he would fall in love with me all over again and dump Crystal or Aura or whatever the hell her name was and I would win. At life. And everything.

I went back home, mad as a hornet, and decided to try to do some yoga, although I really had no idea what yoga even was. What I actually did was produce a stick of roll-on Egyptian musk oil leftover from the late nineties from the bottom of my bathroom drawer, play some New Age music on Pandora, and lie on the floor, trying to put my leg up into the air while Em tumbled and crawled all over me. The cat also decided to join in the fun, and climbed up, sat firmly on my chest, and began to purr like a diesel engine. Realizing this wasn't exactly yoga, I said fuck it and decided to eat some hummus and make a vision board instead. Because that was what yoga people did when they weren't doing yoga. They ate hummus and made vision boards. I had tons of unused craft supplies lying around, and I even got extra points because the New Age music was still playing and I reeked of Egyptian musk. I was totally on the path to enlightenment now, and when Ben got home, he would definitely be impressed with his new wife. Just pasting the pictures onto my vision board made me feel like I'd lost, at the very least, a pound. Maybe two.

I googled images of the things I wanted, pressed print, and cut them out and stuck them to my board. I found the whole exercise very relaxing. I taped a Victorian house beside a photo of a mountain stream. I added a Siamese cat; a big fluffy bed, a cup of coffee and a pile of books beside it, along with an organic vegetable garden and a silhouette of a woman in an absurd yoga pose where she stood on one leg while lifting the other leg over her head and grabbing her foot with her hand. (It was called Lord of the Dance, which cracked me up, because I'm pretty sure that was the name of a PBS special during pledge week.) A massage sounded amazing, so I tacked on a picture of someone's back covered in orchids and river rocks, and then I thought, *Hell, I've always dreamed of going to Japan, so let me find a nice picture of Kyoto with the pink cherry trees in bloom.* And paddleboarding! I wanted to learn how to paddleboard, too. Living in South Florida, I saw people paddle-boarding on the waterways every day, and it looked like a lot of fun. That picture could go next to the yoga contortionist. I looked at my board, and it was beautiful, because it was all the things I most loved and longed for, but it seemed to be missing something. I could go bigger than houses and cats and advanced yoga, I thought, so I asked myself, *What do I really want more than anything else in the whole world?* The truest answer hurt too much. I wanted my family to be whole forever. I wanted them to love me and love one another and I wanted my mom's fantasy, where we piled into the RV and took bus trips to camp in Maine with the kids, to be real: the one where Joel didn't cheat, and Ben and I didn't fight, and I got enough sleep, so I didn't feel completely unhinged 90 percent of the time.

If you do an image search for "the perfect life," you'll find a bunch of lame inspirational quotes and most of them, ironically, will tell you there is no perfect life—that you pretty much have to make do with what you've got. There are also pictures of Tahitian islands, some people drinking Coronas on a tropical beach, and what appears to be a Burning Man drum circle in full swing. I didn't quite get that one, but whatever. The Internet is weird. So for the second time that evening I said fuck it and changed course. If I couldn't pin "the perfect life" to my vision board, and if conventional wisdom seemed to be telling me there was no such thing anyway, I thought of the other thing I most wanted—a book deal. And I wrote myself a fake check, made out to me from a publishing company. In the memo line I put: *Book Deal*.

At the time I realized that getting a book deal was the very pipiest of pipe dreams. I had exactly the same chances of getting an actual book deal as I had of becoming a movie star, but I didn't care. I mean, I didn't even have a book to get a deal for, but writing that fake check felt amazing, and maybe one day . . . well, you never know what the future holds. Hey, maybe one day I'd also be able to stand on one leg and reach back and grab my foot and say, *Lord of the Dance*, without laughing my ass off. Stranger things have happened.

Ben got home a few minutes after I finished pasting. I was standing at the dining room table, admiring my work, imagining the future I was trying to manifest, while Em sat nearby in her high chair, banging a wooden spoon on her tray.

"What's this? Arts and crafts?" he asked, smiling.

"A vision board," I announced. I imagined myself glowing as I told him.

"Oh nice," he said, heading toward the shower.

I lifted Em out of her high chair, and we followed him through the house.

"How was yoga?" I asked.

"Fine."

He turned the faucet and grabbed a clean towel from the cabinet.

"You should try it sometime. I really think you'd get a lot out of it," he said.

"I put it on my vision board!"

"Cut-and-paste is nice, but now you have to actually go to a class," he said. Ben had a point. It wasn't like a yoga teacher was going to magically appear on the doorstep and tell me to bust out a down dog right there in the living room.

"But . . . it's a start, right? It's a goal. I mean, I *want* to go to yoga, but, well, I need someone to watch Em, and I need clothes for it, and I wanted to lose a few pounds before I braved a class and—"

"Stop making excuses and just go," Ben interrupted.

By then he was already in the shower. I listened as his razor scraped against his rough chin and the last splatter of shampoo farted out of the bottle.

"I can't just leave Em here alone and run out and do whatever I want! You work all day and go to class at night, so you're not here to babysit, and I can't ask my parents, because they have so much going on already. They're hardly ever home, and Mom is too stressed-out anyway. It's not that easy for me to do stuff like I used to!" I argued.

"Bottom line is that if you really wanted to do it, you'd find a way," he said.

At that moment, what I really wanted to do was to stab my husband, and I briefly considered "finding a way" to do that.

I'm sure Ben hadn't meant to piss me off. Far from it, actually. Ben was a matter-of-fact person and very literal-minded, which I wasn't, and sometimes he came off a little harsh, and although he hadn't said a single thing that wasn't true, I was mad at his delivery. I took his words as a challenge and vowed to show him up.

I wanted to go to yoga to lose weight. It had been over a decade since I'd been skinny. I'd tried everything—diets, gyms, bizarre nutritional advice doled out by bouncers at strip clubs who moonlighted as personal trainers, dietary supplements, ear candling, Atkins, South Beach—even starving myself, but that lasted for only an hour. I'd done it all, but my problem was that I couldn't stand even a moment's worth of physical discomfort: I'd give up and eat cake. Hunger and physical exertion were painful and, when combined, they were right up there with the agony I'd experienced in childbirth. Besides, there was just way too much temptation around, especially with my parents constantly taking us out to amazing dinners or cooking even better meals at home. All my happiest memories and all the times in my life when I'd felt most loved and most comforted revolved around cooking and eating, so when I was depressed, I would run straight to the kitchen because so many good things began with the words *Cream together the butter and sugar.* Except diets, of course, and I'd been more depressed in the past eighteen months than I'd ever been in my entire life.

Insecurity must feed off fat, too, because the bigger I got, the louder and more insistent Insecurity became. But a couple of days later, my vision board started working. Apparently, all that crap in *The Secret* was true. Who knew? Ashley and I were sitting out in the backyard with the babies, who were staggering in the grass after my sister's dog like two Gymboree-clad drunks, when Ashley mentioned she ran into a friend of hers who had previously been fat and now had the body of a Victoria's Secret model.

"Oh my God, how did she do it?" I asked, desperate to know the magic formula.

"Yoga," Ashley said.

"No fucking way," I replied. The kids were out of earshot. I longed to use foul language as freely as I once had, and I threw in a good swear word whenever I got the chance.

"I asked her how she did it, and she said all she did was start going to yoga."

"You're kidding. Wow. But I mean, look at Ben. Same thing. It's, like, *miraculous* or something," I said.

"Right! I started looking into it, and there's a studio near here that has babysitting twice a day. I think I'm going to go and check out a class. Come with me," Ashley said.

"I don't know," I said, looking down at my belly flab, which now flopped embarrassingly over the waistband of my shorts like over-risen bread dough. "Don't you, like, have to go vegan first or something? I don't know if I'll fit in with the yoga crowd."

"That's ridiculous. Everyone has to start somewhere," Ashley said.

I couldn't ignore the synchronicity, so I gathered the courage to go, and a week later I found myself at the yoga studio, anxiously clutching a mat to my chest with one hand while trying to pick a wedgie out of my ass with the other. I wasn't pretty in my new Lycra gym shorts, but at least I'd showed up.

I hadn't been this intimidated since seventh-grade gym class. I was the cliché kid picked last for every team—the nerdy creative one who covered her face whenever she got within five feet of a dodgeball. Mostly, I'd let the damn thing hit me so I could sit peacefully on the sidelines, daydreaming about a life that didn't involve whistles and competition and dangerous things like red rubber balls. I was proud I'd successfully spent my adult life getting revenge on PE, avoiding gyms and any form of structured exercise, so yoga? It probably wasn't going to come naturally, but desperate times called for desperate measures. I needed my pre-baby body back.

The idea of yoga appealed to me—incense, bamboo, *om*-ing, paisley print—I was down with all that, but when confronted with actually having to set foot in the studio, slap down a mat, and start twisting, I freaked, and oh my God, was it hot. As soon as I walked in, I felt like a water buffalo that had been dropped into the middle of a goddess convention. I mean, who *were* these women?

Until my first yoga class, I'd comforted myself with the common knowledge that the women I saw in magazines—the ones with the perky boobs and shiny hair, who smiled out of Herbal Essences ads and J.Crew catalogs—were not real. Nope. They were airbrushed fiction. Actual human beings did not look like that. Except here I was in yoga, surrounded by women who looked. Exactly. Like. That. My entire worldview was destroyed before the first vinyasa, which I couldn't even do.

I barely got through the warm-up flow before I decided I was suffering from heatstroke and gave up. I then broke every code of yoga etiquette by sitting straight up on my mat and watching the rest of the class dance through the sequences with supernatural ease, but I didn't care. I wanted to at least see what yoga was supposed to look like before I attempted any more of it, and Jesus Christ, the teacher—she was all of about eighty-two pounds—the spitting image of Tinker Bell and full of encouragement. But who wouldn't be positive as hell if they looked like that? Shit, I thought, if I looked like that, I would have no problems whatsoever. Who cares if my parents are going to jail? I am a size zero, motherfuckers. So what if my husband is cheating on me—maybe, according to an online quiz? I can get a new one! I am skinny and beautiful, and I don't give a shit.

The girl closest to me was even tinier than the instructor, and freakishly strong. She did a handstand that lasted at least five minutes, and had a small tattoo of the Olympic rings on her shoulder. Was I really trying to do yoga with freaking Olympic *athletes*? I was out of my league. I thought yoga was about sitting around like Gandhi and inhaling inner peace, not doing pushups in humidity as thick as dal masala.

I stood up and darted to the lobby as quickly as I could, hoping no one would notice. The relief of the air conditioner was practically orgasmic.

"You okay?" the girl at the front desk asked me. She was the studio manager and was filling in for the receptionist that day.

Her name was Susan, and she had sandy hair, eyes as blue as Windex, and an adorable smattering of cinnamon freckles across her nose, and I felt an instant camaraderie with her, because she had a natural, simple beauty and wasn't some Barbie doll plucked off a Fashion Week catwalk.

"I don't know if I can do this," I said, panting.

Susan laughed. "You'll be fine. First time's always hard, but I promise, you get used to it and then it's nothing," she told me.

I had a hard time believing her.

"Go back in there," Susan said.

"I don't think I'm cut out for this," I protested.

She handed me a towel to wipe my face.

"Everyone is cut out for yoga," she said. "Don't get intimidated because you see people in there doing advanced poses. They practice every day, most of them for years now, and a lot of them are also teachers. There are all levels in your class, and you just do what you can, and if you can't, then lie down and focus on your breath. Then tomorrow try to do a little more, and the next day a little more than that. And, eventually, you're going to get better. Seriously, all you have to do is show up. Yoga is about being present."

I supposed Susan was right, that we all had to begin somewhere, but this made me extremely uncomfortable. I'd always hated not being the best: if I didn't immediately take to something, I'd just as soon give up and stick with what I was naturally good at. My whole life, I'd listened to Insecurity snarling in my ear: *No one will love you if you aren't perfect. You suck at this, so you should quit now before you're humiliated.*

But maybe, throughout my life, the universe had repeatedly knocked me on my ass precisely so I would have to keep getting up, exactly like I was doing here in yoga, so that each time I regained my footing, I'd stand a little straighter, find a little more balance.

This time I decided to ignore Insecurity's lies and march back onto my mat. I'd give it one more shot.

My parents hadn't been able to teach me these lessons, because they themselves hadn't learned them and, for that, I wasn't resentful so much as I felt sorry for them. They, too, wanted instant gratification, so they lived their lives believing absolutely that it was possible to make it to the top without having to endure the long rocky climb. Joel always liked to say that if you worked too hard, you'd be too busy to make any money. That was why my parents never got traditional jobs, the kind with weekly paychecks, benefits, retirement plans. They relied on deals and, really, for my whole life, they were always waiting for the next big deal to come along, because that was always going to be the one that would make them rich beyond their wildest dreams.

I guess they'd finally found their "big deal" in the stock market. Penny stocks, pink sheets, over-the-counter trades of D-listed companies so desperate to stay afloat, they were willing to put their businesses into the hands of two street-smart charmers who promised them the world in exchange for a few thousand—maybe even a few million—shares of company stock that was seemingly worthless anyway. At least until my parents got ahold of it.

I'd read a little of the indictment, and my parents were accused of masterminding a pump-and-dump scheme. It said Joel would allegedly take the free-trading stock for himself and issue an even larger amount of "restricted" stock to the companies' owners. Restricted stocks are stocks that can't be traded until certain conditions are met, often until a set date has passed or the company has achieved specific earnings goals. But that didn't matter, he'd supposedly tell the shareholders, because he was going to take the company to the next level, and by the time the restricted stocks were free, they would be worth unimaginable millions. You've waited this long, right? What's another year or so? And then Joel would front them an impressive sum to build the company or pay their debts, and take them out to several costly meals in the meantime. Once, he'd even bought a guy a car, because he was down on his luck and didn't have a ride.

Mom wrote only the press releases. The rest, the real shady stuff, was out of her hands, and if the indictment was true, she probably didn't understand the full scope of the supposed operation, which was why she had fewer and less serious charges. She put out "news" about the companies' upcoming ventures and successes, and she believed in what she was doing. Mom wanted the best for each new company my parents took on. She was genuinely enthusiastic about the products the companies sold—from miraculous heart-monitoring devices to wristwatches designed in honor of African-American historical figures. Her overblown rhetoric is what got her in trouble, and although it may have come from sincere enthusiasm and a lack of real education and understanding of SEC guidelines, it didn't look like the federal government was going to give her a pass for having good intentions.

Once the press releases went out, a "team" got to work promoting or "pumping" the stocks. Groups of individuals who were "in" on the deal created the illusion that the companies were on the rise. First they'd buy up the cheap shares, which usually went for less than a penny. That helped to inflate the prices a little bit.

Then they talked up the stocks on Twitter, in Facebook groups, and in newsletters and on websites they'd designed to look like official tip pages for informed investors. Pretty soon all this activity would start to win public interest and people would start buying the stocks, causing the price to surge and attracting even more buyers, which would jack up the price even more. It seemed like a nearly foolproof way to make a lot of money very quickly, and one could, in the right circumstances, even argue it wasn't really unethical, because all the promoters were really doing was advertising. All companies advertised. Even the CEO of Whole Foods bragged about his stock online.

Next came the "dump." If the team had simply held on to their own stock during these promotions, there likely wouldn't have been a problem, or maybe even a crime. But the point of stock promotion is not to assist a struggling company by increasing its value. The true aim is for those who hold the free-trading stocks to make money, and the only way that can happen is by selling off all the stock, massive amounts of it, while the price is at its peak. Once the stock is dumped, the news releases cease, the online chatter goes silent, and the company is back at square one. The stock goes to its previous, nearly worthless state, and whoever is stuck with the restricted stock is then left feeling conned and robbed, with nothing but a meaningless piece of paper. If that was what my parents had actually been doing, there was no other word for it than *fraud*.

I never wanted to believe that my parents were con artists capable of doing something like this. I knew they had a checkered past, but I figured those days were long behind them. Lots of people do stupid things and get in all kinds of trouble when they're young, but that doesn't mean they can't change as they get older. That was why I took them at face value when Mom said she did Internet marketing and Joel told people he was in the entertainment business. When I read their indictments, I was heartbroken and prayed that Mom was telling the truth and that the charges were all lies. But there was a lot of evidence against them, and I couldn't ignore that.

Mom had been saying for years, though, that she wanted to retire, and the only thing Joel really wanted to do was make movies. The problem was, he'd lacked financing and the right kinds of Hollywood connections, and the indictment said he'd turned to stock scams to pay for his movie. He imagined himself as an influential producer: Hollywood, film festivals, concerts, celebrity parties, the creative energy of filmmaking, recording albums, and hobnobbing with stars. And I wanted my parents to have that dream life, but I wanted them to do it legitimately. I wondered, though, if maybe they didn't know *how* to do things legitimately, or if their desire to prove themselves to the world, and finally have that life of champagne wishes and caviar dreams, was so great, they would do anything to achieve their goals.

As I stepped back onto my mat and lunged my right knee forward, attempting to "exalt my warrior," I hoped that even if they turned out to be totally innocent, getting arrested would become the advanced pose that would finally challenge their balance, expose their vulnerability, and knock my parents on their asses so they'd realize it was time to change.

As for me? I was finally figuring out how to hold on and maintain my balance as unexpected events threatened my stability. One day I would give up my fear of the dark unknown, but that lesson would come later and be hard-earned. I would fall a lot more, and I'd fall hard. Progress would be slow, imperceptible at times, but it would happen. Right now was all that mattered, and here I was, standing tall on my mat, raising my arms high above my head, turning my gaze to the sky, and giving thanks for being here and giving life my best effort.

19

It was yet another stagnant and blistering August afternoon in South Florida. Em and Amelia were playing in the backyard, and I was enjoying a much-needed cup of coffee with extra cream and sugar, while my sister was doing handstands. She could now bend over at the waist, grab her big toe, and then rise to a standing position—still holding her toe, with her leg vertical—so that her body was one straight line of yogic insanity. It was called Bird of Paradise, and it was ridiculous. We'd been going to yoga for only a couple of months, but Ashley quickly excelled and became completely obsessed, while I went about three or four times a week and still struggled to touch my toes without bending my knees. To me, it felt like a big deal that I'd kept going at all, and my current goal was to one day, in the far-flung future, be able to do down dog with my heels flat, or to make it through an entire class without retreating into child's pose in an attempt to hide from the teacher, who might try to coax me into revolving my triangle, an impossible pose that sounded like something RuPaul would say. *Revolve that triangle, girl!*

"You have to remember," Ashley told me, once she was right side up again, "two months before I got pregnant with Amelia, I was training for a marathon. I ran a half marathon on my wedding day, so I started yoga in a different place than you. Let's just face the facts here. I've always been the athletic one, and this is totally new to you. You just have to keep trying. You'll get there if you don't quit."

We sat quietly in the grass for a moment, watching our daughters splash in the water table my mom had recently bought them. Amelia put a stone in her mouth, and Ashley fished it out, while Em ran headlong into a cherry tomato plant growing along the fence and began plucking off the red tomatoes and eating them. Amelia followed, and soon both kids were laughing, their chins slimy with tomato seeds. It was a perfect moment, and I wished it could last forever. I took a sip of coffee, savored it, and told Ashley my news.

"I'm going to Delaware in two weeks, just me and Em, since Ben has to work," I announced.

"Nice! Did you tell *her*, though? Did she freak?"

"She wasn't thrilled," I said.

We were talking about Mom. Because she was actually her half sister, Ashley didn't really call my mother Mom, and we just referred to her as *her* or *she*. The relationships within our family were so complicated, it was hard to find names or titles for people that felt appropriate, so a lot of the time Ashley and I just avoided calling our parents anything but pronouns.

"Why does she do that? Why does she always get mad when we want to travel?" Ashley asked.

"I think she feels like she might lose us if we go away, or something might happen to us," I said, but I didn't really know. "Maybe she misses us. She seems to feel threatened by my going to Delaware for some reason."

Ashley nodded. "Because she hates it there, maybe, and she can't imagine someone feeling something she doesn't?"

"She wants to believe she 'saved' me from the life I would've had if I stayed there, and you can't really 'save' someone if they love the place, you know? Plus, I have a whole other family there that doesn't involve her."

"She doesn't want you to like them more than her?" Ashley asked.

"Something like that," I said. Then I added, "I want to see my half siblings on this trip. I've been communicating with them online, but I feel like it's finally time to see them in person."

"I get that. I'd want to see them too if I were you, and you want Em to know the rest of her family. Did you tell *her* you're planning to see them?" Ashley asked.

"I conveniently left that part out. I don't have the energy to get into it with her, and I don't want to hurt her feelings," I explained. "I told her I need to see Mommom Alice and Mommom Marie. They're not getting any younger, and it's easy to visit them both at the same time since they live all of five miles from each other."

"I hear you," Ashley said. She checked the time on her phone. "We need to get ready for yoga," she added.

"I don't know. I'm tired this afternoon. Plus, I want to finish this coffee, and ugh, maybe I just need a break from yoga. I don't know. I feel like I should've lost some weight by now. Maybe I'm not cut out for it," I said.

"Stop making excuses! Get off your ass and go!" she said. For good measure she arranged herself into an impressive straddle split, and then grabbed both feet with her Silly Putty arms.

"Show-off," I muttered.

I herded Em inside and changed into my yoga shorts and a tank top. After I braided my hair and filled my water bottle, I loaded Em and my mat into the car, letting out a resigned sigh. When class was over, I'd be glad I went, like always. The hardest part was actually getting up and going, but thank goodness, I had Ashley to motivate me.

Yoga was always tough, but that day was particularly challenging, and I couldn't concentrate. Every time I tried to hold still, some unreachable part of my body would start to itch. Sweat stung my eyes. I couldn't stop thinking about how earlier that day Mom had called me, frantic, and ranting about a miracle—a piece of paper that would break open her entire case had been missing, and she'd finally found it. For some reason she believed Allie had taken the paper but had snuck in the house and returned it.

I asked Mom what the paper was, and she told me it was a contract that would prove she was innocent, but I still didn't get how the part about Allie fit in. It didn't make sense to me, but Mom was insistent.

"Can't you see?" Mom said.

I couldn't, and I'd lost my patience with her, ending the call as fast as I could.

My parents' case had continued to plod forward. Lately my parents had been spending long hours with their lawyers, poring over thick, tedious stacks of paperwork—transcripts of similar cases, statements, investigations, and legal motions. They were building their defense by going through piles of reference materials, but the work was draining my mother. She couldn't focus or understand the legal jargon, and her emotions often overcame her composure. During that time, in every phone conversation she had with me and over every dinner we shared, she'd rail against the injustice of the current administration, parroting the outrage she heard from the mouths of pundits on the news shows she watched constantly. Mom thought her arrest was based in jealousy. She believed we lived in a culture that reviled the rich. People were lazy and wanted handouts, and were out to take money from people like her who had nice things, and she blamed everyone but herself for her predicament. She even said old friends who weren't successful envied her big house and luxury vehicles, and had put the evil eye on her, causing this bad luck.

Joel, though, was her rock. He'd drive her home from their lawyer's office, musing about their future successes and big projects he had coming up, like a documentary of a famous doo-wop group's current reunion tour. To calm her down, Joel would tell Mom about all the places they were going to go when this was all over—Israel, Spain, Uruguay. When they got back from meeting with their lawyers each day, they'd hit the living room bar. Wine for him. Belvedere on ice, splash of cranberry, just a faint blush of juice, twist of lime for her. Two cocktails, then three, then dinner out to celebrate their upcoming courtroom victory, over and over, whenever that day came. We still didn't know. Joel doubted they'd ever go to trial.

I wished I didn't think about my parents while I was in yoga, but as I moved through the strenuous poses, my mind tended to wander a lot. I figured yoga was supposed to help me focus better, so I was surprised when the instructors explained that it was normal for the drama in our lives to come up during practice. They told us to observe our thoughts without reacting to them, and to let them go, so I tried to release my worries about my parents that afternoon, but it was hard, because my mind kept returning to my worst fear—losing my family, being alone.

Toward the end of class, the teacher led us into a torturous flow. My arms ached and my legs shook, which she said meant I was burning off old karma. Whatever. Some students swiveled into complicated arm balances. They were thin and gorgeous— perfect—and I wished I could be them because I wanted out of my own life, where it seemed like I was losing everything except weight.

I'd actually *gained* a couple of pounds doing yoga, and it was becoming yet another opportunity for me to bash myself—where I could run through my exhaustive mental catalog of failures: my failure to be a nurturing mother, a supportive daughter, a hot wife; my failure to make a career out of writing, or even to clean the house; my failure to enjoy kale; and my failure to put my leg behind my head. These were all simple things, yet I couldn't manage any of them. Not a one.

The teacher today (not the one who looked like Tinker Bell), led us into our final savasana, where we got to lie motionless on the floor and listen to Radiohead's "Karma Police." It was easily the best part of class.

"Beauty is not what you see," said the teacher. "It's who you are. Do you get that? It's not about your flat stomach or your perfect ass, so just stop with that. You are beautiful already."

She paused. My eyes were closed, but the tears were already flowing.

"No one is responsible for your happiness but you. You have the power and you have to reclaim it and you can do that right here on your mat. You think yoga is about tricks? No way. That's the circus. Real yoga is about quieting your mind, stopping that inner dialogue that holds you back. It's about sticking with the hard parts, the uncomfortable parts, and learning the tools you need to keep going, to face your fears and your emotions and stop running from them. It's about writing the happy ending to your own story."

She stood without speaking for a moment and then shouted: "YOU HAVE TO FUCKING LOVE YOURSELF!"

Well, that came out of nowhere, I thought, but that was when I got it. My yoga before and after wasn't something that would show up in photographs. Yoga was going to be about learning to fucking love myself and that was when I really started to cry, because that was going to be a lot harder than balancing on my elbows.

20

Two weeks later, Em and I flew from Florida to Philadelphia. I'd been a nervous wreck, flying alone with a toddler for the first time, but she was surprisingly relaxed on the flight, and easily placated by cheese puffs and scratch-and-sniff stickers, which ended up all over my T-shirt and even in my hair. Although she wasn't quite two, Em could speak well now, and that made her much easier to deal with, so I felt a lot more comfortable traveling with her. Before she could talk, I always felt like some kind of failed psychic, trying to read her mind, searching for clues to what she might want, but never quite succeeding. *Do you want Cheerios? A diaper change? Your sippy cup? You want to rip my earrings out and swallow them? No? What is it you want, for the love of God?* But now she shouted her demands articulately: "Give me juice boxes, Mommy!" And I became her dutiful lady-in-waiting.

My first cousin Alex, the daughter of my bio dad's older brother, picked us up at the airport. It was great to see her again, after over a year. We hadn't grown up together, but we'd reconnected as adults and were now good friends. She's a few years younger than I am, but already the mother of three teenagers, and I respected her take-charge attitude and independence. Alex was one of those women who took it as a compliment if you called her a bitch, and proved all those stereotypes about fiery redheads. She didn't just wear the pants in her family—she carried the gun, too.

We left the airport and drove south from Philly, racing past cornfields along the rural back roads of my home state in Alex's Durango. The earthy, ammonia smell of fertilizer filled the car and brought back memories of summers spent barefoot and sunburned, hiding in the pole beans and running into bleach-scented bedsheets, cold and wet and billowing on my grandmother's clothesline.

"It's great to be home." I sighed.

"We're glad to have you back, and Mommom Alice is beyond happy you're bringing Em to see her," Alex answered.

"I missed my family here a lot," I admitted.

Alex took a long swig of Mountain Dew from a bottle she lifted from the truck's console.

"How are your mom and Joel holding up?" she asked. Alex didn't know my parents all that well, but since Alex and I were close, I trusted her, and I'd given her an overview of their situation before I came.

"You know what they're like. Mom's gloom and doom one minute and ecstatic the next. Joel's more even-keeled, but I think he's overconfident. He thinks there's no way they can lose because they have money, and he's always saying money is power and the one with the most money wins."

"Pft," Alex scoffed. "I'm sorry, Vic, but I've read their charges, and this is serious. Besides, no one has more money than the government."

Alex had worked as a paralegal for years. At work she had access to federal court databases, and she knew how to read legal jargon. She'd done her research on my parents' case and knew what she was talking about.

"Just don't tell anyone else in the family, please. I came here to get away from it all, and I don't want it taking over every conversation like it does at home. I don't want to have to explain it to Mommom Alice," I said, leaning my face against the cool glass of the passenger-side window.

As we drove farther south, we passed miles of forests and

farmlands, peach orchards, and lonely trailer parks, and I lightened the conversation by remarking about how little the rest of the country seemed to know about Delaware.

"They know Joe Biden's from here, but a lot of people don't even realize Delaware's a state! They think it's part of New Jersey or something," I joked.

It was true. My home state was a bit obscure, likely due to its size (Delaware is the second smallest state after Rhode Island). Its northwestern shoulder sidles up to Pennsylvania and New Jersey, and that region is wealthier and more urban, but the farther you travel from New Castle County, the more rural Delaware becomes. The part where I'm from is affectionately called Slower Lower, and is downright country—a different world from South Florida for sure. Milford, the town where Mom and I were born and raised, is home to a little more than ten thousand people, and over the years not much has changed. As Alex barreled down Route 113, the main stretch through town, I saw a couple of new fast-food joints and noticed that a popular grocery store had gone out of business, likely displaced by the new Walmart Supercenter. The important things were the same, though. Milford had a real main street, a Dairy Queen that served sundaes through a screened window, and the fireflies still lit up the country twilight just the way I remembered. They were just beginning to flicker greenish-gold among the trees when we arrived.

Whenever I visited Delaware, I always stayed with Mommom Alice at her condo. She was my bio dad's mom—the woman who'd raised me until I was nine. It was good to wake up in the morning and have her pour me a mug of Folgers while I rifled through my hometown newspaper, which was filled with tales of busted meth labs and ads for used farm equipment.

Each morning, when I was done with my coffee, I'd get into Mommom Alice's car (she let me borrow it since she didn't drive much anymore) and head over to Mommom Marie's house. She was my other grandmother, Mom's mom, and she lived on the opposite side of town in a little brick house with a big yard filled with meticulously tended flowers. It might sound like a long drive, but in Milford, the other side of town was only about five minutes away, seven in the beach traffic the locals bitched about.

Em and I visited Mommom Marie every day, and as soon as we'd arrive, she'd try to stuff us half to death with food, buckwheat pancakes crisped alongside sizzling sausage links, while she moved around her tiny kitchen, slicing farm-fresh cantaloupe and plucking grapes from their stems to pop into Em's mouth.

"You want some cheese? Let me fry you up an egg, too," my grandmother said. "I have bacon!"

I laughed. I was going to weigh three hundred pounds by the time I made it home.

After our feast that first morning, Mommom Marie and I relaxed on her back patio. She smoked, something she managed to do with an old-fashioned elegance, while Em scampered in the soft grass beneath a huge maple. I reclined on a chaise so I could close my eyes and remember how much I loved the electric buzz of cicadas. I couldn't remember ever hearing them in Fort Lauderdale.

Mommom Marie brought up dinner plans for the weekend, and I immediately tensed. I told her I'd already made plans for Saturday with my cousin Bailey, which wasn't a total lie, but it certainly wasn't the whole truth, either. Bailey would be there, but Saturday was the big day. I was reuniting with four of my five siblings.

I was nervous, excited at times about meeting them, yet apprehensive, too, and I certainly didn't want it getting back to my mom that I was trying to build a relationship with them when I still wasn't sure how much I even wanted my half brothers and sisters in my life. I didn't know who these people were. They'd been sheltered and raised with a lot of beliefs I disagreed with. Besides, five years earlier my siblings had watched their mom die a slow death from inflammatory breast cancer, an aggressive and brutal disease. They'd been through a lot lately—their dad had just remarried, and they were dealing with a new stepmom. I couldn't help but wonder how their experiences might affect our developing relationship. I had my own scars too. After all, I didn't even have a relationship with our father.

Mommom Alice had known about the reunion for weeks, and was overjoyed because, for the first time, she'd have nearly all her grandchildren in her condo. She had pushed for the big get-together, and had never understood why I was estranged from my father, her son. In the past, Mommom Alice and I argued a lot over this, because she held us equally responsible for the rift. She believed I should reach out to the man my mom called my "sperm donor" and thought my reticence was rooted in pride and stubbornness, or some undeserved loyalty to Joel. But the truth was none of those things. My father was a stranger who didn't share my beliefs and values. Worse, he was a stranger who'd abandoned his daughter. When I was only eleven, I'd told him I wanted to live with my mother instead of with him and my stepmother. I missed my mom and needed her, but he told me my decision betrayed him, and if I went, that meant never seeing or speaking to him again, and he'd kept his word for more than twenty-five years. I knew I was better off without someone like that, but his kids? That was more complicated.

Saturday came, and rain put a damper on what was supposed to be a party at Mommom Alice's community pool. My cousin Bailey arrived early to help set up. Bailey and I had grown up together. During our childhoods, Mommom Alice babysat her while her mom worked, so she was like a little sister to me. I remembered sitting in my grandfather's easy chair and being allowed to feed Bailey a bottle when she was a baby, and we had a strong bond. She'd grown into a responsible, fun-loving woman, who worked in banking but was obsessed with Disney movies and Harry Potter. She had a tattoo of an elephant on her foot and wore her blond hair in a playful flip, and was the closest thing I had to a best friend, besides Ashley. After Ashley and Ben, Bailey was the first person I'd called after each of my parents' arrests, and she'd kept her promise not to tell anyone, even her parents. She never judged, and I was going to need some serious moral support that day, so I was glad to have her around.

"Stop pacing!" Bailey told me. "You're making me nervous."

I folded and refolded a stack of paper napkins on the kitchen counter.

"Do you think they're going to like the salad I made?" I asked.

"Of course! Everyone loves taco salad. Calm down. There's nothing to freak out about," Bailey reassured me.

"What if it's weird?" I asked.

"What if *what's* weird?"

"You know, hanging out with my siblings," I said. I took the salad out of the fridge, tasted it, and added more cilantro, but then remembered that a lot of people hate cilantro. I was afraid my sisters and brother were anti-cilantro and they'd think I was some kind of cilantro-loving maniac.

"Weird never killed anyone, and if you don't like spending time with them, you never have to do it again," Bailey said, and I loved her for her laid-back attitude. Plus, she had a good point—I was in control of who I spent time with.

The knock finally came a few minutes later. I took a deep breath and then hurried to answer the door, Em toddling close behind me. When I had tried to imagine this moment, I'd thought it might be awkward and filled with nervous silences—the conversational equivalent of when you're walking toward someone and you both move in the same direction to get out of each other's way, accomplishing the opposite of what you'd intended. It wasn't that way at all. The first thing my half siblings did was grab me and Em, and fold us into a big group hug. It was happy chaos. Everyone was shouting at once, trying to get a look at one another, lifting up Em and her cousins Audrey and Isabella and kissing their adorable cheeks.

"I can't believe we're finally together!"

"Em is even cuter in person than on Facebook!"

"So is Audrey!"

"Look how much Isabella grew! Her curls are gorgeous!"

"This is amazing, seeing you in real life!"

Meeting my siblings wasn't like meeting strangers. There was no small talk to get through, no formalities to get out of the way, and I found we had a natural sense of comfort and ease with one another I couldn't explain. Right away we got to work setting up folding card tables to accommodate our big group. My siblings had brought KFC with all the sides. My aunts and uncles arrived next with Jell-O salads and veggie trays, and Cousin Alex showed up last. As soon as she put her purse down, she got on the phone and began ordering pizza, so within an hour we had a full-on bacchanal of junk food. None of the dishes went together, and it was nothing like my parents' fancy get-togethers back in Florida, but I didn't care. Diet, be damned. Fried chicken was good, and the company was even better.

My youngest sister, Grace, a tall blonde who was majoring in elementary education, fixed Em a buttered biscuit and sat at the kid's table during dinner. Ellen, who looked so much like her mother, had made a special road trip all the way from Ohio with her husband and daughter, Audrey, just for the visit. Audrey was only four months older than Em, and the two cousins hit it off immediately and set to work spreading as many toys across the living room floor as they could manage. I paused to watch as they moved on to stacking towers of red plastic cups, and realized Em could have cousins, real first cousins, to visit and grow up with. This could be amazing.

My younger brother, Thaddeus, quickly joined the kids on the floor. He delighted them with a complicated train track he built from a set Em had brought along from home. It made perfect sense. Thaddeus was in his last year of college, an engineering major, and he told me that after graduation, his dream was to get a job designing amusement park rides. His blue eyes disappeared when he smiled, which was often, and I loved him instantly. Before the evening ended, Em was following him around adoringly and calling him Uncle Thaddeus. It was how he'd introduced himself to her.

It was good to see Sarah again too. She had a baby now, and everyone said the baby looked exactly like Sarah had when she was that age, but I didn't know one way or the other, because I never got to see her while I was growing up. Sarah's daughter, Isabella, was eight months old and learning to crawl, and her big cousins Em and Audrey encouraged her to scoot across the floor to retrieve the toys they held out for her.

Pretty soon Ellen uncorked a few bottles of wine she'd brought from a farmer's market on the way down, and poured glasses for everyone, making the day feel even more celebratory. When one of my cousins made a poop joke, everyone cracked up at the same time, and it was nice to know my siblings shared my lowbrow sense of humor. Not only that, they shared my sweet tooth. We did some serious damage to the desserts, laughing about how we'd have heartburn later. Turned out, we all had sensitive stomachs too. I'd always wondered where my chronic heartburn came from, and now it appeared it was actually genetic.

"It's a shame Lucas couldn't come," Mommom Alice mentioned.

I took Sarah aside and asked where he was.

"I don't know," Sarah said, and I sensed she was exasperated about his not coming, so I didn't press the issue.

Lucas was the youngest, the only one of us who hadn't turned eighteen, so he was still under his father's rule. No one said so, but I wondered if Lucas had been forbidden from visiting, though his absence could've been due to a lot of things. Maybe, like most teenage boys, he'd rather hang with his friends instead of his grandmother. I knew I'd meet him someday, though, and for now this was more than enough.

Time flew that day, and when everyone had finally gathered

up their belongings and we finished saying good-bye, it was almost eight P.M. Em and I went to bed immediately. We were worn-out, but we were full and happy. For the first time in my life, I felt fully included in my biological father's family.

Mommom Marie called early the next morning to check up on us. The phone roused me out of bed, and I answered groggily.

"Hey, honey," she said. Her voice was musical, and I could hear her smile.

I asked her if she still wanted to have dinner that evening.

"Well, we've had a little change in plans." She laughed, and from her tone that sounded like a good thing. "Guess who drove up late last night?"

"Who?" I asked, totally confused.

"Your mother and Joel! Dogs and all."

Before I could register my shock, I heard my mother call out in the background: "Tell her to bring that baby over here! I can't take another minute without her!"

"I'm so confused. Did they come in the RV?" I asked.

"Mm-hmm. Sure did. I was confused too, believe me. So are you coming over, sweetheart? I've got scrapple frying."

"I guess I am. Let me get dressed."

I hung up, threw some clothes on, put Em in an eyelet romper, and headed out the door. We were at Mommom Marie's house within five minutes.

Mommom Marie's small kitchen was fogged with cigarette smoke when we arrived. She and my mother were enjoying coffee, Marlboro Lights, and scrapple, a horrifying local delicacy made from ground pig guts mixed with cornmeal and spices. Scrapple was the haggis of Delaware, the sort of thing out-of-towners might try on a dare, but only if they were really drunk. It was gray and looked like a gelatinous slab of concrete, and I wouldn't eat it for a thousand bucks, but Mom loved it. I'd smelled it and the cigarettes from the driveway, and had left Em outside in the yard with Joel, who was throwing sticks to the Doberman.

She'd wriggled out of my arms when I unbuckled her from her car seat and had run to her grandfather, shrieking, "Papa J! Papa J!" as soon as she'd spotted him.

That night Joel took us all to dinner at a popular seafood restaurant on the beach. My parents had towed their Hummer behind the RV so they'd have a vehicle to jaunt around in, and when we pulled up in that huge gleaming black monstrosity, Mom said we may as well have been movie stars, and she laughed proudly about how the most popular girls she'd gone to high school with in Milford, the ones who'd made fun of her for being poor back in the day, had all grown up to drive used Chevrolets.

"I showed them. Nobody around here drives something like this," Mom said as she tucked her hair behind her ears, making her two-carat diamond studs even more obvious. "Look how we're dressed. People here don't look like us."

Tourists waited for tables on benches outside. They wore shorts, tanks, flip-flops, fanny packs, and visors while Mom sashayed past them in black palazzo pants and a sequined tank. Joel strutted inside in a black straw trilby, a studded rocker tee, tailored jeans, and Prada loafers. He slipped the host a wad of cash, who knows how much, and instantly we were seated at a roomy table. The server brought us a complimentary appetizer while everyone else waited hours for their names to be called over the loudspeaker.

"Always a charmer," Mommom Marie said, and laughed, pressing her hand against Joel's shoulder.

He leaned over and kissed her cheek.

"Anything for you, Mom. And order whatever you'd like," he said.

When our entrees arrived, my grandmother lamented that, at eighty, her gnarled, arthritic hands had a hard time cracking open the king crab legs she loved so much. Joel slid her platter toward him and opened each orange shell for her—all she had to do was take a fork and dig in. Mommom Marie was thrilled because she could enjoy her favorite meal without hurting her hands cracking shells.

After he finished opening the king crab legs, Joel had to go to the bathroom to wash his hands. Joel was allergic to crab, and while it was safe for him to handle, if he accidentally ingested even a small amount of it, he would spend the rest of the night itching, wheezing, and puking his guts out. Mom smiled and remarked about her husband's selflessness, putting himself in danger to help out his mother-in-law.

She drained her vodka cranberry and ordered another. "We found out something important this week," she announced. "We got our trial date."

I rested my fork in my plate of mahimahi.

"When?" I asked.

"Second week of March," Mom said.

Joel had returned and was entertaining Em by lifting her high above the table and pretending he was about to drop her. I ignored them.

"Oh, honey," Mommom Marie said, "that's so soon. I'm so sorry."

"Six months. Half a year. Could be worse, I guess," Mom replied.

"They're bullies," Joel said, referring to the government, "and I don't let bullies push me around. You know what I do to bullies?"

Joel started to tell us about his school days, and what it was like when he'd come to America from Israel when he was just fourteen years old.

"I was little, skinny, and nerdy with huge black glasses. Big, curly hair. I looked like a social reject, and my family was religious. We didn't speak the language. Imagine I came to America and didn't speak a word of English, and in 1967 they didn't have all these immigrant programs like they do now. It was sink or swim. Nobody gave a shit. You had to learn English, and since I didn't know it yet, they put me in the class with the morons and juvenile delinquents."

He described the teacher of that class, and as he talked, I pictured the principals from every high school movie I'd ever seen. He said the guy would come down the rows of desks and twist students' ears or drag them by their collars up to the front of the class, where he'd find all kinds of ways to humiliate them. Joel was ridiculed for being a foreigner. The other kids in the class thought he was weak, and picked on him, too: stealing his books, kicking and tripping him, cornering him in the boys' room, and flushing his head down the toilet for laughs, like a rougher version of the T-Birds from *Grease*, with Joel as some poor little Eugene.

"One day," he continued, "I had had enough. I said, if they're going to put me in this class of juvenile delinquents, I'm going to beat them at their own game. I'll be the biggest delinquent they've ever seen, so the next time Mr. Green comes by and starts twisting ears, I make my plan. Next day he tells me to come up and pass out the textbooks, so I calmly get up and grab the books off his desk and go over to the window."

Mr. Green started barking his head off. But Joel ignored him and opened the third-story windows of his classroom, and dumped all the textbooks onto the concrete below. This caused a bit of a riot, because all the other students wanted to follow suit, and pretty soon all the windows were open. The bigger kids started tossing the desks and chairs out too, and they had just about hurled Mr. Green out with the furniture, but he was a total coward, and when he realized he couldn't control his class, he took off down the hallway, loafers skidding and slipping like crazy on the ugly institutional linoleum.

"He was running for dear life," Joel said, and by this time he was laughing so hard at the memory, tears were streaming down his face. We were all laughing, even Em.

"That's what I do to bullies. I beat them at their own game. And that's exactly what I'm going to do to the federal government," Joel said.

We skipped dessert that night. Joel said he wanted to clear out and that he and Mom wanted to take Em to Funland.

"I don't know. I think she's too little. She's not even two yet. Maybe in a couple of years," I said, but then I realized we didn't have a couple of years.

There we were at a nice restaurant, in our fancy clothes, me with the Coach purse I'd gotten for Christmas, Em all ruffled up in Janie and Jack, Joel in Prada shoes. We'd ordered expensive champagne and king crab legs. We had every luxury but time. So I changed my mind—now that the trial date was set, I knew this would be the first of the lasts.

"You know what? Who cares? She'll love the boardwalk and the lights. It'll be fun," I said.

Sunset over the choppy Atlantic Ocean streaked the dimming sky cotton-candy-pink and blue as we arrived. Mommom Marie had driven herself to the restaurant and had gone home, so it was just the four of us now. My parents walked hand in hand down the boardwalk. Em bounced with delight on Joel's shoulders, and as we headed toward the games and rides, I took it all in—the flashing lights, the dings and bleeps of the arcade, the nose-burning creosote of the treated wooden planks beneath our feet. Kids streaked by, slinging green glow sticks. I'd done the same thing at their age and, with any luck, in a few years that'd be Emmeline, too. Tourists in cheesy T-shirts ambled past, carrying buckets of beach fries soggy with malt vinegar, and I wanted some even though I was full from dinner, just because I remembered how delicious they were.

Joel took Em on the carousel, and she shrieked and waved each time she spotted Mom and me in the crowd. After the ride stopped, she wanted more and pointed at the little boats that cruised around a green concrete mermaid in a shallow pool, then the baby swings and the bright red fire trucks with clanging bells. She wasn't too young to appreciate Funland after all, I supposed.

"Copter, Mommy!" Em begged, reaching out of my arms toward a more grown-up ride.

I could tell Mom sensed my apprehension. "Go ahead and take her on that," she said.

The helicopters held two people, usually a parent and a child. I'd ridden them a hundred times when I was little, and I loved swooping up and down as the little choppers circled on long metal arms around the center axle. It always felt like we were really flying.

"You don't think it's too scary?" I asked, but Mom said Em wasn't scared of anything.

"She's not like you, remember."

Joel went to buy us tickets, and after a short wait Em and I whizzed around in a helicopter of our own.

"Higher, Mommy! Higher!" Em shouted over the buzz of the rickety ride.

I panicked for a second. Em could fall out. What if the arm holding our helicopter broke off, and we crashed onto the concrete? This thing had to have been around for at least thirty-something years. That ride was exactly the same as it had been when I was a kid, and that was ages ago.

"Look!" Em said. "Mommom and Papa J on the ground!"

We waved at my parents and they waved back. Joel snapped photos with his phone.

"Please, Mommy. Higher!" Em pled, and I let it go. I released the handle so the helicopter jerked up way over Funland's gray-shingled rooftops. We could see everything up there, the Ferris wheel, the misty ocean, and for a minute it was just the two of us, Em and me, and we were soaring above everything, laughing and whooping and pointing at the stars that were just beginning to poke through the twilight.

"High as the sky!" Em demanded.

"We can't go any higher," I said, and laughed.

"Yes, Mommy. Higher," she repeated, and pointed straight up.

My parents were so far below. Two teeny, smiling, happy grandparents, waving like mad every time they spotted us whiz by, and it reminded me of a song I used to love long before any of this life existed, back when I was a single undergrad:

They will see us waving from such great heights.
"Come down now," they'll say.
But everything looks perfect from far away.
"Come down now." But we'll stay. . . .

And as we flew, I started to sing.

21

"Pink," Emmeline said.

"Come on," I argued. "What about purple? Green is pretty. Look at this red. Red is beautiful."

"Pink," Em repeated.

My child could hold her ground, that much was certain. As ridiculous and futile as it was, I was arguing with an almost two-year-old over what her favorite color should be, because she'd recently become completely obsessed with the color pink.

This was, of course, my karma: when I was pregnant, I'd arrogantly tempted fate by eschewing all things pink and princessy. *My daughter wouldn't conform to gender stereotypes*, I'd bragged. *There will be no body-dysmorphic Barbies in my house! My daughter will play with wooden trains and balls of felt and whatever random junk she can find out in the yard. Because that will nurture her imagination, and she can grow up to be a chef or an engineer!*

But now here I was, two days home from Delaware and awake way too early, trying to convince my child that pink really wasn't all that. At the time it seemed like a righteous battle because, in my mind, pink was common. Those awful pageant kids from Kentucky who had names like Capri (as in pants) loved pink, and so did Mary Kay ladies. Pink was the signature color of strippers for God's sake. I wanted Em to be a little more original, but children, I was now convinced, come to Earth to humble their parents by doing the opposite of everything their mothers and fathers want.

I'd barely been a mom for two years, but I already laughed at the naïve expectant parent I'd been, who'd envisioned herself gardening, a peaceful infant strapped to her back in an organic cotton sling. I was going to be the no-TV mom too, and have the kid who ate lots of fresh vegetables because I fed her the French way, whatever that even was.

The child in front of me had never been a blank page waiting for me to write her personality upon. She'd arrived with her own agenda, or so it seemed, and because I'd struggled so hard with postpartum depression, I didn't have the energy to garden or cook French food, and I'd quickly given in when I found that the TV— the wonderful TV—allowed me to eat a meal or take a shower or even doze off on the couch for a blissful twenty minutes at a time. Em loved cartoon animals. She played with plastic toys that made a racket and lit up and were supposed to cause ADHD and Lord knows what other neurological defects in developing brains. Relatives had bought them for her in spades, and the toys kept her entertained, so I hadn't had the heart to trash them in favor of wooden animals that were handmade in Germany and cost approximately ninety dollars per set. She wore T-shirts with characters, and sneakers that flashed, and she'd now entered a terrifying phase in which she wouldn't leave the house without a tutu on. I had one of those kids who worshiped at the shrine of sequins, tulle, and strawberry lip gloss. She had the taste and style of a Vegas cabaret performer, and her will was like a force of nature, so I waved my white—er, *pink*—flag, and decided to let it be. Maybe the pink obsession was temporary. My phone was ringing anyway, and it was Mommom Marie, probably checking to see if we'd made it home okay, and I was all ready to fess up about how I'd plied Em with chocolate Tastykakes so she would sit quietly until the plane landed. Something in my grandmother's voice, though, immediately told me this phone call wasn't going to be about cupcakes.

"Honey, have you heard from your parents?" she asked.

"Actually, no, but they were supposed to have left last night, so that would probably put them somewhere in the Carolinas by now, I'd imagine."

"They didn't leave, sweetheart. There's been a terrible accident."

My stomach lurched into my throat, and I felt like I was trapped inside a broken elevator that had just dropped three floors in less than a second.

"They were going to leave Milford and head back to Florida last night, but first they decided to take the Hummer out and get some dinner. They were heading through town on their way back to the RV and someone ran a red light—"

"Are they okay? Where are they?" I cried.

"I don't know." Mommom Marie sighed. "Joel called me last night and said they were headed to the hospital, but I haven't heard from them since, and I was actually hoping you had."

"I'll let you know as soon as I do," I said.

When I called, Joel's cell went straight to voice mail. I tried Mom's, and it rang and rang. Nearly sick with worry, I checked for them on Facebook and even called Milford Memorial, only to be told that they had no patients with my parents' names. I googled "Milford, Delaware, car accidents" and checked the websites for local newspapers, but found nothing. I could only wait, queasy with adrenaline, and expecting the worst until someone called with an update.

Hours later Mom finally did. They'd been T-boned at a major intersection, and the force of the collision had slammed the Hummer into a light pole, which had crashed down on them and crushed the SUV's hood.

"It missed the roof by inches," Mom said. "And, if it hadn't, we wouldn't be here. We would not be here."

She praised her guardian angel and then the Hummer itself

for keeping them alive. As it stood, the car was totaled, but she and Joel were okay. Sore, cut up, bruised, and shaken, but still here. Knowing her phobia of medical procedures, I asked if she'd actually gone to the hospital.

"Oh, they wanted me to, those paramedics. My blood pressure was off the charts. They thought I was about to have a stroke, and I told them it was just because the accident had scared me half to death, but they insisted we go to the emergency room and get checked out. Of course Joel was fine. You know how calm he is all the time, and he didn't have a scratch, but they wanted to check him out anyway. So they took us in the ambulance. Hooked me up to all kinds of shit, monitoring my heart. They made us sit there all night long, and finally I said, 'This is ridiculous. I don't go to doctors. I haven't been to a damn doctor since I was twenty, and I'm not about to start now.' I told Joel we were leaving, unhooked myself, and walked straight out that door," she said.

"Are you nuts?" I asked.

"I'm completely fine. If I wasn't fine, they wouldn't have let me sit there by myself."

Maybe she had a point, but still, after a serious car accident, you don't just get up and walk out of the hospital. It was irresponsible, and Mom's flippant attitude about her health got on my nerves. Ashley and I always laughed that one day Mom was going to suddenly drop dead of something completely preventable, but it was never really a joke.

"We ended up taking a taxi back to Mommom Marie's, and had some breakfast. We're just going to rest in the RV till we feel better, and then we'll head on back to Florida in a couple of days, but believe me, I don't want to spend another second in this shit hole. I need to get back in my house with my baby girls."

"Just come home to us safe," I said.

I'd imagined losing my parents for the past two years, but in a different sort of way: I worried about them going to jail, but until now I'd never stopped to consider that they could die, that their loss could be whole and permanent, and what that sort of grief might look like. I'd taken for granted that my parents would always be around—I'd seen them as superheroes my whole life. As a kid, it had seemed like they stood formidable in the face of every challenge, that they'd always be there to save me, but now I saw that they were as fragile as the rest of us, maybe more so. There were no superheroes, least of all Mom and Joel. If they couldn't even protect themselves, they certainly couldn't be expected to rescue me, or even serve as a buffer against bad luck, random accidents, and all the challenges the world might throw in my direction.

Em was watching *Wonder Pets!*, a show for toddlers about a resourceful guinea pig, a talking turtle, and a lisping duckling who teamed up to rescue animals trapped in perilous situations. *Where are you, Linny, Tuck, and Ming-Ming too?* I thought. *This is serious. You have to help me.*

22

My parents recovered quickly from their accident, and once they returned home from Delaware, they bought a new Hummer identical to the one that got totaled, and went back to hosting Sunday dinners every week. The house was always packed. They fired their old cleaning lady because she hadn't been reliable, and hired a live-in housekeeper to deal with all the mess. She was a Lithuanian immigrant with rotten gray teeth, and she smoked so much, I wondered if she actually needed a cigarette to breathe, but Liszka was gentle and unassuming. As nice as she was, though—and as great as it was having someone to help clean the kitchen—the timing still seemed weird.

"Why would condemned people hire a maid?" Ben asked one day as we stood in our kitchen, getting ready to go to yet another feast at the House of Dreams.

"Denial? Or because they're confident in their innocence?" I speculated. "You know, there's still a chance. They have good lawyers. They aren't automatically *condemned*, and that's a dramatic word. It's not like they're on death row!"

"I'm just being realistic, Victoria. Most people don't beat those kinds of charges, and I don't want you to be disappointed," he said. He ran his fingers through his hair until it stood on end. "This is affecting me, too. You don't seem to get that," he added, uncorking a new bottle of Chardonnay.

"I don't know what to say. I'm sorry. I don't know how to make it better," I said.

"I could lose my job," he said. "Do you get that? If someone suspected?"

"But you were never even remotely involved."

"Doesn't matter. Reputations are everything."

He took his glass of wine and went out into the backyard.

His family knew the truth now, and we were humiliated. Earlier in the summer Ben's cousin had been in town with her husband and sons. We'd met them at their hotel for an afternoon at the pool, and later that day my parents had generously invited them to one of their Sunday barbecues. It seemed like they'd enjoyed themselves. Mom made the kids a sundae bar, and Joel had played with them in the pool. The cousin went home, and we hadn't heard from them since, but apparently Mom and Joel had made an impression on her husband. He wanted to know what they did for a living—how they got that fancy house, the boat, the Bentley, the Hummer—so he'd taken to the Internet, and when he'd found out the truth, he'd copied and pasted several choice tidbits into a mass e-mail he sent to the rest of the family. Just a heads-up, you know. Ben married into a family of criminals. He hadn't even considered our feelings, or how doing something like this would affect Ben or me. But as embarrassing as the situation was, Ben's parents had been gracious and understanding.

"It's not our business," Ben's mom had politely said to me over the phone one day as I tried to apologize for the terrible things I knew she'd read about my parents. "We've always liked your parents, and this won't change that."

It had been kind of her to say that, but her words didn't make me feel better. I'd googled my parents, and I knew what Ben's family had read about them. Besides the indictment and a few brief news stories, there were several scathing posts on penny stock message boards. They said my parents were grifters and referred to stock promoters like my mother as "scums of the Earth." Someone had even devoted an entire blog to exposing their alleged crimes. I'd scrolled through website after website, reading posts written by people who claimed that my mom and Joel had ripped them off. Afterward I hid my Chanel shoes and Kate Spade bags in the back of the closet. I couldn't bear to think that my nice things might have come at someone else's expense, and I had no use for them anymore.

Right after the e-mail incident with his cousin, I noticed that Ben had removed his marital status from Facebook. At first I'd assumed it was because he was cheating on me, but the truth, I feared, was worse. Adultery would've stung less than shame, and I believed my husband had severed his online ties to me because he didn't want anyone else snooping around and finding out he was associated with my notorious family. I never let on to him that I had noticed or that I understood why, and that afternoon I didn't run after him, though I wanted to. I just stood at the kitchen sink, leaning over a pile of dirty pots, and watched him standing in the yard, his back to me as he drained his Chardonnay and stared blankly at the fence.

He came back in a while later. He poured another glass of wine, and we pasted on smiles so we could walk hand in hand over to my parents' house for another party. He didn't mention his thoughts about the charges again.

That fall we collected memories like souvenirs from a vacation that was almost over, gathering as many as we could before the trial, just in case. No one wanted to say what the "just in case" was, and we never actually brought it up, but it was always there like a silent, menacing presence, reminding us that time was running out.

My memory of those few months is a movie montage of perfect moments: pumpkin patches, birthday parties, Em turning two, the perfectly pink strawberry cake I made for her. On Halloween, Joel took her trick-or-treating, Em dressed as a furry kitten (pink, of course). Then came Joel's birthday and mine, only a day apart in early November. We celebrated at our favorite Italian restaurant, at a big table crowded with my parents' friends, and there was pasta with fresh white truffles shaved on top for everyone. Mom decorated early for the holidays that year and hired a photographer to come to the house and take family portraits. We must've taken a thousand photos that fall. It was like we knew that in the past we'd taken our time together for granted, and now we were desperate to document each second we had left.

When Ashley and Andrew made their announcement, they chose to share their good news at a Sunday dinner.

"We're having a baby!" There was a champagne toast, and mazel tovs all around.

I knew they'd been trying for a second child, but I didn't think it was a good idea. We'd talked about it right after I got back from Delaware, during one of our afternoon playdates.

"You'll be due around the trial," I'd told her, but Ashley had shrugged it off.

"We want our kids to be close in age. We can't put our lives on hold because of them," she'd said.

"But they may never get to meet this baby," I'd said.

"Then that's their consequence for committing crimes," Andrew had interjected. We'd all been in the backyard. He'd been planting a papaya tree by the shed and had overheard our conversation.

"Exactly," Ashley had said.

"They're innocent until proven guilty," I'd mumbled.

Then I'd tried to segue into a more pleasant topic because the conversation was making me uncomfortable.

"I have a little news of my own," I'd announced. "Em and I are going to preschool this fall!"

Starting that October, Em and I went to a Mommy and Me class at an alternative preschool. It was my weapon against pink. The Barbie army was gaining on us, and I was determined to battle it with something called "organic play." It seemed to involve a lot of recorder music and non-GMO raisins, but I was ecstatic when I found the place. A decade earlier, before I'd moved to Florida, I'd actually worked as a kindergarten aide at a similar school in Atlanta. I thought the school's philosophy was slightly wacko (they believed in gnomes), but I found their aesthetic, with its dedication to pastels, natural materials, and a homelike classroom setting, healing and incredibly comforting. It would be a good contrast to the chaos of Casa dei Sogni and would give Em a solid foundation for her education, I thought. More than anything, I hoped we could find a community there that would embrace us. I wanted Em and I to make some friends.

Finding other mom friends had been hard. We'd attempted a couple of playdates with parents we met at the park or the library, but each of them ended in disaster. We'd had two experiences from hell before I'd given up. One of the moms was interested in nothing except bragging about what a genius her kid was, and it made me want to stab her in the face with a fork.

"When did Em say her first word?" she asked, and before I could answer, the woman was yawping about how her little Taizlee had waved and said *bye-bye* at six months old, and how no one could believe it but it was totally true and they even had it on video.

Our second nightmare playdate involved a child who was so perfect, I thought she was one of those robot kids from *A.I.* We'd met Camilla and her mom at a weekly story hour at a toy store, and I'd invited them over because they seemed nice. They *were* nice—a little *too* nice. Camilla always shared and smiled. She had blue eyes like an old-time china doll and allowed her mother to clip pretty bows in her golden curls. She even loved broccoli. Em, by contrast, lived on Goldfish crackers, had hair like Chaka from *Land of the Lost* because she wouldn't let me brush it, and spent the entire playdate forcefully ripping toys out of Camilla's hands and yelling "No!" at the top of her lungs. By the time they finally left our house, Em and I were both in tears, and it wasn't a surprise when they never called us to play again. I hoped the moms at the alternative preschool might be a better fit.

There were about eight of us in the class, and our teacher was a soft-spoken grandmother who'd raised four children of her own. She'd taught for many years and seemed to hold the wisdom of the ages, probably storing it in the crystals she wore on hemp ropes around her neck (because leather isn't vegan). On the first day, the mothers sat outside in a circle on the "free-range" playground while the children explored their new surroundings. We introduced ourselves, and at least five of the moms called themselves *doulas*, and I think *all* of them were yoga teachers. After everyone had said their names, the teacher asked us to discuss what had surprised us most about motherhood.

"The love." The first mom sighed. "I've been awash in universal love. I didn't know, before I was blessed with this star child, that I could feel so intensely."

The other mothers nodded in understanding, and one whispered reverently about how overwhelming that sort of happiness can be, and then the next mom said she was surprised her home birth (in a kiddie pool) had been like having multiple orgasms because she was connected so intimately to the goddess energy— which then led to a detailed conversation about placenta eating. That was when I knew I wasn't going to fit in. When my turn came, I mumbled something about being surprised at how tired I was all the time, and was met by blank stares until the orgasm mom chimed in and told me I should co-sleep: then all the world's problems would be solved. If this bunch had a clue what I was dealing with, they'd want nothing to do with me and my kid, I realized. We were already highly suspect, because Em was the only toddler there in Huggies. Most of these moms proudly sewed their own cloth diapers, but the real valedictorians boasted that they practiced "elimination communication." They mysteriously knew when their babies had to pee and poop, and would hold them over a toilet when they needed to go.

"Diapers are unnatural. Such a *Western* practice!" one of the moms scoffed with a tittering laugh. "Mothers in third-world countries have been *undiapering* for centuries."

But that was just the beginning. The next several weeks

blurred into a series of awkward and embarrassing situations, like the time Em rifled through my purse and pulled out a package of nonorganic, dye-filled fruit snacks. The gasps were audible.

"Oh gosh, I-I-I think we got those trick-or-treating," I tried to explain, and, of course, as I attempted to throw them away, Em ran after me screaming, "Gummies!" because my child would sell her soul to the devil at the crossroads for a single pack of fruit snacks. So serious was her addiction to princess-shaped gelled fruit, I thought she was going to need a toddler twelve-step program to kick it.

Em also had it out for one of the other little girls in the class, and if she were allowed within arm's reach of this child, Em would bite the shit out of her for no apparent reason. Em hit and pushed and obsessed over the preschool's only pink dress-up dress, and melted down if any of the other little girls wanted it, and when she got mad, I could feel the other moms judging me, thinking that Em's appalling behavior was my fault because I fed her fruit snacks and let her watch Disney Junior—the equivalent of using live grenades as toys. I got mad when I felt like they judged me, asking repeatedly if I'd tried her on a gluten-free diet or if I allowed her the nemesis of crunchy moms everywhere—*screen time.* I wanted to yell at them and tell them I'd spent 70 percent of my childhood on the floor, too close to the TV set, eating Oreos, while mesmerized by *Scooby-Doo* and *The Brady Bunch*, and that I still managed to grow up into something other than a burger-flipper at Wendy's, but it wouldn't have done any good, and part of me—okay *most* of me—believed that Em's issues *were* my fault because I was distracted and lazy and watched *The Bachelorette,* and even more so because Ben and I would sometimes fight in front of her.

The other moms definitely didn't fight with their husbands. How could they? They were all married to their soul mates and were too enlightened to argue. Besides, they were right about everything anyway. They sounded like the world's dullest radio show, and reminded me of that old *Saturday Night Live* skit where

they used to make fun of NPR for being monotone and boring. I
wanted to shake them and yell, *Inflection! Intonation! Speak the
fuck up! Show some emotion!* But the thing was, these soft-spoken,
(almond) milquetoast moms, with their whispering robotic tones,
were actually the most quietly hysterical women I'd ever met. The
most passion I ever saw them express was over a strawberry.

We arrived late one morning, so I showed up midconversation.

"Yes, so I had to end the friendship because I simply cannot
be friends with someone who doesn't share my values and who
would endanger my son, Poet, like that," Marilyn, who sounded
the most like an NPR show, was saying.

The moms all nodded in apparent sympathy.

"I was honestly appalled," she continued, "that I was friends
with someone who would give Poet a nonorganic strawberry."

"I mean, how did she not know?" Jennifer (one of the five
doulas) said. "Strawberries are on the dirty dozen list."

"Exactly, exactly. And ever since, I can't shake the feeling that
Poet has been contaminated in some way, that he has lost his innocence. I was terrified. I watched him for several days for signs
of a reaction." Marilyn sighed.

"Did you notice anything?" Jennifer asked.

Marilyn shook her head tragically. "He isn't the same child."

This is where I had to butt in because, seriously, come the
fuck on.

"So let me clarify: Poet had one nonorganic strawberry? That's
it?" I asked.

"Well, she would have given him several more had I not stepped
in, but alas, I was too late, and he'd swallowed it," Marilyn confirmed.

As much as I wanted to shout, *Are you kidding me?* I needed to
know how Poet (for the love of Jesus F-ing Christ) was "not the
same child" as he had been pre–nonorganic strawberry poisoning. My curiosity was killing me, because by that point in her life,
Em had probably eaten hundreds of nonorganic strawberries.

"He's grabbing things. Constantly grabbing and getting into things around the house," Marilyn said.

"How old is your son?" I asked.

"He's seventy-three weeks tomorrow," she said, "not counting his gestational age."

"So he's a year and a half?" I asked.

"Yes. Seventy-three weeks." She nodded.

"And he's getting into stuff and grabbing things?" I asked. She nodded again.

"You do know that's what toddlers do, right? I mean, my two-year-old spends her entire waking existence trying to grab, get into, climb on, and consume things that will kill her. If she could play with nothing but fire, poison, and knives, she'd be thrilled," I said.

"Poet is also climbing."

"My child is, at this very second, climbing," I said.

"Have you looked at her diet? Are you feeding her gluten? She could have wheat belly." Marilyn looked genuinely concerned. I had to get up and walk away.

That day we held a "blessingway" for Ellie, my favorite mom of the group, who was about to give birth to her second daughter. Jennifer initiated this event, which was basically a New Age baby shower, and at first it was nothing short of ridiculous. Jennifer began to chant over a bowl of water. That lasted about two seconds before Em wandered over from the sandbox and plunged her hands in the water yelling "Splash!" I was mortified, but Jennifer just nonchalantly moved on to burning some sage, and after that we read Ellie our favorite verses from a book of birth poetry, a genre I must've missed in grad school. Jennifer wove flowers into Ellie's long blond hair, and then we went around and shared our wishes for the new baby. As my turn approached, I started to lose it.

I couldn't cry in front of them and cause some drama queen scene. Ellie deserved every bit of the group's good energy, but the enormity of my own situation overwhelmed me. I excused myself and walked quickly across the playground to the organic garden before anyone could see my tears, and stood by the picket fence in a patch of sweet potato vines to catch my breath.

I'd been cynical about the blessingway because I was envious. I wished Em could have been welcomed into the world with this same gentle joy. My pregnancy and birth had scared me. So much trauma had clouded Em's arrival—renovating our house, the raid, the arrests, my postpartum depression. Her first few years had been hard, and I worried I could never be the calm, nurturing mother she needed. I felt guilty, but also angry, because most of this wasn't my fault. In fact, none of it was my fault, and all of it was entirely beyond my control, but something else was on my mind that morning.

The blessingway had reminded me I was about to become an aunt again. I couldn't stop thinking about Ashley's second pregnancy, and how sad I was about it. I *wanted* to be happy for her, but it was as if I'd lost my ability to truly celebrate or even feel much of anything. Something like envy had surfaced when Ashley told me she was pregnant, but that wasn't it exactly. *I* certainly didn't want to be pregnant again, nor did I want another C-section, and I *never* wanted to go back to the harrowing first months of caring for a newborn, especially not while trying to manage Em's terrible twos and the upcoming trial. Rather than envying my sister's second pregnancy, I wished I wanted a bigger family, that I had the mental capacity to deal with two kids. I wished I could set better boundaries and separate myself from the turmoil of my parents' indictments with a little of Ashley's "life goes on" attitude, but I couldn't. I couldn't bear the thought of having a child who may never meet his or her grandparents.

23

It was December, and I'd signed up for the thirty-day yoga challenge for the certificate I'd get if I completed it. My self-esteem was at an all-time low, so each day when I finished a class, I was thrilled when the teacher gave me a literal gold star. In the lobby, the studio manager had hung up a big chart, which looked exactly like Em's good behavior chart at home, and worked the same way. Every time I went to yoga, I got to put a gold star sticker on the chart by my name. It was absurdly motivating—if I got thirty stars in thirty days, I won a week of free classes, plus the certificate, which at that point seemed harder to obtain than another college degree. I planned on framing it and hanging it in the living room next to my bachelor's and master's.

I know I was the last person anyone would expect to do yoga for thirty straight days, but I was determined to get the last laugh on my husband. Also, I hoped that by some miracle of God, thirty straight days of yoga might fit me into a size four again. It had certainly worked for Ashley. She was three months pregnant and in better shape than ever, because she went to yoga twice a day, every single day of the week—she even talked about becoming a yoga teacher.

I, on the other hand, was still a remedial yogi and still trying to get through a class without comparing myself to the skinny bitches around me while trying to love and embrace my muffin top. Yoga might not have taught me humility yet, but I was starting to learn what it felt like to relax, and to live in the present moment, without always trying to predict the future and defend myself against whatever awful thing I thought might happen next.

One day in mid-December, I was struggling through a particularly hard class when I finally enjoyed a moment of triumph. I got my foot in the crook of my elbow. *Yes! I am strong!* I thought, but then the teacher came over and adjusted me, because it turned out I was actually doing the pose wrong. There were women literally twice my age in that class who were, at that moment, upside down, but I couldn't even manage what looked like a simple pose, so I began to feel very sorry for myself again, which was not yogic at all.

We always began class by setting intentions, and that day mine had been to stop fighting. I was a fighter, and up until then I thought that was a good thing, that it meant I was determined and perseverant, and that fighting would make me tough, and that the more I fought, the less I'd be hurt. I argued and squabbled with everyone, especially Ben. He was too loud and too messy, I griped. I complained he didn't spend enough time at home and that it was wrong for him to hang out at his best friend's house, and then when he *was* home, he got on my nerves. He'd get defensive and hurl insults back at me, which hurt my feelings and pissed me off so I had to be even nastier to get the last word. Then he'd withdraw and become cold and distant, at which point Insecurity would show up and shine a spotlight on my very worst fear—abandonment. I'd become completely hysterical, raging at him to love me, until he withdrew more or just left the house.

We moved through a long floor sequence that afternoon, and it felt good. The yoga room was dim, lit only by flickering candles, and the heat, for once, felt amazing. Instead of fearing that I was about to succumb to heatstroke, I welcomed the warmth. It softened my muscles, letting me stretch a little farther past my limits. I exhaled and folded myself into pigeon, and as I touched my

nose to my mat, it occurred to me that in fighting, I was creating
the exact opposite of what I wanted. The more I fought, the more
hurt I got and the more hurt I caused. It had become a vicious
cycle, and I was working on it as best as I could. The truth was,
all this fighting was wearing me down.

I realized I needed to learn to let everything go, like those
beautiful paper lanterns whose fire lifts them up to the sky until
they vaporize, but I didn't know how to detach. That day I
heard another message in my head. *You will get through this*, it
said. *You are going to be okay. One of these days, you will look back
on all this and laugh, one day, when the things you most want are all the
things you have.*

The funny part was that, back then, I already had a lot of *things*.
I just didn't want them. My mother bought me purses and shoes
even when I'd asked her not to. She never made a trip to Ross without bringing me back at least a couple of cute tops. Em's wardrobe
was on par with the royal family's, and she had heaps of toys at
home *and* at her grandparents'. I was always grateful, but it was
all clutter, and I still felt empty. Pining and longing and loneliness
consumed me, and I'd look at the objects my parents had generously
piled on us and wonder how I could possibly have so much expensive stuff I didn't even care about, while the things I *did* want, like
romance, human connection, acceptance, time, and *sleep*, eluded
me. And all these things were free.

I wanted more memories, too. I couldn't get enough, so that
December I made sure we did everything. I dragged my parents
out almost every day. Long lunches blended into tours of holiday
light displays and Christmas festivals. Even though we were exhausted, Ben and I hosted a Christmas party at my house and
invited everyone on the block. We couldn't believe how many
people showed up, bearing bottles of wine, trays of cookies, and
presents for Em. That night was a blast—everyone singing carols,
dipping mulled wine from a big pot simmering on the stove, and
reminiscing about old times. Mom and Joel gave Barbara and

Arlo a puppy. Their beloved Yorkie had died a few weeks earlier, and she and her husband were grief stricken, so my mom searched long and hard to find them "a new baby." She'd tied a bow around the puppy's neck and presented it to them in front of everyone. Barbara had sobbed with joy.

Mom bought everyone presents that Christmas. She shopped like never before, and I couldn't believe how much she'd bought Em. *Where am I going to put it all?* I wondered. Some of the stuff was huge—a pink play kitchen set; a miniature piano made from real cherrywood; trikes; bikes; a three-story dollhouse. It was nuts. She even bought her an artisan potty chair! Who even knew something like that existed?

On Christmas Eve, after a seafood and pasta feast, I went home and began trying to organize some of the gifts. A lot of the toys, puzzles, and games Mom got for Em were for older children. She'd bought clothing up to size five when Em had only just turned two. That was when it hit me: my mother was making sure Em was well stocked, that she'd have everything she needed for the next few years in case she and Joel were gone for the rest of her childhood.

As Ben and I played Santa Claus, arranging Em's gifts beneath the tree while she slept, I remembered the stories my mom had always told me about her childhood. She grew up one of four, and when my mom was little, her father had owned a successful trucking company. When business was good, her mother made sure her family was beautifully dressed.

"I was a girly girl like Em. I loved ruffles and lace," Mom had told me.

People complimented their family wherever they went, and my mother had delighted in being called *precious, darling, gorgeous.* She said it made her feel proud when people raved about what a pretty little girl she was. But then my grandfather's business went bankrupt, and they were left penniless. Mom's self-worth disappeared with the ruffled dresses.

"We had to wear hand-me-downs. Ugly shit. Clothes that were too small. I was so ashamed of myself. My mom had to sew our clothes, and we had to wear the same outfits to school every single day. Nobody ever said I was pretty anymore," Mom told me.

Her words helped me make sense of her behavior. Even as a small child, my mother attached her self-worth to outward appearances and material things. She needed something, like a fine blouse or a brand-name purse (even if it was a fake one) and a big gaudy house, to prove she was important, beautiful, and successful. She loved giving others the things that made her feel good, and perhaps that was the only way she could believe that others would love her back. I couldn't help but wonder what my mother would have left if the money, the clothes, and the fancy dinners were suddenly gone. Could she value herself without jeweled shoes and access to an American Express black card? Would all her friends disappear?

They certainly showed up on Christmas Day. Casa dei Sogni was practically filled to capacity that year. Every guest room jammed with out-of-town visitors. Some people even slept on the floors. Corks popped, and the kitchen filled with the delicious scents of rosemary, garlic, and the caramelized onions Joel served with his delectable prime rib. That year we'd given him a black polo shirt and a new baseball cap, both embroidered with the words PAPA J in bright yellow letters. He wore them proudly as he cooked, stopping every now and then to turn up the volume on the sound system when a song he liked came on. I always turned it back down.

The revelry got on my nerves. All that rockin' around the Christmas tree, the red glitter *everything*, candles, ornaments, blinking lights, smells, food, bodies blocking every open space—it was sensory overload, but what could I say? I knew it would be the last big Christmas our family ever saw, so I tried to pretend everything was fine. But all day, amid the cacophony of small talk and drunken laughter, I constantly caught words and snippets of conversations that wouldn't let me forget: *trial date, charges, witnesses, fraud, testifying, market manipulation.*

Later in the evening several of the neighbors showed up for the celebration and ended up camped out at the bar. Half of the people there I barely knew, including the girl Baron Von Bod showed up with. He'd arrived just in time for dessert with a surprise announcement: his date, Layla, was his new fiancée.

Baron Von Bod was the last person on earth I'd ever expect to get married, and his bride was even more shocking, mostly because she was actually normal. Since he'd once been the boy toy of a madam who was close to fifteen years his senior, I'd always imagined the love of his life as a trashy-looking porn star, but nope—Layla was a quiet, innocent girl. She was Lebanese, pretty and petite, with long layered hair the color of hot chocolate, olive skin, and green eyes. She wore skinny jeans and knee-high boots and liked accessorizing with bulky scarves. Nothing about this woman even remotely suggested she would go for a reality-show pimp. I was feeling more charitable than usual that evening (maybe the thirty days of yoga was working), so I felt genuinely happy for the couple. Layla was nothing but smiles, and Baron was obviously smitten with her. *A nice girl would be good for Baron,* I thought.

Mom was ecstatic about their engagement, and shocked everyone, especially me, when she spontaneously announced, after popping open yet another bottle of Gloria Ferrer Sonoma Brut, that she was throwing Baron and Layla's wedding right there at Casa dei Sogni.

"Valentine's weekend!" Mom told everyone. "It's going to be the most beautiful wedding you've ever seen in your lives, and you're all invited. It's going to be one hell of a party! The whole cast of *Stud Muffins* is going to be here!"

Ashley and I shot each other horrified looks across the room. Was Mom serious? That was less than a month before their trial. What was she thinking?

"Even better?" Mom continued, sloshing champagne out of her glass. "Em and Amelia are going to be the flower girls!"

Her revelation was followed by whistles and applause.

Ben whipped his head around and narrowed his eyes at me. *What?* he mouthed.

I shrugged and looked at Ashley. She seemed as bewildered as Ben and I were.

"Did you know about this? Were you keeping it from me?" Ben asked.

"No! I swear! This is the first I've heard of any of this," I said.

"Your mother just gets to decide that our child is going to be in the wedding of a guy who owns an escort service? And she doesn't even ask before making an announcement in front of fifty people?"

I shook my head and threw up my hands. My eyes filled with tears as I pleaded with my husband to believe that I had no idea, and that my mom, under the influence of champagne and caught up in the moment, had probably come up with the idea on the spot.

"Over my dead body is my daughter going to be in this wedding," Ben said.

24

My parents finished building Casa dei Sogni in 2005. The week they moved in, Ben and I got engaged, and the first party they ever threw there was to celebrate us. They'd had a sushi chef come to make fresh rolls to order, and it had been awesome. I couldn't believe that after all these years, this was finally our life. For a long time I forgot what they say about things that are too good to be true, because the decadence was new and intoxicating—I hadn't forgotten what it was like to screen calls for my parents so they wouldn't have to talk to a collection agency. I remembered when we lived on a street full of row houses in the bad part of town, and I knew what it was like to live in an empty house because we couldn't afford furniture and to have the utilities shut off all the time because the bills were late. For years my parents told me and everyone else who'd listen that they were going to be multimillionaires someday. They watched *Lifestyles of the Rich and Famous* like it was an instructional video and kept stacks of the *Robb Report* piled in their bedroom—at night they would flip through the magazine's glossy spreads and imagine which luxury cars and yachts they would someday buy. Now someday was here, and that was why they'd named their waterfront mansion their "House of Dreams."

That house had a special joy and a magnetic energy, or maybe I just imagined it did because I knew how much it meant to my mom and Joel. In just a few years, we'd filled that home with so many memories. Ashley and Andrew had gotten married there right before Christmas 2009, and I'll never forget the image of my beaming parents escorting my little sister, magical in the white drifts of her wedding gown, down the grand marble staircase to the refrain of Annie Lennox's "There Must Be an Angel." That had been Ashley's favorite song when she was a little girl, and I'd broken down completely when she took her vows under a chuppa of pink roses in the backyard.

And now this reality-show pimp, Baron Von Bod, was going to do the exact same thing. I thought it totally cheapened the significance of Ashley's wedding. Mom had even offered to pay for most of the event, and said she was going to use all the same vendors—basically repeating the exact same affair, just with different people, who happened to be on a cheesy reality show about sex workers.

Ashley and I were disgusted. Ben was upset about the wedding for a different reason.

He explained that he used to be able to laugh at all the characters at my parents', and he'd even thought it was funny when my parents filmed porn at their house, but something changed when Em was born. It wasn't just a big joke anymore. He had to think about his daughter now, and he didn't want her exposed to stuff like that. Besides, by deciding that Em would be the flower girl in this wedding, Mom was totally disregarding his role as Em's father. He felt like she'd always done this to him, and that I'd never stood up to her. It was the biggest point of contention in our marriage.

When we argued, Ben had a way of making me feel like I was being cross-examined. He would question me relentlessly, and I, just wanting him to stop, would try to explain myself, but he would interpret that as me pitting myself against him. He wanted concrete facts, black-and-white yeses and nos, but I could only offer indecision and ambiguity. We'd become more and more frustrated with each other until he'd end up fleeing the house to escape while I sobbed on the bathroom floor. We never accomplished much except causing each other pain, and this time he was right. I couldn't stand up to my parents and tell them I didn't want Em to be in the wedding—well, at least I thought I didn't. Sometimes it seemed okay, like when I was talking to my mom. Then, when Ben brought it up, I'd rethink the matter and realize that, no, I actually didn't want my daughter to be in the wedding of a guy who ran a male escort business.

The trial complicated what should have been an absolute no into an "Uhh, I don't know, maybe." I didn't want to disappoint my mother because I saw how very much it meant to her to see her granddaughter in a puffy dress and a crown of roses, scattering petals down an aisle. My mother was living in an elaborate fantasy where she had this beautiful, perfect life, with a beaming, close-knit family, and my kid was part of an illusion that helped her deny the fact that in a couple of short months she might be losing everything if the jury found her guilty. To me, that was tragic and I felt so much grief and compassion for my mother, but what was more important? Making my mother happy, or going with my gut and making a decision that was right for my husband and my child even though it would royally piss her off? As Ben put it, I needed to grow the fuck up already.

"Start making decisions like a parent instead of a child," he said.

That night I said a desperate prayer. I didn't even know who I was praying to—maybe that Virgin Mary statue. I begged for a solution that would make everyone happy, and I didn't want to face the fact that there simply was no way to please everyone.

The next morning I decided to defer to Ashley, because if she and I could agree, then perhaps we could present a united front, but Ashley's decision actually surprised me.

"I don't really care," she said. "I'm pregnant and I'm tired and if she wants Amelia in it, it's not a big deal. The whole thing will probably last fifteen minutes, and then we'll come home and it'll be over. Besides, Amelia's two. She's not going to remember this."

She had a point.

"We have more important things to worry about right now," Ashley said.

I rested my phone in the crook of my shoulder as I made a wide right turn in my car. I'd called her as I was taking Em home from story time at the library, and she was napping in her car seat, snuggled up in a fleece blanket. (It was mid-January and chilly for South Florida.)

"Seriously," I agreed.

"No, I mean, right this second, not like, in general," Ashley said.

"What do you mean?" I asked.

"Umm, like the car that's been parked out in front of our houses all morning."

"What?"

"Yeah, ever since you left. This car has been parked on the street, in between our houses," Ashley told me. "I can't see inside. The windows are tinted."

I made a left turn onto our street and approached slowly until I could see the mystery car. It was a shadowy sedan, nondescript, and through the windshield, which was facing north as I drove south, I could just barely make out a figure inside.

"Someone's in the car," I told Ashley. "I'm coming down the street right now, and I'm stopping. I'm going to say something to him, because this is creepy."

"Are you crazy? What if it's the Feds? What if they arrest you?"

"They're not going to arrest me," I said, but it was all bravado. I was petrified that they were camped out, waiting for me, and that they were going to haul me off to jail even though I'd never done anything wrong. But I was more scared of not knowing, so I inched up alongside the vehicle and rolled down my window.

For a long time the other driver ignored me, probably hoping I would give up and go away, but I didn't. I was mad. I felt violated and I wanted answers. Finally he rolled down his window, and then I realized I had nothing prepared to say.

"Umm, I heard you've been sitting here in front of my house all morning, and I was wondering why," I said.

The man smirked. He was wearing those big mirrored sunglasses that cops always seem to have on, and I stared at my reflection in them while I waited for him to respond. I noticed I looked a bit hysterical. My ponytail was coming undone, and the top of my head was full of flyaways. I had to resist the urge to fix my hair as the man produced a badge.

"I'm doing some surveillance in the neighborhood," the man said. "I'm a federal investigator."

Though he confirmed what I'd dreaded—expected even—I was still kind of taken aback and, for God knows what reason, I decided to challenge him.

"Who are you surveilling?" I asked. (Was that even a word?) "Because honestly? It's really freaking creepy to have a man in a dark car parked out in front of your house all day."

He smirked again. Why was this so funny to him?

"Can't tell ya," he said.

"Well, can you leave? Because this is my sister's house and that's my house and we both have little girls and this is disturbing. We aren't doing anything, so I don't know what you think you're going to see here. You know, one street over we have a bunch of derelicts living in all those beachfront motels, selling drugs. How about you go investigate them?"

"I can't tell you what I'm doing here and I can't leave right now, but I can tell you I won't be here much longer, and rest assured I'm working on a case that's going to make the neighborhood safer," he said.

"What does that even mean?" I demanded.

"Look, just calm down. It means what it means."

"Well, I don't like being watched!"

He shrugged and offered a curt "Sorry?"

Sometimes I imagined having a day without consequences, where I could say and do outrageous things and express my true feelings and act on my worst impulses without getting in trouble for them. That morning, if I could have done what I'd most wanted, I would've rammed my well-worn, seven-year-old Saturn SUV repeatedly into his vehicle until his car looked like a crushed soda can. But as that would probably get me more jail time than my parents were currently facing, I instead practiced some breathing exercises from yoga and drove away. About a half an hour later I peered out the window and the car was gone, just like the investigator had promised.

I called Ashley again. Like me, she wondered why, if they were following my parents, they would want to camp out in front of *our* houses? It wasn't like they'd see much more than the two of us buckling our toddlers into their car seats and taking them to Target—pretty scandalous, right? Ashley said she'd called Joel and he'd practically flipped out on her and made her swear she'd never talk to the investigators if they knocked on the door. I called Joel too, and like always, he said the Feds were still trying to intimidate them into making a plea bargain and forgoing a jury trial. As he did with my sister, he warned me never to speak to them. I knew I had to tell Ben, but I dreaded calling him, especially because he was at work. As soon as I told him the story, I regretted mentioning it at all; he became angry and defensive and blamed my parents for putting us through all this. He said they owed us an apology. But I knew they'd never say they were sorry. An apology would've been an admission of guilt, and my parents believed they'd done nothing wrong.

I called my mom last, right after Em woke up.

"I need you to come over right now," she said.

There was some sort of crisis going on, but Mom refused to discuss it over the phone, which I was used to by now. I figured whatever it was had to do with my earlier run-in with the investigator, and I was scared to death I'd done something wrong. Mom insisted I come over immediately, so, begrudgingly, I buckled Em in her stroller and took a brisk walk over to my parents'.

Allie greeted us at the door. She'd always been a fixture at Casa dei Sogni, but lately she'd been around even more, often sleeping over for four and five days at a time. Mom said it was because she had no money, something she'd never admit, and she stayed at my parents' house so she'd have something to eat.

Allie whisked Em out of her stroller to play with her dog in the backyard. Before she went out the back door, she shot me a warning.

"Your mom's in her office," Allie said. "It's not good."

"What happened?" I asked.

"Just let her tell you." Allie shook her head in exasperation and trotted off with Em.

I found my mom hunched over in her desk chair. Though it was past noon, she was still in her pajamas, rocking rhythmically and pulling her nose to her chin. Her hair was unwashed, and her face wasn't made-up. An ashtray overflowed on the desk, with one butt still smoldering, but she lit up a new one, inhaled, and stared into space, oblivious to the Fox News blaring on the flat-screen TV across from her. She didn't acknowledge my presence or seem to notice when I switched the television off.

"What is going on?" I asked. "Does this have to do with the guy camped out in front of my house all day?"

She shook her head. "You didn't talk to him, did you?" Mom asked.

"No!" I lied. "But is that what you're upset about?"

"Something else," she said.

"What?"

"You don't wanna know," she murmured, and turned to her computer, where she began scrolling through her Facebook feed while I stood behind her, looking at her computer screen over her right shoulder.

She was silent for a while, then said, "She's been sending me Facebook messages since last night."

"Who?" I asked.

"Ruffina," Mom said. "She's lost her shit over Joel. She's going crazy." She showed me the first message. "She's from Italy, so she doesn't write good in English."

I bent down closer next to Mom so I could see her monitor more easily, and began to read.

Hi, Cecily. Joel is been dating this woman in the neighborhood for over a year. I want help you, the message began.

He travel with this woman everywhere, good friend told me he pay for everything for her, she live somewhere close to you. He take her everywhere all your friends from Cali know about her and Baron Von Bod is with her every day at gym, all your neighbors know about her. Joel want to leave you, sorry, Cecily, give me few days to get strong enough to call you. She Russian, he is getting divorce from you after the trial, pig bastard. Put him on the street with nothing, get his ass off the house. I see them together. He was kissing her on the street. I call my neighbor last week, she told me it's all true. That bastard.

"Jesus fucking Christ," I said. "So the gist is that Joel has a mistress here in the neighborhood, and everyone knows about it except you? Including all your best friends and even Baron, whose wedding you're hosting and paying for?" I clarified.

She nodded. "Ruffina is in love with him," Mom said. "She's jealous and trying to get back at him."

"I thought that years ago," I said. "All those fancy gifts for him from Neiman Marcus that she'd leave on the front step? I'm sorry, Mom, but that wasn't normal neighborly behavior. I've thought he was having an affair with her for a long time."

I hesitated. "And I think maybe he does have a mistress in the neighborhood."

"How do you know?" Mom demanded.

"Because Ashley caught them together."

My mother looked like I'd thrown a glass of iced tea in her face, but I knew what was coming: she wasn't going to believe me. Her reaction, though, completely shocked me.

"Yeah." Mom sighed. "He's been fucking both of them. I confronted him after I read the message, and he admitted everything."

I sat down so hard in the other office chair, it rolled halfway across the wood floor and almost crashed into the wall.

"He said a few years back Ruffina was stalking him," she continued. "That woman's crazy. She threw herself at him—"

"So you're blaming *her*?" I interrupted.

She ignored me and went on. "He told me the truth. When I ask him, he always tells me the truth."

Even after a revelation like this, Mom still defended him. She gave standing by your man a whole new meaning.

"So what did he have to say for himself?" I wanted to know. I figured it had to be good.

"He was sorry. He didn't know what he was thinking. He said he has a problem he can't control, especially when he's stressed out, and it was just an escape that meant nothing. It was just some European girl who lives in the neighborhood. Calls herself a massage therapist. They go to the gym together. He bought her a Jaguar. Ruffina's jealous, so now she's threatening him."

"Wait, wait—you don't buy someone who means nothing to you a Jag. Let me get this straight: Joel's mistress is mad because she caught him with his other mistress and got jealous and decided to tell you to get back at him?" I asked.

"You can call it whatever you want."

"What are you going to do?" I asked.

"There's nothing I *can* do. You want me to leave him? I can't. I have a trial in two months. And, Vic, this is nothing new. All men cheat, don't you know that?"

"No, they don't," I muttered, but I said that more out of hope than conviction. After all, I was still obsessed with the idea that

Ben might be cheating on me. I'd never confronted him, never found any concrete proof, but the fear that he might give in to temptation was always in the back of my mind.

"You'll learn," she said. "All of them do it."

I prayed she was wrong. I worried all the time I'd lose Ben to someone younger, prettier, skinnier, more fun. If Ben cheated on me, that would mean I was unlovable and, worse, if my parents went to jail and Ben left me for another woman, I'd have no one left at all. Just Em.

My mother was trying to put on a brave face, but she looked devastated, and how could she not be? She was haggard, her expression was hollow, and I knew she was hurt, and yet she defended him and pretended to be dismissive of Joel's behavior. She gave me a pleading look.

"I do everything for everybody, and I get shit on," she said. "It's nothing new. Don't judge me, though. I have a trial we can't go into divided, and that's the most important thing to me right now. We have to be strong together if we want to win this, and I have this wedding to deal with. The invitations are already sent out."

"I don't know what to tell you," I said.

She grabbed the remote and turned the TV back on. After a few minutes she turned to me again.

"After almost thirty-five years, you don't just turn around and throw your whole life with somebody away, not after the incredible times we've had together. Maybe one day you'll understand," she said. There were tears in her eyes.

"Maybe," I whispered.

I left my mother as I'd found her and grabbed Em up off the living room floor where she and Allie were playing with blocks. As we were getting ready to leave, I commented to Allie how messed up this whole thing was.

"I told you so," Allie said. "But it's probably best to stay out of it. Be supportive, but don't give your mom any advice, because she's not going to take it anyway, and hopefully, in a week or so, this will all blow over. Maybe they can deal with it after the trial. Either way, it's not anyone else's business but their own."

The drama raged on for a few more days as Ruffina tormented my mother through every channel she could. At first she was the concerned "friend" who just wanted my mom to know the "truth" about Joel, though she conveniently left out her own role in the story. She even told my mother that Joel and his mistress were plotting to flee the country before the trial, leaving my mom alone to take the fall. With each e-mail, Facebook post, and instant message, Ruffina became more unhinged, until she was sending several furious rants a day that weren't much more than poorly constructed strings of cuss words aimed at Joel. It was hard to tell what sort of reaction Ruffina wanted from my mother, but whatever it was, she wasn't getting it. Mom blocked her e-mails, and when she did the same to Ruffina's Facebook, Ruffina simply made new accounts in different names and continued her onslaught. I told my mom she'd better keep an eye on her mini pin before Ruffina tried to boil him, because the bitch had gone full-on *Fatal Attraction*. Several times I caught her milling around on the street in front of my parents' house. She paced the neighborhood all day in her stilettos under the pretense of walking her yappy Pekinese, dragging it haplessly behind her as she stalked our family. She would loop the dog's leash around her wrist so she could hold her iPad in one hand while she clutched her phone in the other, shrieking unintelligible nonsense into it. I didn't know who she was talking to. All I knew for sure was that this woman was insane. I mean, for the love of God, who wears five-inch heels to walk a damn dog?

That whole week my mother stayed the same. I don't think she ever got dressed, and I never saw her without a cigarette, rocking in her office chair, eyes fixed on her computer screen. I went to her every day, wanting to comfort her, but each time I'd leave pissed off and frustrated because when she spoke, her words were a tangle of contradictions.

How could he do this to me?

What the fuck was he thinking?

He was a good father to you and Ashley.

He was the best husband in the world.

She showed me the mystery woman's Facebook profile. She and Allie had done some stalking of their own, based on the small amount of information Mom had from Joel, and they'd managed to find her. Her name was Agnés, and she had long spiraling dark hair, blue eyes like a Siamese cat, a Tang-tinted spray tan, and a tattoo of a great white shark emblazoned across her chest. I wasn't impressed, especially when she posted pics of her vanity tag. It read GR8 WHT—I guess because every adulteress should have a license plate to match her tat.

"I've seen that car," I said. "It's always parked in front of that big condo building, the Silver Seahorse, across from the playground we take the girls to. That must be where she lives."

"That's right across from Ruffina's house too, because Ruffina lives next to that park," Mom added.

"Right. What kind of an asshole has mistresses who live across the fucking street from each other?" I asked.

"Don't you know men are idiots?" Mom said.

I had to give her that one.

Throughout all this, Joel spent very little time at home. Mom said he came home at night, that they were having long talks and working through this, but the few times I ran into him, usually as he was coming in and I was leaving, he acted like nothing had happened. It was so awkward, I had no choice but to play along with the "everything's fine" routine, mostly because I was afraid to unleash my true feelings at him. So I smiled and said hey and let him take Em on bike rides, when the sight of him made me want to vomit all over his impeccable Prada driving shoes.

The next Friday I decided to take Em over to see my mom. I wanted to cheer her up, and planned on seeing if I could make her get dressed so I could drag her out of the house. I wanted to go to lunch, but as usual, Mom was firmly planted at her desk, and I couldn't get her to budge. She told me that the night before she'd called Barry, Joel's partner in a record company out in L.A., and that Barry had confirmed what Ruffina said in her original message: Joel had been taking Agnés on his "business" trips out West. All their Los Angeles friends had met her, probably had dinner and partied with her too. As Mom told me about her conversation with Barry, Em grabbed a handful of papers from the messy desk and tossed them onto the floor. I scrambled to pick them up and get them back into some semblance of order and realized Em had actually gotten her hands on a stack of RSVP cards for the Von Bod wedding. One in particular stood out because someone had scrawled all over it in ballpoint pen.

Shame on you! You disgusting pigs! How dare you have a cele-bration at your home, knowing we are unable to pay our bills! the card read.

"Well, I guess this one goes in the no pile," I remarked. "Who sent this?"

"Don't even ask." She sighed, rolling her eyes. "It's from the wife of one of the producers of Joel's movie. She's trying to say we owe her money, but we don't owe that bitch shit. She's crazy. Her husband screwed us!"

Of course he did, I thought. Why had this woman been invited to the wedding in the first place if it was true that her husband "screwed" them, and if her family wasn't owed money, why was she so angry? Mom became enraged when I asked her to explain.

"Do you think I need this bullshit right now on top of every-thing else? Don't worry about it! Why don't you get out of here and let me be? I don't want to go to lunch. I can't take this!"

I left, feeling more confused and dejected than ever, but mostly, I felt alone. All afternoon I circled the neighborhood sidewalks with Em in her stroller, and as I walked I thought about how the events of the past few years had isolated me. Be-fore the raid and before parenthood, everything had been con-stant fun. I never had a chance to be bored because there were boat rides, parties every weekend, Sunday dinners, barbecues, and exciting new deals and projects always on the horizon. We celebrated everything. My family had been my whole life and, sure, I had some friends when I was in grad school, but after we graduated, those friendships fizzled to little more than the occasional Facebook comment. Most of my friends had gone off to Ph.D. programs or teaching positions in other states, and I hadn't been too sad about it because Casa dei Sogni dominated my social life. Ashley was my best friend, and I was married to my soul mate. I was teaching and writing, and life was pretty much fine, but my parents' arrests proved our lives weren't as glamorous as we'd imagined. It had been easy to laugh and get along when things seemed good, but when we were challenged, we'd failed to truly band together. Instead we'd each withdrawn and succumbed to our own weaknesses as a way to avoid dealing with the difficult situation at hand. For Joel it was the thrill of affairs, for my mom it was the distractions of the Internet and shopping. Ben shut down emotionally and spent more time away from me, while Ashley overexercised and grew cynical. As for me? I was a slave to my hair-trigger emotions, screaming and crying over everything that didn't go according to my expectations. I turned into a madwoman and proceeded to metaphorically burn down my attic, and I had to get away from the drama so I could clear my head.

That night, when Ben got home from work, I told him I was leaving.

"I'm taking Em away from all this," I said. "It's too much. There's too much going on right now—investigators in front of the house, Ruffina, Agnés, Joel's whole mess. My mom's crazy, and Ashley is wrapped up in her own life."

My voice fractured into sobs. I wanted Ben to put his arms around me, but he stood still, a few steps away from me in the kitchen, arms crossed over his chest while he leaned against the countertop.

"Where are you going?" he asked, expressionless.

"Delaware," I said through my tears.

He cleared his throat and sipped his vodka soda, and after a minute he said he thought it was a good idea.

"And the best part is that we won't be around for the wedding. Em will be safe in Delaware. She won't be Baron Von Bod's flower girl."

"How long do you want to stay?" Ben asked, and I told him at least a month. He suggested I stay longer, if possible, and leave my return date open so maybe I could go to the trial in New York, which was about four hours away. I said that sounded like a good idea.

"We can leave as soon as you want," he said. "I'll drive you up so you have a car."

I was scared shitless to tell my mom about my plans, so I procrastinated a couple of more days while I packed and ran back and forth to Target, making sure I had enough warm clothes for Em. Finally, once the suitcases were packed (the week before the trip, because I was an overachiever like that), I dropped the bomb. Mom was just as mad as I'd predicted. She laid a guilt trip on me about depriving her of Em, the one good thing in her life, and tried to tell me I'd be missing out on all the fun of the wedding. I told her I didn't care. The wedding meant nothing to me, and I didn't want Em in it. Mom tried everything to make me change my mind.

"I saved you from that miserable piece of shit state, and now you want to go back there in that freezing cold hick town? Em's going to get sick in that weather, and forget driving anywhere. You never drove in ice before! And you know you can't breathe in the cold. You'll be coughing your ass off. Your body can't handle the cold air!"

Even Joel, who was not confrontational and usually played good cop to Mom's bad cop, looked at me in disgust.

"I'm disappointed in you, Victoria. That you could do this to your mother at a time like this," he said.

For a second I felt like a twelve-year-old again—like I'd dis-obeyed and was about to get grounded, or have my phone privi-leges taken away for two weeks, but as I looked at my parents, in their disaster of an office, papers and dirty ashtrays everywhere, something shifted inside of me. The tectonic plates in my brain were rearranging themselves. I'd always been afraid to disappoint them. I wanted to be perfect for my parents, and over and over it seemed like I'd found new and pathetic ways not to live up to their expectations—dropping out of that expensive college when I was eighteen, running off to Atlanta with my friends, dating guys they didn't approve of, and then living at home when I was twenty-six—the way I'd struggled with anxiety and depression since I was a kid—but that day it occurred to me that I didn't really care if they were disappointed in me. I was infinitely more disappointed in them.

For the next couple of days I felt better because of my deci-sion. Ben was happy I'd finally stood up to my parents, and that I'd found the way to keep Em out of the wedding. Besides, I needed a break, and I believed going to Delaware would give it to me—a slower pace in a simpler place, with my grandmother there to help me, just like she had when I was little. I didn't think I was running away. I believed I was going home.

25

There must be a tenth circle of hell that Dante forgot to include in his *Inferno*, where the punishment for some horrendous transgression involves taking a road trip with a two-year-old. With constant stops, it took nearly two days to get to Delaware, and by the time we crossed the state line, a flaming tomb and a boiling river of blood sounded downright relaxing. *Freeze me in an icy lake any day*, I thought. Just get this kid out of her car seat. Em's frustrated screaming, the endless loop of children's videos I hoped might appease her boredom, the stench of the Taco Bell burrito wrappers wedged somewhere under the floor mats—it was nearly unbearable. The worst part was that I had to jam myself in the backseat under all the junk I'd packed, because Em threw a fit if I tried to sit in the passenger seat while Ben drove. She wanted me next to her at all times.

We left at six in the morning on January 30, and before we'd even made it to Palm Beach County, we had to stop because I had diarrhea. Then, as if that weren't enough, I got my period, too. I was a crampy, nauseated, hormonal disaster the whole way, through seven very long states, and because we had to make so many pit stops we barely made it past South of the Border, a tacky tourist trap of a rest area right under the North Carolina line, before we decided to call it a night and get a motel room. I've never been so happy to see a giant yellow sombrero towering over a highway in my life.

We were back on the road again before dawn, hurtling up the highway through an uninhabited stretch of North Carolina countryside. An unfamiliar morning show murmured on the radio, and the sky turned the color of a burnt sienna Crayola at the horizon. Ben pulled off at the next exit and headed down a dirt lane before pulling the car over beside a frost-covered field as the sun rose over a red barn. He jumped out of the car and walked a few paces into the furrows, his breath making clouds that floated back toward the car where Em and I stayed in the warmth of the purring heater. He was taking pictures of the sky.

My husband loved sunrises. He always got up early at home and took walks to the beach so he could catch the glory of the sun coming up over the waves on his camera phone. I loved that he made space to appreciate the beauty of the world. It reminded me of when we fell in love. The first night we spent together, we stayed up until dawn and raced barefoot across an empty road until our feet hit the sand. Hand in hand, we ran to the shore and embraced as the sun's pink rays bloomed across the sky. It was everything I imagined true love would be, and I thought about that first sunrise as I watched him that morning, snapping photos in an icy tobacco field. We'd be apart from each other for a long time, so I wanted us to share this last sunrise, to have a special moment together.

I got out of the car and went to him. I wanted to hold him and kiss him, to feel in love again, but as I approached, he held out his arm to prevent me from coming any closer. I touched his sleeve, and he shook me off.

"Go back to the car. I'll be there in a second," he said.

I cried four times that day. The first was when I got back in the car. I cried again when we crossed the Bay Bridge and I saw the Chesapeake Bay for the first time in years. It was snowing by then, and the flakes were falling into the choppy gray surf. Later I cried when Ben snapped at me because he was hungry, tired, and angry he'd accidentally broken one of the lights on the car's ceiling. The fourth time, I wept silently, locked in my grand-mother's bathroom while she amused Em, because I didn't know exactly when I'd see my husband again, and I didn't know what our lives would be like whenever he came back for us. So much can change in a short period of time, and so much did.

My first few days in Delaware were a relief, though. I'd suc-cessfully removed myself from the wedding chaos and the drama over Joel's affairs, and I was getting a much-needed break—at least at first. I also felt like I was doing a good deed by keeping my grandmother company. I did her grocery shopping, helped her run errands around town. I even cooked dinner for her every night, and in exchange she'd read to Em and tickle her and give me a couple of minutes here and there to stop and do nothing. I needed that.

But Delaware in the winter is nothing like Delaware in the summer. The resorts become windswept ghost towns. The Dairy Queen closes until Memorial Day because no one's much in the mood for ice cream when there's a twenty-degree wind chill. Be-tween November and April, the lush green landscape of towering trees, wildflowers, and fertile fields becomes a flat patchwork of gray-and-brown desolation. I'd envisioned idyllic snowy after-noons, but the winter of 2013 let me down, delivering a soggy chill that was just cold enough to make me miserable without being cold enough to snow. After three straight days of being trapped inside Mommom Alice's condo, with evenings at Fun-land and boardwalk fries still half a year away, I began to regret my decision to come north. At home, at least we could go to the park, but swings and slides aren't much fun in sleet, and Em was going stir-crazy, trapped in a small space that was decorated with at least a hundred priceless glass knickknacks and decorative china plates, all just out of reach.

Things quickly went to pieces, as everything in my life was wont to do. We weren't even in Delaware a week when Mom-mom Alice slipped on the steps at the entry of her building and took a hard fall on the concrete. We were headed to the library when it happened, and I couldn't lift my grandmother from the sidewalk, so I called my cousin Bailey's parents. My aunt and uncle, who lived about fifteen minutes away, came as soon as they could, and rushed Mommom Alice to the ER. Nothing was broken, but her ankle was badly swollen, and at four the next morning, she woke me up to let me know she'd called an ambulance: she was having chest pains and thought maybe the tumble had triggered something. She'd already had one heart attack a couple of years earlier, and she had had an aortic aneurysm that scared her to death. If that thing burst, nothing would save her, her cardiologist had warned. The paramedics came and took her back to the hospital, and Em slept through the whole event, but once they were gone and I knew my aunt and uncle were headed to the ER to be by my grandmother's side, I couldn't fall back to sleep. I called Ben, woke him up, and made him listen to me cry.

By the grace of God, it turned out my grandmother was having only a panic attack. Her heart was fine, so she was discharged late that same morning. I made her a pot of homemade vegetable soup and picked up some new prescriptions for her, but I couldn't help but feel guilty. This was my fault, coming up here, thinking I was doing the right thing keeping an old widow company, when all I was doing was disrupting her household and making her anxious. It was a miracle I *hadn't* given her a heart attack.

I tried my best to create some sense of rhythm for Em each day, to give her a sense of normalcy, whatever that was. I found an inexpensive Kindermusik class she loved, plus a Mommy and Me class that met one morning a week at a nearby elementary school. These activities were lifesavers, but they didn't take up nearly enough of our time. The rest of our free hours were spent with my other grandmother, Mommom Marie, who was visibly distraught about my parents and pressed me for information I didn't have.

Some days I drove Em forty minutes north to the nearest mall.

There was a Chick-fil-A close by, with a play area we frequented, and other times we'd get in the car and drive aimlessly along lonesome roads. I had no idea where I was going. I just needed the time to pass more quickly until I could put Em to bed, because the task of engaging and occupying her often seemed as insurmountable as my sadness. As I drove, I kept my eyes on the rearview mirror, terrified that the Feds knew where I was, that they'd followed me, and that one morning, when I least expected it, I'd wake up to the sound of them pounding on my grandmother's front door.

Mommom Marie knew, of course, but Mommom Alice had no clue why I'd come up or what I was running away from. For a long time I'd feared that my grandmothers' paths might cross and that Mommom Marie might assume Mommom Alice knew, and mention something about my parents' case. A couple of times a year, they'd run into each other in the Walmart and make polite small talk, usually about me, since I was all they had in common anymore, but it hadn't happened lately. Mommom Alice, as far as I could tell, still knew nothing about my parents' arrests or their looming trial. It was a tremendous elephant in the room, and I was desperately trying to hide it—to stuff it, trunk and all, into the closet of my grandmother's teeny apartment.

"What do you mean you didn't tell her?" my cousin Bailey exclaimed.

"You have to tell her," Alex said.

My first cousins and I were having dinner at the Olive Garden, and I'd confided my situation to them over a plate of mediocre eggplant parm. They believed, quite adamantly, that I needed to tell our grandmother the truth about what was going on.

"I don't think she needs to know," I said. "It'll upset her first of all, and second of all what does she care what her son's ex-wife from almost forty years ago is up to? It doesn't affect her."

Bailey swirled a long strand of fettuccine Alfredo around her fork while Alex sucked down a glass of Coke.

"But it affects *you*," Bailey said, plucking an olive out of her salad to give to Em.

"She has a right to know. She's worried about you, Victoria. She already told my dad something's up with you. The whole family's saying it. I mean, it's not normal to leave your husband and your house and your cat and all your friends and family and come up here in the middle of winter and not even know when you're leaving. Everybody's wondering why you're here. It looks fishy," Alex said.

"So just tell them I needed some time away, or tell them I felt badly for Mommom being all by herself!" I argued.

Alex rolled her eyes and stabbed a tangle of fried calamari with her fork. She shook the crispy tentacles at me to emphasize her point. "Nobody's gonna believe that for a second."

Bailey agreed. "Nobody *does* believe it."

But I ignored my cousins' advice and continued to drag my secrets around with me like a diaper bag loaded with shit-swollen Huggies, until one day that shame-stuffed bag finally gave out and burst.

I'd caught a bad cold our first week in Delaware, and it had led to a hacking case of bronchitis. My doctor at home had been kind enough to call in a prescription for a Z-Pak and some cough syrup, and I was ecstatic to go and pick up the meds, because that meant I had something to do besides dust my grandmother's extensive collection of *Gone with the Wind* commemorative figurines. I also planned to pick up a frozen cherry pie from the grocery store on the way home and bake it for dessert. I had a cozy, peaceful evening planned, but my cell phone rang while I was in line at the pharmacy drive-through. It was Mom.

"Hey, I'm picking up my medicine. Can I call you right back?" I said.

"Victoria, wait!"

I thought she was going to go off on me and point out that she was right, that I'd gotten sick just as she predicted, but her voice was urgent, and I knew it was an emergency.

I paid quickly, pulled out of the parking lot, and headed toward the grocery store.

"They took Joel this morning," my mom told me.

"*Who* took Joel? What are you talking about? Where is he?"

I turned down the nerve-grating Elmo CD Em was listening to.

"The Feds came yesterday to take our stuff," she said.

"What stuff? How can they come take anything before you've even had a trial?" I asked.

I was confused and kept on going past the store and way out into the country, beyond the city limits.

"They can do anything they want. Don't you know that?"

I asked her again what they took, and she said they'd taken Joel's cars and the RV.

"They do it to scare you," Mom said. "Before a trial, they can come seize your assets and keep them locked up somewhere, so in case you're found guilty, you can't sell them off ahead of time and squirrel the cash away somewhere they can't get to."

"I've never heard of such a thing. Do you get them back if you're found innocent?" I asked.

"Hopefully."

She told me they'd created a big scene the day before—cop cars and armed officers flashing badges and shaking paperwork in their faces. The dog had been so scared, he'd peed on the floor, and Liszka had hidden upstairs in her room and burned through a pack of Parliaments, terrified. Mom said she'd known there was nothing she could do. She threw her hands in the air and pointed to the car keys on the table in the foyer.

"Take it all," she'd told them.

Joel had finally cracked. He hadn't offered them espresso this time. He'd laughed in their faces, sneering at them, and called them pussies and losers.

"I will destroy you in court," he told the Feds. He pointed at the lead investigator. "I will crush you like the filthy cockroach you are."

Mom had been mortified. She said she couldn't believe Joel was acting like that, but part of her understood.

"It's been almost two and a half years of this, of constant stress, of us not being able to enjoy our lives and our grandchildren, of our family being tormented and destroyed by these evil bastards, and it finally got to him, you know what I'm saying? *It got to him.* He couldn't stand to see them taking away everything we built up and everything we worked so hard for, and he stood up to them. But at the same time, I said, 'Joel, you're a fucking asshole, and they're going to come after you hard now because you made it personal.' I knew it too. I knew he was done for after he said that. I knew he didn't have a chance in hell."

And he didn't.

"They picked him up this morning." Mom sighed.

"Oh my God," I said.

She described the scene. Joel was walking the dogs in the neighborhood like he did every day, stopping to chat with the neighbors or answer a text. It had been unusually warm—sunny, the perfect vacation day—and he was wearing his red shoes. Back at the house, the vendors had already begun to set up for the Von Bod wedding that was going to take place that weekend.

First Mom heard the sirens. Police cars squealed to a halt, blocking the street and the gated driveway of Casa dei Sogni. They made Mom stay inside—they weren't interested in her. Joel's bond had been revoked, and he'd been declared a flight risk. The Feds said he was going to flee the country before the trial and that he'd been planning to for months. He'd turned in his American passport when he was arrested the previous Christmas, but they believed he thought he could get one over on them by keeping his Israeli passport. (He had dual citizenship.) They said they even had proof he was going to use it to escape.

"They really don't, though," Mom said. "It's a pack of lies."

"But they can't revoke someone's bond and declare them a flight risk without probable cause, or whatever it's called," I argued. "They have to have something to base it on."

"Oh no. No, they don't," she snapped. "They can do whatever they want. They're the government. They're liars. They have nothing but the passport, which he forgot about. He forgot to turn it in, is all. It was an honest mistake."

"Was it?" I asked.

"Of course it fucking was! Do you think for a second he'd leave this family? His grandchildren? He would never do that!"

"I know. He would never do that," I said, but a poppy seed's worth of doubt had already been planted.

If Joel could keep two mistresses who lived across the street from each other—and a block away from his wife, no less—essentially living an entire life of lies, then where would he draw the line? How could he really love us if he was capable of doing something like that? Joel had broken my trust, so I couldn't help but wonder. *Was* he planning to abandon my mother and let her take the fall? There would be no way of knowing now, but Ruffina's e-mails had certainly said so, though she clearly wasn't a reliable witness.

"If he was going to leave the country, he would've done it already," Mom insisted. "I know my husband like a book, and he would never abandon me."

I kept driving. A semi full of chickens passed me, thundering down the two-lane road on its way to the slaughterhouse. Em began to whine for more Elmo songs, and I tossed a package of fruit snacks to her.

"Where is he now?" I asked.

Mom didn't know. They had a team of lawyers getting ready to unleash an arsenal of writs and motions, but even my mother had to admit it was unlikely he'd be released before the trial ended. His only hope was to be found innocent.

"They'll hold him in Miami for a little while until they can get him a flight to New York with a U.S. Marshal. The lawyers told me he'll be at the Metropolitan Correctional Center in New York for the trial, and then we'll win and they'll let him go. We'll come home. Oh! I have an incoming call on the other line. I have to go. This might be him."

Mom hung up on me, and when I lost the connection, I was overcome by an overwhelming sense of helplessness and isolation. The feeling was like slamming into a telephone pole at seventy miles an hour. I was alone. No one could fix this. No one could make me feel better or offer reassurance, and I lived for reassurance. My throat was closing, and I began to cough and couldn't stop, so I pulled the car over beside a drainage ditch and took a swig of the codeine syrup straight from the bottle.

I left the Saturn running, my crying child buckled inside. I needed air. I needed to get out of the fucking car so I ran, still coughing, the bitter cherry syrup burning my throat, and came to a stop in a cold fallow field.

It was really just twenty or so steps from the side of the road, but it felt farther. It was getting dark; the sky was enormous, wisped with cirrus clouds as the sun set behind the bare trees that bordered the field. The wind swept the frozen ground, and from some far-off place came the sad lowing of cows.

What had I done? What hideous mistake had I made in leaving my parents at a time like this? I had deprived them of the last few days we could have had together as a family, and left my mother when she needed me most. I would never get to say goodbye to Joel. I would live the rest of my life knowing that the last time I saw my stepfather as a free man we'd been disappointed in each other. Now I worried we'd never have the chance to work things out.

I didn't know what it was like when the Feds took him, but I wanted the scene to be as I saw it in my head. "'It's better to burn out than to fade away,'" Joel always said, and I didn't want him to have gone down without a fight. I wanted to believe he struggled, his chest stuck out, as he strained against the handcuffs behind his back. I wanted him to be yelling something heroic to my mother as they pushed his head into the backseat of the cop car.

All at once a flock of snow geese—hundreds of them—flew up from the field and into the sky. Something had startled them, and their wings gleamed a metallic white. I turned to watch them, and there was Em, her little hand pressed against the car window. I could see her face, haloed by the pink hood of her parka. Her mouth was open, and she was crying for me.

"Mommy! Mommy! Don't leave me! Mommy, come back!" I heard her screaming. I ran back to the car and flung open the back door.

"I'm here, Em. I'm so sorry. Mommy's back, okay?"

"Stop crying, Mommy!"

"I can't, baby girl. I can't."

But gradually I did stop crying, because I had to. Em was scared, and she needed a mommy who at least *tried* to put on a brave face, so in an act of absolute desperation, I turned to Taylor Swift. Sometimes, when you are completely going to pieces inside, you just need to blast the car stereo and sing, "'Wee-eee are never, ever, ever, getting back together," at the top of your lungs. It was better than fucking Elmo, for crying out loud, and when the song ended, I played it again and again until we pulled into the driveway, because it made my daughter smile, and watching her big grin in the rearview mirror as I messed up all the lyrics gave me the strength to drive back to my grandmother's condo.

When we got home, Mommom Alice was worried.

"You were gone for two hours," she said. "You look like you've seen a ghost. What's going on?"

"I don't know. I got bored, so we took a drive. Then I hit a patch of black ice and skidded. Scared me to death," I lied.

She gave me a lecture about being careful on the roads, and I nodded obediently. I wished I could tell her the truth.

"I thought you said you were getting a cherry pie," she said.

"I forgot."

The evening deteriorated from there. It was like I was living in a mash-up of *Three's Company* and *Breaking Bad*—a disturbing and surreal black comedy in which I found myself telling ever more ridiculous lies to my grandmother, fumbling over my untruths, and losing track of what I'd previously said as I made up new stories in a desperate attempt to keep that elephant crammed in the closet while also looking after Em, because motherhood doesn't give a shit that your dad just got hauled off to prison. You still have to convince your kid to eat something other than Teddy Grahams for dinner, and you still have to drop everything when she craps her Pull-Ups, and as much as you'd rather wallow in your despair alone, you're not getting out of reading *The Lorax* for the seven hundredth fucking time before she goes to bed.

On top of caring for my child, I had phone calls to make. I wanted information, but the problem was twofold. Cell service was spotty everywhere up here, and nonexistent inside my grandmother's condo. She had a landline, but her place was so small, she'd hear everything I said, so my only option was to put Em with Mommom Alice in front of a DVD while I bundled up and took my calls outside, but every time I tried to do that, Em would go hysterical, and Mommom Alice would stand at her door and call me to come back in. This happened at least six times, and I was jonesing for a gin and tonic by Em's third tantrum, and I wasn't even a drinker.

I called Ben first, of course. When he got home from work that evening, investigators had been waiting for him on our front step. They asked him if he'd like to discuss his relationship with Joel and Cecily Gold. He told them he didn't and they left, which I found completely bizarre. They already had Joel, so what more could my husband possibly have offered them, and why did they think he'd want to talk to them in the first place?

"It's harassment!" I told him.

"They're just covering their bases, I think," Ben said, but I could tell he was shaken and I felt guilty. He hadn't been prepared for this, no matter what he tried to tell me.

I tried Mom next, but she was of little help—she could do nothing but wait for Joel to call. Allie was there for support, and I was thankful for that, but it was wrong. She had taken on the responsibility that I, Mom's daughter, should have shouldered, and when I called Ashley to see if she'd gone over to help, she told me she was staying away from the chaos. She'd gone to yoga instead.

"I can't have my kid around that kind of bad energy," she explained. "It's not like I can do anything to fix it."

"Obviously, you can't fix it, but your presence would show you care," I said.

"I'll try to go check on her tomorrow," Ashley promised, before telling me she had to hang up because it was already three minutes past Amelia's bedtime and they didn't want to get off schedule, which reminded me that I had my own child to bathe and wrestle into a pair of fleece jammies.

As much as I longed for the peaceful alone time that came when Em finally went to sleep, I dreaded the bedtime ritual. So did she, because she fought me tooth and nail, proving to me daily that adults and children are wired very differently. My ultimate fantasy as a grown-up was to have someone force me to take a bubble bath and get twelve hours of sleep, but Em always acted like she was terrified she was going to miss something—like the second she closed her eyes, the real fun would begin. She probably thought that after her bedtime, adults had rowdy foam parties with all the Disney princesses while eating piles of cotton candy and playing Hot Lava on the living room furniture. The reality was a lot different, though. Mostly I slumped on the sofa, too tired to hold my head up, and tried to make it through an episode of *Modern Family*.

That night it seemed like Em resisted bedtime even more

than usual, but after two hours, seven stories, three books, what seemed like sixteen drinks of water, three pee breaks (probably from all that water), and two Pull-Ups changes, I did finally manage to get her to sleep. Afterward, considering the day I'd had, all I wanted was a shower and some me time with a good book (okay, and maybe a hot stone massage, a Xanax, and a chocolate cupcake), but that was when Mommom Alice confronted me.

"Something's going on, young lady, and I'd like to know what it is," she said.

I tried to pretend I hadn't heard her and grabbed the remote off the pink damask footstool and switched on the ten-o'clock news. The local news in Delaware cracked me up. In Florida there were always murder/suicides and people turning into real-life zombies, but here the headline of the week was a deer rescue. This was followed by the gripping tale of a tree that had fallen on some train tracks, which was such big news, a reporter had been dispatched to the scene to interview three separate eyewitnesses who couldn't seem to agree on what kind of tree it was.

"I'm purty sure it was a spruce," said one witness, while another argued that it was definitely a fir, because that was obviously an important distinction.

I couldn't help but laugh as the news cameras zoomed in on a man dragging the branches off the tracks. I swear, I saw him rolling his eyes. But my grandmother wasn't about to let me off the hook, so she asked me again what was going on.

"Mommom, it's nothing," I insisted.

"My ass, it's nothing," Mommom said.

I couldn't fool her, so I had to come clean. I told her everything that had happened since Em's birth as simply as I could.

"I wondered how long you were going to keep this from me," she said when I finished.

"You already knew?" I asked.

She nodded.

"How?"

"You forget how fast news travels in a small town like Milford, don't you? Your mother has friends and family here. People get to talkin'. You know how it is. I'd heard some rumors, so I asked your uncle to doodle it."

"Doodle it?" I asked.

"You know, on that Americans Online. He looked it up on his key punch machine."

"I see-ee," I said. "So . . . everyone already knows?"

"We knew for a long time that they were still messing with drugs. When we all came down for your wedding and saw that house they live in, we knew it was all drug money."

"Mommom, it's not drugs," I insisted. "These charges don't involve drugs at all. It's white-collar crime they're accused of. It's completely different!"

"Don't you tell me. Your uncle looked it up, and it's drugs."

"Mommom, no, it isn't." But there was no point in trying to argue with her.

My grandmother had a very limited idea of Florida, and nothing was going to change her mind. To her, there were only two versions: Disney World and *Scarface*, and once you step off that monorail, your ass had better duck the gunfire. Over the years I'd tried to convince Mommom Alice that what she saw in the movies wasn't real life, that there actually were normal people with families and respectable jobs, but she wasn't having any of it. She'd seen the outrageous stories that came out of the Sunshine State ("Florida Woman Causes Car Crash While Shaving Vagina" and "Naked Florida Man Jumps off Roof onto Homeowner, Knocks Television Over, Empties Vacuum Cleaner, Masturbates"), and since 1979 my mother and Joel had proved her right. I often wondered what she thought my life was like—if she thought we all strutted around poolside, snorting blow and wearing low-cut, polyester jumpsuits like Michelle Pfeiffer while my parents played with the pet tiger they kept in the backyard. *Sorry, Mommom*, I wanted to tell her, *when I said, "Say hello to my little friend," I was talking about Em.*

"I don't know what to do," I confessed.

My grandmother set down her pencil and the crossword puzzle she'd been working on. She removed her reading glasses and placed them on the end table next to the couch.

"I can't help you, Victoria," she said. "I know you probably came up here thinking I could help you out, but I'm an eighty-year-old widow now. I've got heart problems, and I'm not as strong as I once was. There's not much I can do for you anymore, but there's one thing I *can* tell you. You need to live your own life, no matter what your mother or Joel or Ben or any of them's got going on. This is *your* life. You and Emmeline are all you need to worry about. Their problems are not yours to fix, just like your problems aren't mine to fix. All I can do is love you."

A little later I tried to go to bed, but lately I hadn't been able to sleep. I'd make my best effort, but as tired as I was, and as much as I wanted to sleep, my mind wouldn't shut down. As soon as I'd begin to drift off, my head would fill with horrible visions—a film reel of my worst fears in Technicolor. I imagined my parents in orange jumpsuits, their ankles shackled, and Ben and I going through a bitter divorce, me ending up on food stamps, losing my home and everything I loved because I couldn't afford to support myself, while Ben danced with a hot young girlfriend. Then I worried that seeing my depression had irreparably damaged my daughter, and I'd picture her in eighteen years, half naked and wrapped around a metal pole, wearing five-inch Lucites and blaming her bad childhood. Sometimes I even fantasized about what it might be like to end my life. In my saddest, loneliest moments, sometimes it seemed like death might be the only way I'd find peace.

One night I dozed off and woke from a particularly terrible nightmare. My heart was racing, and adrenaline coursed through me like the dream had really happened, and try as I might, I couldn't calm down.

That was when I remembered that my mother had told me that when she was younger, to calm down, she'd lie in bed and fantasize about the house of dreams she'd one day have and how she would decorate it down to the last detail. It motivated her and raised her spirits during her toughest times, so I decided to give it a try. My house, though, didn't have stainless-steel appliances or granite countertops, and I wasn't concerned with painting murals on the ceilings. My house of dreams was filled with people I loved, so instead of imagining paint colors and wallpaper patterns, I soothed my nerves by envisioning the celebrations I'd like to have someday, and how my home would be filled with Em's cousins and friends running in and out, playing tag and dashing through the sprinklers in the backyard. There'd be good food, and my house would smell like cookies. I still felt heavyhearted, grief-stricken even, but in the middle of the night, thinking about hosting holidays and entertaining loved ones helped to keep my demons a little more at bay. Mom was right.

That weekend I admitted to my cousin Bailey that I was having a hard time managing my depression. She lived an hour and a half north of Milford, closer to Philly, and she drove down to see me because she knew I was in a bad place. Bailey and I had always been close, and I knew when I told her my secrets, she'd never judge me and she'd never tell a soul. She wouldn't invalidate my feelings or call me crazy and tell me to get my shit together or say I was trying to get attention. People like that were rare in my life, so I treasured Bailey, and always felt a little better after we spent time together.

Saturday afternoon we decided to take Em and go out for chicken and dumplings at a roadside diner west of town. It was a brisk but sunny afternoon, and I was glad to drive, to get out of the condo. Mommom Alice had come down with the flu, which she probably caught from me, and being in poor health, she took it hard and was bedridden. I couldn't get her to eat, so on top of my other stress, I was now even more worried about my grandmother.

"The shit keeps piling on, and I feel so alone. It's like trying to carry all the grocery bags into the house at the same time and you're dropping everything and the bags are ripping open and you can't hold them all at once. I just want someone to come and take a few of the bags away. I need someone to help me carry it all," I said, staring ahead at the long road in front of me.

"It's not going to last forever," Bailey said. "And you aren't alone. It might feel like you are, but you have me. You have a *real family* here, Vic. You have five brothers and sisters!"

"I haven't called them," I said. "They don't know about this. Apparently the rest of the family does, but they don't."

"You might be surprised how they'd react. Look, the rest of us know about it, and no one is judging you."

"I feel so ashamed, though. I know that people my mom grew up with are gossiping all over town. I was at the grocery store the other day, and I saw a couple of her old friends. They didn't even say hi to me, but I saw them whispering," I said.

I told her how I finally understood why my mom hated this place so much, and why she'd wanted so badly to escape. Small towns don't let people change. As long as you stay, you can never get away from your past. To everyone in Milford, Mom would always be a drug dealer, and they'd probably always look at her suspiciously—hell, maybe they had good reason to. Mom might have thought she was proving she'd made it big when she came back for visits, driving a fancy Hummer, flashing her big diamonds, and peacocking around in her elegant outfits, but she wasn't impressing anyone. Old friends, acquaintances, and even family members might smile and compliment her, but I had a feeling they were tearing her to shreds behind her back. And me, too, for that matter.

"What do you think they're saying about me?" I asked Bailey. "Probably, there's Cecily's kid—the poor thing. Her mom's going to jail again, and her dad abandoned her. No wonder she's so strange."

"First of all, Victoria, who cares? They can say whatever they want, but that doesn't mean it's true. They could call you a big pink elephant, but would that make you one?" Bailey said.

I shook my head, and she went on.

"And second, yes, people do look at you everywhere you go in Delaware. I've seen, but do you know why?" Bailey asked.

I shrugged.

"They're not staring at you, thinking your parents are criminals. They're looking at you because you don't look like the typical southern Delawarian who goes to Walmart in her Marvin the Martian pajama pants. They're looking at you because you're pretty!"

"What are you talking about?" I asked, blushing.

"How do you *not* know you're pretty?" Bailey asked.

"I look in the mirror, and I see tired and haggard. I see someone totally broken," I said.

"That's not what everyone else sees," Bailey told me. "You're not as broken as you feel."

"So whenever I look like shit, you're saying I can always go to a Walmart in Delaware and feel like a supermodel?" I asked, almost laughing.

"Whatever works. Sometimes you gotta set the bar a little lower," Bailey said.

We stopped talking for a few minutes to listen to Em singing along with her Kindermusik CD, before pulling into the diner's gravel parking lot behind a pickup truck full of hunting gear and a dead deer strapped to its roof.

"You know, your mind is a really powerful thing, and it can trick you sometimes, especially when you're under a lot of stress, and believe me, I know you can't control it on your own. I know how scary it is," Bailey said before we got out of the car.

It was true. Bailey had OCD, and she knew what it was like to have your brain go haywire. She never told me to stop acting crazy, because people had told her the same things in her worst moments, and she understood that some people can't "just stop."

Seriously, those comments made me the angriest, because if people could "just stop," they obviously would. It wasn't like I loved feeling desperate and overwhelmed, or that Bailey enjoyed being late because she had to check each of her doorknobs forty-four times before she left her house.

"Vic," Bailey said, "have you thought about going on antidepressants again?"

"I have, actually. I've talked to my doctor about it, but I decided not to," I confessed.

Ten years earlier Zoloft had gotten me through a traumatic breakup and a bad case of social anxiety that had made me fearful of going back to college. The drug worked, but it made me gain weight, and weaning myself off it had led to two intense, nausea-filled weeks that felt like the worst case of PMS ever. I'd even had tremors in my hands from the withdrawal, and I never lost all the weight I'd gained, so I wasn't enthused about having to repeat the experience.

"I just don't know if I need it," I lied.

"If you are so stressed out right now that you can't count your blessings and see how amazing you really are, then you need it, at least for the time being," Bailey said.

I tried to argue about weight gain and withdrawals. I told her I was scared that the meds could make me feel worse.

"If you feel worse, call your doctor or call me. I'll help talk you off the ledge. Look, I am here. I know you think you're alone, but I am telling you that you're not. Even if you have no one else on this earth, you know you'll always have me and that I don't care how crazy you are or what your parents did or what anyone else thinks, okay? Please try the medicine, and don't even give me that shit about your weight. Em would rather have a chubby mom who's happy than a mom wearing a size-six dress who cries every day."

She reached across the car's console and hugged me tight.

"Thank you," I whispered in her ear.

The next day I went to a small get-together at my other cousin

Alex's house. It was mostly just for Alex's immediate family and close friends—my siblings wouldn't be there, which was a relief. I'd still been apprehensive about going, because I'd be facing a lot of family members who'd apparently done extensive Internet searches on my parents in the past few weeks, and I felt like some kind of a freak, like I should be wearing a T-shirt that said, KISS ME, MY STEPDAD'S IN PRISON. But I went anyway, because it was better than being lonely, and because it would definitely entertain Em. Plus, it gave me a reasonable excuse for making a huge pan of chocolate chip blondies. I've always been a champion stress eater.

A fire was crackling in the fireplace when I got to Alex's house. She'd decorated for the festivities with balloons. There was no bar, and no one was making espresso martinis, but if you wanted a drink, there were some cans of soda in a cooler on the linoleum floor in the kitchen. None of the guests were sex workers or reality TV stars. Nobody was a millionaire. Heavily augmented trophy wives were noticeably absent, and not a soul had a platinum hair weave or mink eyelash extensions. At this party there were regular people with nine-to-five jobs. They lived in homes with wood paneling. These were people who'd never heard of Manolo Blahnik, who were just hanging out—joking around with one another, watching Beyoncé on TV, and trying to figure out how to pronounce *edamame*.

Soybeans have been grown in Delaware for decades, but I guess the people in my home state never thought to actually eat the things, so they were considered exotic fare. But lower Delaware was slowly modernizing. There was one Japanese restaurant that a few brave souls had actually tried and liked, and Alex's friend had seen edamame dip on the Food Network and miraculously found the ingredients, made a bowl, and brought it to the party. I thought it was freaking fantastic, but some of the other guests were apprehensive, and not one of them knew how to say it, so I had to intervene.

"It's *eh-duh-mah-may*," I enunciated.

Blank stares, but God bless 'em. At least they tried it, and who even cared? We were having a blast. Somebody even got out a board game. *A board game!* It felt like I'd traveled back in time to the 1950s, like I was in *Pleasantville.* I hadn't had that much fun in ages. While Em giggled and tormented Alex's cats and I stuffed my face with cupcakes and buffalo wings, I forgot that a week earlier I'd imagined ending my life might be the only solution to my sadness. That night, I forgot I felt alone.

My parents' parties stressed me out, but here I didn't have to worry about what drunk asshole was going to cause a scene, and I didn't have to fret about what I was wearing or whether I fit in with the "beautiful people." Hell, I wore a saggy pair of jeans, a flannel shirt, and a pair of ten-dollar, knock-off Uggs I got on clearance, and I felt perfectly comfortable. It was like a revelation. People were sincerely interested in having a conversation with me (about real things!), and they thought it was cool that I wanted to be a writer even if it *was* a little weird. At home, no one talked to me. I couldn't even count how many times my parents' guests mistook me for the maid and handed me their drained cocktail glasses stuffed with dirty napkins. Every once in a while someone would try to say something to me in Spanish, and I'd want to answer back: *How do say 'fuck you' en Español, dickwad? I'm Joel and Cecily's daughter!*

It's a miracle I'm not crazier, I thought as I drove back to the condo that night. I'd always wondered how my life could encompass so many contradictions. On one hand, I was a small-town girl who'd come from people who partied hard with Yahtzee and Dr Pepper, but with my parents I had a life of champagne, speedboats, and Bentleys. I supposed I'd always straddled the fence between the two, torn, never really choosing one side or the other. When Florida overwhelmed me, I'd run to Delaware, and when Delaware bored me, I fled for Florida. Sometimes it was metaphorical and, sometimes, like now, I literally bounded back and forth.

The party had exhausted poor Em, who was out cold five minutes into the drive home. As I carried her inside to bed, a few snow flurries brushed my cheek, and after I'd tucked her in, I drew the bedroom curtain aside to see the flakes, now falling heavily, illuminated against a streetlight. Snow had already glittered the tops of the cars parked along the street.

I missed the snow so much in Florida. When I lived up north, I'd always loved sitting at the window and watching the snow sift down from a silent, orange-black night sky. I never wanted to move to Florida. I still held a grudge against my parents for uprooting me and transplanting me to the flat, hot, dull, seasonless Sunshine State, with its ugly grids of strip malls and blinking neon tourist traps. Every winter I'd watch the Weather Channel and see it snowing in all the places where we used to live, and my heart would ache like I was going through a breakup I could never get over. I'd wonder why I kept staying in a place I hated, but I always knew the answer. I stayed for my mom, because of those years when I was a kid when we weren't together and the stories she told me about how she'd fought so hard to get custody and how much she missed me. She'd fallen in love with Joel because on their first date he'd promised he would help her get me back, and he had. He'd fought beside her for seven years and they'd finally won, so after that, how could I leave them again?

I snuck outside, so as not to wake Em or my grandmother, and stood in the middle of the street. I stretched out my arms and caught flakes on my mittens and opened my mouth so the flurries could fall on my tongue as I shuffled my boots along the icy asphalt. It was so goddamned beautiful. What I needed, I realized—besides a weeklong spa vacation alone with a stack of good books and some chocolate chip cookies—wasn't what I thought. All this time I felt like I had to make a choice between the lives that Florida and Delaware represented—my mother or everything she hated. But this was something new. The universe was urging me not to pick one of two but to create a radical third option: to make my own life with my own dreams instead of trying to live up to everyone else's expectations.

Step one—tame the brain.

So the next day, I called my doctor and asked her to call me in the prescription for antidepressants we'd discussed.

"I think you're going to feel a lot better, Victoria," my doctor said, and I prayed she was right.

26

When Mom and Allie stopped in Delaware for a few days on their way to New York for the trial, it had been about a month since I'd seen them. Mom looked awful, but as haggard as she was, she couldn't help but gloat that for the first time in our lives, she actually weighed less than I did. Whatever. I'd been trapped in chicken-and-dumpling land, comforting myself with pie while Mom had been trying to make it through the worst four weeks of her life. To recap: first she found out that her husband had been cheating on her with not one but *two* skanky-assed, psycho-bitches who lived across the street from each other. Then said husband had been picked up by the Feds the day after all her assets had been seized—the same week Mom was supposed to host a wedding for her favorite reality star, a wedding in which most of the groomsmen would be gigolos. Luckily, that was about the only thing that had gone off without a hitch, and apparently there had been some *Magic Mike*–style entertainment at the reception, thanks to the wedding party, so I was glad I missed it, because lately, I hadn't been much in the mood for body rolls and windmills.

More information had surfaced about why Joel was considered a flight risk. Turned out, Ruffina had written a letter to the investigators telling them that Joel was plotting to run off with the Great White Shark before the trial. Supposedly he had bragged all about his plans and about how many millions he had secretly hidden away overseas that no one, not even my mom, knew of. Even skeptical me cried bullshit on that one. Joel would never have told Ruffina something like that, especially knowing how angry and jealous she was of Agnés. It was pretty much a given that Ruffina was making shit up to get revenge.

"That woman has derailed our trial," Mom said. "She's made Joel look so bad, it's not even funny, though of course, it's his own damn fault. I can't defend him there. What he did with those women was stupid."

"It was beyond stupid," I added.

"Victoria, you don't even understand. We would've had almost six weeks left to plan our defense with our lawyers, and we have a marvelous team, let me tell you, but Joel had the papers, the contracts. He had the evidence to prove the government is lying about us, but now we can barely talk to him. We can't get access to his information. No one knows where anything is or how to get to it and we're fucked. We're going to lose this case because of it. We needed that time to put our argument together."

"Where is Joel now?" I asked, wondering why, if Joel was allowed phone calls, he couldn't just tell her over the phone where to find this supposed "evidence." Surely he could speak with his lawyers and tell *them*.

"He's in New York. He's fine, but you know how he is. Nothing gets him down," Mom said.

"He's probably like the governor of jail," I said, and laughed dryly.

I sprawled out across the bed. Mom and Allie were staying in a hotel on the highway out of Milford, and I'd come to spend the last few days there with them. Allie had taken Em to run through the hallways, and I was so thankful to have even a short break from entertaining a two-and-a-half-year-old, I could've made out with her. There might even have been some tongue.

We didn't have much time together, and I'd decided not to attend the trial. Mom understood my decision. She'd told me she didn't want me there anyway, because she knew what a burden a trip like that would be with a toddler who was in the throes of potty training angst. They didn't allow children in the courtroom, and no one knew how long the trial would even last, so if Em and I went, we'd basically be stuck in a downtown hotel room all day every day for weeks. We were better off staying put at Mommom Alice's.

"I only have three days here," Mom said. "Let's make them fun. Let's just play with Em and have slumber parties here in the hotel and try to have a good time."

We did exactly that. The time passed more quickly than anyone wanted it to, but had the circumstances been different and had we not been in, well, *Delaware*, it might have felt like a vacation.

I didn't see my mom a lot when I was little. When I lived with my paternal grandparents, Mom lived in Florida, where she'd met and married Joel, but once a month or so, she'd drive all the way from Fort Lauderdale to pick me up at their house. We'd stay in a hotel together, usually someplace at the beach, and spend the whole weekend ordering room service. I always had a single scoop of lime sherbet in a frosted metal dish. Mom painted my nails, let me wear her fur coats (that she bought at the Salvation Army), and taste her Fu-ki plum right out of the bottle. We'd take bubble baths and watch cartoons in bed and have pizza delivered to the room. Those weekends with my mother were pure kid heaven, nothing like life at my grandparents', where weekends were predictable and regimented: fish sticks for dinner on Friday, *The Love Boat* on Saturday night, and Sunday School the next morning. With Mom, though, anything could happen. She was *Fantasy Island*, and I loved the sense of wild abandon I felt when I was with her, but somehow I was always relieved to get back to the order of my grandparents' home when it was over. Even as a child, I had trouble reconciling the opposite sides of my life: Snow White and Tony Montana.

The time we spent at the hotel that week, before Mom and Allie drove off in the Hummer to New York for the trial, reminded me of the weekends when I was a kid all over again, except this time it was Em with the tacky pink nail polish, jumping on the beds wearing nothing but fairy wings, sugared-up, and smelling like bubblegum.

They left late in the afternoon on the last Wednesday in February. The trial would begin on Monday, but they needed to get to the city early for last-minute meetings with lawyers, and Mom hoped she'd be able to see Joel again. Allie also had to take her shopping, but this time it wasn't for fun.

"Your mother needs to get it through her head that she can't wear aquamarine sequins and hot-pink rhinestones in a courtroom!" Allie exclaimed. She was right. Mom's affinity for leopard print would most certainly give the wrong impression, but it was nearly impossible for me to imagine my mother dressed conservatively. She'd recently freshened up her platinum hair extensions (for the trial, of course) and was currently sporting pink suede Yves Saint Laurent sneakers. She just wasn't a suit-and-chignon kind of woman, so I hoped Allie's makeover would be successful.

We took Mommom Marie to lunch that day, but since Allie and Mom were running late, we had to stay in Milford, and our only choice was a Bob Evans. My grandmother and Em were thrilled, but Allie stabbed her fork into her salad like she was re-enacting the shower scene in *Psycho*.

"Jesus, do they have anything other than iceberg lettuce in this state? Haven't they heard of field greens yet?" she complained.

I'd lost whatever appetite I'd had, but I swirled my spoon in my bowl of congealed orange chili and dumped in another pack of crushed saltines. I didn't even bother to take a bite.

"At least there's good news," Mom said.

Good had become a relative term for us, and the "good" news was that if she were found guilty, she wouldn't be hauled off to jail immediately. The prosecution had agreed to let her come home to wait for her sentencing.

"Don't talk like that," Allie said. She'd given up on her limp salad and was twirling a straw in her club soda.

"Maybe that won't even be important," I said, trying to sound upbeat and encouraging, although I was feeling anything but.

"Joel seems to think we'll be found innocent," Mom said. "He made me pack a case of 1980 Jordan in the Hummer so we can celebrate together. Can you imagine all that expensive vintage wine sitting in the trunk? But we decided if we get off, we're having a party in New York City, and then we're going on vacation for a couple of months, maybe to Israel."

Mommom Marie sighed loudly.

"I just wish you'd stayed off that Internet, sweetheart," she said to my mom. "I tried to warn everyone. That computer is evil. I saw it on *Dateline*. It's nothing but pedophiles on there, and the government can see every single thing you post. You'll never convince me that this president didn't come after you personally because you spoke out against him online."

Allie and I rolled our eyes at each other, and I wanted to smack my head on the table, but Mom seemed to agree.

"That man has a vendetta against the wealthy!" Mom said.

"You think you were arrested because of politics?" I asked.

My grandmother interjected, "Well, *I* most certainly do!"

"Victoria, don't be naïve. We don't live in a free country anymore. Have you ever heard of redistribution of wealth? This administration despises rich people. They hate entrepreneurs, and they want a welfare state, so they come after people like me and Joel," Mom said.

Mommom Marie shook her head sadly and pushed away her platter of baked cod.

"I wish you two had never built that fancy house or bought those cars," she said.

"It was like putting a target on us," Mom agreed. "But I'm

proud of my accomplishments, and Joel and I are fighting for what's right. We took risks, but I have zero regrets. Most people don't get to live the life we have, and I wouldn't trade it for a thing. I wouldn't settle like these assholes here in Milford have, because it's safe and easy. I dreamed bigger, you know what I'm saying? I wanted more, and *I got it*."

No one spoke for a moment. Mom pushed her turkey and dressing around on her plate, while she sat Em on her lap and plundered the bread basket. I stared outside. Seated next to a window, I had a prime view of the parking lot and the water tower across the highway. It was a bleak gray day, and we were expecting an ice storm that evening. The roads were going to get treacherous fast.

"It's starting to sleet," I remarked.

"I wish you didn't have to drive all the way up to New York in this," Mommom Marie said.

"We'll be fine. I've got to get up there and, truth be told, I'm ready to go. I'm ready to fight for my life," Mom said.

That was when I realized. This moment in a generic roadside Bob Evans, over meals that no one felt like eating—*this was it*. This could be, this probably *would* be, the last time we were ever together again. Four generations of Tuckers. My grandmother, my mother, me, and Em. Our future together depended on the outcome of this trial, and without a not-guilty verdict, Mom wouldn't be able to spend the last years of her mother's life with her. Mommom Marie shared her daughter's fear of travel, but worse than Mom, she refused to travel under any circumstances. She wasn't fit enough to fly (plus she was convinced that terrorists were going to take down whatever flight she was on) or able to make a long drive, especially not alone. The world outside of Milford had grown too enormous and terrifying, so she stayed home, making it clear there'd be no exceptions. If my mother went to prison, they'd exchange letters and phone calls, but Mommom wouldn't visit, so a shitty last lunch and a looming ice

storm was all we had left. No more king crabs. No more Funland.

Mom paid the check, and we got our coats on and went outside.
Allie started the Hummer and waited for us to say our good-
byes. The sleet kept it brief, but I held Em, and the four of us
hugged there in the icy parking lot. Mommom Marie told Mom
to take care of herself, and hurried off, saying she didn't trust the
roads. I promised her I'd come by for breakfast the next morning
and Mom and I watched her light a cigarette as she drove away.

"Give me that baby," Mom said.

She grabbed Em out of my arms and squeezed her so tight,
Em coughed and wriggled in protest, but my mother didn't want
to let her go.

"Mommom loves you, Emmie. Mommom's gonna fight for you,
baby girl," Mom said. Her voice cracked, and she began to sob.

Allie honked the horn.

"You got this," I told my mother. "You're strong."

"And so are you," she said, pointing at me. "Now get the baby
out of the cold. Go ahead and let me go."

I buckled Em into her car seat and then turned around. Mom
was already climbing into the passenger seat of the Hummer,
but I ran to her across the parking lot and caught ahold of her coat
and pulled her back, so I could wrap my arms around her one last
time before she left.

"I love you," I cried.

"I love you too."

A minute later it was over, and Mom was gone. The Hummer
made a left while I turned right in my Saturn and sat at a stop-
light, watching the hulking, black vehicle in my rearview mirror
until it cleared a northbound overpass and disappeared.

The sleet fell harder now, mixed with a few wet snowflakes
the size of chicken feathers. I didn't care if the roads were haz-
ardous. I didn't want to go back to Mommom Alice's condo yet,
and once again I was struck with the feeling that I was trapped in
a life I didn't want to be living.

I hadn't chosen this—the raid, the trial, my stepfather's adultery. My parents' life was like a 747 at takeoff, and I was a crop duster who'd gotten swept up in its turbulent wake. I didn't feel guilty about missing the trial, and that day I was able to let my mother go. I was finally learning to set a boundary. I could be supportive from a distance: loving my family didn't mean I had to forget me. Like my yoga teacher said, I had to fucking love myself, too, and while I couldn't control my circumstances, I could control how I reacted to them.

Maybe the Zoloft was starting to work, but that day, for the first time, I made a conscious decision to be a little kinder to myself. I decided to stay away from the desolate country roads, to head in a different direction, and made a left turn toward downtown instead.

"Let's go get hot chocolate together, Em," I said.

"Yes! Mama! Chocolate!"

My favorite thing about my hometown has always been its real, old-fashioned main street. When I was little, it was all there was. It was where people went to shop, but then they built a plaza on Route 113 and then another, bigger plaza across from that, and businesses started moving out of downtown. By the time I was a teenager, the downtown area was all but deserted, but a recent revitalization project had finally restored its charm. Pretty streetlights, a health food store, a riverfront theater, some new boutiques, even an eco-spa—it was lovelier than ever now. Pretty soon I bet someone would even open a restaurant that served field greens, and while there was no Starbucks for at least thirty miles around, there was something better—a bakery with a coffee shop.

It almost didn't feel right to sit on the cozy, plush sofas of the café, munching oatmeal cookies and sipping hot chocolate with Em while my mother was headed to trial, but I knew I had to do this. Experiencing pleasure did not mean I was betraying my mother. Em deserved a happy mommy who did fun things with her, and I hadn't spent nearly enough sweet moments simply enjoying the company of my little girl. I pulled my daughter onto my lap, snuggled her close, and kissed the top of her head. Her presence wasn't a hassle or another burden I had to carry, and together we sat for a long time, watching the storm outside while we were safe and warm in the cinnamon-scented bakery.

When I got home, Mommom Alice was out of bed, finally recovering from her flu.

"Sarah called for you, Vic," she said. "You know, this is the fourth or fifth time she's called since you've been here. She said she and Grace and Thaddeus wanted to see you. She doesn't understand why you haven't called her back."

It was true. My half siblings had all reached out to me since I'd been in Delaware, and Sarah had been the most persistent. She'd e-mailed me and even posted on my Facebook wall, but I'd ignored her. I didn't have the energy for new people, and I didn't want them to see me like this, when I wasn't strong enough to pretend everything was happy and fine. I texted Sarah back and apologized. I blamed the ice and my lingering bronchitis along with my grandmother's health, and I felt guilty because part of me wanted to see my brothers and sisters, but a bigger and more powerful part of me still wanted to say no.

Later that night, after Mommom Alice and I had polished off a couple of chicken potpies, Allie rang me on my grandmother's landline to tell me they'd made it to New York. By that point I'd given up facing the elements in order to get one bar of cell reception, so I traded my privacy for the comfort of the heater and a pink velveteen easy chair. I asked Allie how the drive had gone and if Mom was okay.

"Ugh, I can't even tell you. Not good," Allie said. "Bomboclat passed away today. Liszka was watching him, and he had a seizure and couldn't breathe, and since Liszka doesn't have a car, she had to call Ashley to come get him and take him to the vet, and they ended up just putting him down."

"Oh my God, no. That's terrible," I said.

In all honesty, I wasn't really that upset that my mom's mini pin had died, because I had little love for his nasty ass. I was sad for my mom, because she adored the despicable dog and, dear God, could the timing have been any worse? Like, seriously, she's on the way to a trial in an ice storm, and the dog dies too? I mean, his death wasn't exactly unexpected, though—Bomboclat was so old, we'd sort of lost track of how old he actually was. I seemed to remember him appearing in our lives around 1998, which would have made him about fifteen, but Mom, with her penchant for hyperbole, might tell people he was anywhere between eighteen and twenty-seven. In any case, the fucker was as old as he was disgusting, and though I'd never held much affection for him in life (he was a vicious snapper), I'd miss him as a fixture of Casa dei Sogni. He was one more quirky constant in our world that had slipped away.

"Well, at least we won't have to smell his infected anal glands anymore," I snarked in an attempt at humor.

Bomboclat, who'd been named for an unmentionable Jamaican curse word, possessed a legendary odor. I often described him as hot garbage on a choke chain. He was also blind, deaf, and obese, and he compulsively humped threadbare stuffed cats (always in front of guests) until he rendered himself breathless, which resulted in terrible coughing spells. He'd walk around honking like an asthmatic goose, but Mom never seemed to mind. It was like she couldn't even see that he looked like a decaying, portly gargoyle. To her, Bomboclat was adorable, and because he was such a wreck, she loved him all the more. He was her baby and now, at the worst possible time, he'd died and she hadn't been there to hold him as he faded away.

Allie put me on the phone with my mother, and I managed to get her to laugh as I reflected on all of poor Bomboclat's shortcomings—the time he yanked an entire pumpkin pie off the Thanksgiving buffet and scarfed it down before anyone caught him, another when he tried to claim our grocery bags as his own personal property and stood in the kitchen, bristling and growling at anyone who dared come near. Once he almost ripped my throat out over a package of filet mignon, and Joel finally had to lure him outside with a raw hot dog so we could get the food in the fridge.

"Oh Lord, we've had some funny times." Mom sighed.

"And we'll figure out how to have more," I said.

Ben was working in New York that same week, so I called him at his hotel later and told him it was time for me and Em to go home. I didn't beg, and I didn't pose it as a question. This time I was firm.

"Are you sure you don't want to stay until the end of the trial?" he asked. "What if they get off? Don't you want to be there to celebrate?"

"I don't know how I'll feel about celebrating, but I know I've been through enough and that I'm not putting my life and my desires on hold anymore just to wait to see what happens next with my parents. I want to be in my own home, and I want to be in the warm weather. I'm ready for spring."

"Fair enough. I'll come down next weekend and we'll drive home," Ben said.

The day before Ben arrived, I wanted to take Em for one last drive out in the country. I wanted to take her for a hike in the winter woods I once played in.

Outside of town there was an old sawmill that had been turned into a nature center, complete with forest trails and wooden bridges over a trickling brook that emptied into the cold mirror of the millpond. The mill was surrounded by maple trees, and each tree was fitted with a spile and a bucket for collecting sap. Around here, sugar season was one of the first signs that warmer weather was coming. The sap was already running, and the syrup would soon boil.

Bundled in our heavy coats and scarves, Em and I ambled through the silvery woods. The trees were still bare, but the branches were budding. Birds were returning and building their

nests. At the edge of the forest, we squatted to admire a magnificent cluster of bright purple crocuses in a patch of ice, pushing
miraculously out of the frozen ground. Em called them snow
flowers.

Closer to the road, we even found a clump of daffodils emerg-
ing from the frost. One of them, in the sunniest spot, had already
bloomed, and was nodding its happy yellow head in the cold
breeze.

"Mommy, it's saying yes!" Em shouted.

I laughed. "Maybe you're right," I told her. "Maybe it's telling
us not to give up. Spring is right around the bend."

PART 3

27

"I missed you guys," Ben told me. We were just pulling into our driveway. It was sunset, and the line of palm trees across the street from us was silhouetted against a salmon-colored sky. Before we parked and got out of the car, I rolled down the window and breathed in the warm, humid air for the first time in two months.

"We missed you too." I smiled and rubbed the back of Ben's head.

"Home again, home again, jiggity jig," Em sang sleepily from her car seat.

It had taken three days for us to drive home from Delaware. Em had come down with a respiratory virus, the car had overheated twice, and Ben and I were physically and emotionally drained, but we'd made it back in one piece. It was now the middle of March, and I was looking forward to April and Easter bunnies and having Mom back home. Even more, I was ready for the closure that would come when the trial was over, whatever the verdict was.

Mom called me every night with updates after court adjourned, but it was often hard to make sense of her reports. I desperately wanted real, concrete information that might help me predict the outcome, or at least give me a sense of how it was going, but one day Mom would be wildly optimistic, and the next she'd swear they were going to lose. From what I could tell, the trial was like a boxing match. One side would throw a punch and send the opponent flying into the ropes, only to have the other side come back the next day, swinging harder. But so far, it didn't sound like there'd been any knockouts.

Perhaps if I'd been there I could've understood the proceedings better, but I never regretted my decision not to go. Em was the main reason I hadn't, but I couldn't help wondering what I would've done if she hadn't been a factor. Could I have handled listening to the allegations against my parents, or sat there, emotionless, while the prosecution detailed my family's decadent lifestyle, turning them into sneering, palm-rubbing, cartoon villains?

Mom had plenty of support without me, though. Allie was by her side every day, and Baron Von Bod came too. Ben was even there for part of the trial when he was working in New York, and so was my mom's friend from New Orleans—Elva Foxworth.

My only impression of Elva Foxworth was questionable at best—it involved cake. She had brought an enormous home-made German chocolate cake to a Casa dei Sogni barbecue one year, and had slipped and fallen flat on her ass at the front door. Luckily, Elva had ample padding so she was okay, aside from her bruised ego. The cake didn't fare as well—it went flying across the travertine, but never one to waste chocolate, I scraped it off the floor and we ate it anyway. Elva was one of those bossy, buxom Southern types who liked to brag about how she was into younger dudes, but aside from that, I knew very little about her. All Mom ever said was that she met Elva online and she was supposedly "in the business" and she "knew a lot of people," and was sure my parents were going to win this case.

During the trial, I often questioned my reality. My parents certainly weren't cartoon villains—a real-life Boris and Natasha, cackling over their evil schemes. The Joel and Cecily Gold I knew were far more complicated. Above all else, they just seemed to value family, loyalty, generosity, and tradition, yet I had to admit they had a dark side—just like everyone else. But was their dark side powerful enough to make them do the terrible things they were accused of? Though this was possible, it was hard for me to imagine. When I'd read the indictment, it had felt like I was reading about total strangers. I'd puzzle to myself for hours, usually in the middle of sleepless nights, trying to figure out if I even knew who my parents were at all, and if they were truly capable of masterminding elaborate cons. If they were, then that made a mark, because I hadn't suspected a thing. Or maybe, I thought sometimes, I just didn't want to see the truth, and because I loved my parents so much, I may have even fooled myself.

In Mom's mind, she was the angel to the prosecution's devil—a grandmother, dedicated wholly to her family. She and Joel helped people, for God's sakes, and all those companies they took public? They were helping them, too, because they believed in their businesses and wanted them to succeed. Mom said she and Joel were good, honest people who'd scraped their way to the top without privilege or education, trying to make their way in a world dominated by elitist Ivy Leaguers who resented their success.

She and Joel were the only ones who fought back. When Mom was first arrested in October of 2010, she wasn't the only one who went down that day. Four other South Floridians were busted as coconspirators. Ian Greenberg, the guy who came over that first Thanksgiving right after Em was born, was one of them. Several longshoremen in New York—Carmelo's guys—were arrested too, but Mom didn't know any of them. The point is, everybody else pleaded guilty in exchange for lighter sentences. But Mom and Joel, without hesitation, maintained their innocence, and let their cases go to trial.

When I asked my mother how she could plead not guilty when everyone she worked with had done the opposite, she told me it was because she had to stand up for what she knew was right. She hadn't done anything wrong, and she wasn't going to be a pussy like those other guys and make cowardly deals with the government. She wanted to fight for her reputation, even if she lost.

"They did it because they were scared. They let the Feds intimidate them and coerce them into making false confessions. I don't even blame Carmelo for setting me up. He wanted a family. He wanted to keep trying for a baby with his wife, and I think he knew if he worked with them, they'd let him off, but if he fought, he could get ten years and they'd never be able to have kids," Mom said.

"What about Ian Greenberg?" I asked. "I see him all over Facebook, Twitter, like nothing ever happened. What's up with that?"

"All I know is he was broke on his ass and had no money to defend himself. He was just a kid, Vic. He had nobody to help him, so I don't know, maybe he made some kind of a deal because he had no choice."

"Why didn't you make a deal if you could get off or get less time?" I asked.

Mom didn't hesitate. "Because *I'm not guilty*. Because they'd want me to set people up and rat people out, and I'm not going to do that. Most of these people have families, you know what I'm saying? I'm not going to let the government tear apart any more families. I'm not going to be part of that."

The first week of the trial, Mom usually seemed fairly hopeful, with stories about witnesses breaking down under cross-examination. When the prosecution called up a kid who claimed to have lost everything on penny stocks, Mom's lawyers had supposedly torn him to shreds and made him look like a moron. Mom said he didn't even know who my parents were, and like a gambler, he was addicted to day trading. He made the decision to bet his life savings, Mom told me. My parents hadn't put him up to anything. At one point another witness—the CEO of one of the companies Joel took public—asked for a break and, according to Mom, he told the judge off the record that he didn't even know why he was there.

"The Golds are good people. I'd do business with them again if I could," he'd apparently said off the record.

That night Mom, Allie, and Elva had gone out for cocktails to celebrate, but most of the time Mom wasn't that confident. On the hardest days, Allie was the one who'd call with updates. She recounted how Joel had sat stone-faced throughout the proceedings, but that Mom had a hard time containing her emotions, especially when she was forced to sit quietly and listen to a prosecutor spin a tale that painted her as a snake. She wanted a chance to tell her side of things, but her team wouldn't let her on the stand.

It was even more difficult for her to hear the testimonies of people she'd once considered her best friends, people she'd welcomed in her home and cooked our favorite family recipes for. *This guy blew all his earnings on strippers and whores,* she wanted to say. They'd loaned him money to pay his bills. And how about this jackass, who was practically homeless until he met her and Joel? They'd fed him, bought him new clothes and a car, helped him get his life back in order so he had a chance to be somebody, and he squandered everything they gave him because he was a mooch.

The biggest shock came when the prosecution called Chuck Prince to the stand. I couldn't believe it when Allie told me. Had Joel not been around for our weddings, Chuck Prince would have walked me and Ashley down the aisle. He was a well-to-do Orlando cardiologist, close to seventy, and the last person any of us would have expected to testify against my parents.

Mom and Joel had been friends with him since the early nineties, when Mom had met him in the Florida Millionaires chat room on AOL. He was divorced and lonely, always soft-spoken and sheepish, and she and Joel had finally met him in real life at a meet-up at the Ritz-Carlton in Naples. They hit it off, and before long Dr. Prince was driving to Fort Lauderdale most weekends to hang out with our family. Since he didn't have one of his own, he spent every holiday with us, and always showed up with bags of gifts. He was funny and kind, different from my parents' usual crew, and Ashley and I liked him.

But the man in court wasn't the Dr. Prince we knew and loved. He was angry and bitter and said Joel had forged stock certificates in his name, meaning that Joel was buying the stocks himself but pretending Chuck was the purchaser, supposedly without Chuck's knowledge. Chuck came off as someone who my parents had courted because he had money.

I never believed that though. They'd been friends with this man for almost twenty years, and he was like family. Mom and Joel had been there for him when he was lonely and had had bad luck in love. Most of the time they were the ones treating him to dinner on the weekends. If they'd had ulterior motives, I doubted their friendship would've lasted as long as it did.

Mom blamed Georgia, Chuck's new girlfriend. Mom was never a fan of Georgia, and she accused her of having been a prostitute before she managed to rope Chuck. She said Georgia was the one who was really fleecing him, and that Georgia was jealous of her and Joel.

Ashley and I had met Georgia, and we concluded she was indeed an unusual individual. The first time we had dinner with her, she'd giggled uncontrollably and told us she ate literally nothing but pills and 3 Musketeers bars (she inhaled several, which she pulled out of her Michael Kors bag while the rest of us ordered steaks), and that she'd bleached her teeth so many times, they'd turned as blue and transparent as little panes of glass. She was also an obsessed pageant mom. *Toddlers and Tiaras* seriously missed out on filming her spray tanning her five-year-old daughter Pacific while she frantically searched for the kid's "flipper" before the little girl went onstage in garters and fishnets to sing "Don't Cry for Me Argentina" in a Wyndham hotel somewhere in Tennessee. Pacific's pageant career, according to Mom, was funded by Chuck, of course.

Mom believed Georgia wanted to drive a wedge between Chuck and our family, and by turning my parents in, she also stood to gain a thirty-thousand-dollar reward. After she called the investigators and they showed up at Chuck's office wanting more information, Mom said he was probably scared shitless.

"Because he's always been a pussy," Mom said.

According to her theory, he started singing whatever tune he thought the Feds wanted to hear.

The trial dragged on for three weeks. During that time, Em and I enjoyed being back in Florida, sleeping in our own beds, frolicking in the tropical weather again—I didn't realize how much I'd taken eighty-degree afternoons for granted. After the long, bleak winter in Delaware, I had a new appreciation for where I lived, and each day, I tried to keep myself busy as the trial slogged forward. Em and I went to every children's museum within a fifty-mile radius of our home. We visited farms and botanical gardens and attempted dance classes—anything to pass the time, but it was more than that. I was genuinely enjoying being a mom for the first time. Em and I were having fun.

When we got home, I'd started making some positive changes. I gladly went back to yoga, where I found I still couldn't stand on my head or even do the beginning of a split, but you know what I could do? I could give thanks for the privilege of being present. I wouldn't be performing in the next Cirque du Soleil (unless the new show was entitled *Spazzy Housewives Mildly Stretching*), but my body could walk and knead dough, it could pick strawberries and push Em on the swings. I had a hand that could reach out and provide a butterfly with a safe place to land and a mind that could tell stories and make people laugh.

In yoga, the teacher had told us about the lotus flower, which manages to bloom beautifully even as it hovers over stagnant ponds. The lotus lives in a muddy world, as we all do, but it isn't affected by it. Its petals don't get dirty because, ultimately, the lotus is detached from the mud. It's not scared. It doesn't make itself crazy trying to figure out how to clean up the pond. It blooms with no worries whatsoever. Maybe I could learn to be like the lotus too.

No matter the outcome of the trial, no matter what happened to my parents, I wouldn't freak out. I would keep on living and growing, and when the verdict came, I would deal with whatever changes it brought.

The prosecution presented its closing arguments toward the end of March. Mom said they showed the jury glossy, poster-size photos of their house, cars, and boat—that they were trying to make the jurors jealous. According to Mom, when it came time for Joel's attorneys to make their closing statement, Joel's lawyer got sick and almost fainted in the courtroom, forcing the judge to adjourn. The next day, he came back (Mom said he was fighting off a stomach bug) and presented his final argument. Mom told me that the prosecution was allowed a rebuttal, which flabbergasted me, because it seemed unfair that both sides didn't get equal chances to address the jury. I hadn't realized it worked that way, but I supposed that the prosecution got the home court advantage. After that, it was time for the jury to deliberate.

I would've sucked as a juror. I would've been reluctant to make a decision on the off chance I was wrong, and wouldn't have wanted that kind of power over someone else's life. On the last day of the trial, I took Em to the park for several hours to distract myself, and while I sang nursery rhymes, Em on the swings, I couldn't help but wonder what the jurors on my parents' case were thinking, discussing, or maybe even arguing. I tried to imagine what sort of impression my parents had made on them. How did other people, *normal people*, see Joel and Cecily Gold?

By six that night, I still hadn't heard from anyone, so I reluctantly packed up our things and left the park. Em was getting hungry, and soon it would be time to start our bedtime routine. At home Em played with blocks on the kitchen floor while I robotically prepared a box of macaroni and cheese for dinner. I'd been making it so often, I'd memorized the instructions, and I tried to forgive the transgression of not making it homemade anymore by telling myself that at least I bought the organic one with the bunny on the box, which had to count for something. I was whisking the neon-orange cheese powder into the milk and melted butter when Allie finally called. I snatched the phone off the counter without even bothering to wipe away a drop of milk that had splattered on the screen, and answered on the first ring.

"Guilty on all charges. Both of them," she said, sighing.

I paused for a moment, not knowing what to say. I felt nothing. Truthfully, I'd expected this and had prepared for this moment for a long time.

"Is Mom okay?" I finally asked.

"She's fine. She just wants to come home, so we're packing up right now and heading back tonight."

"What about Joel?" I asked.

"He took it a lot harder than your mom. His knees gave out when they read the verdict. His attorneys had to hold him up, and he turned white as a sheet. He really thought he was going to walk, but your mom was always a lot more realistic. She said this morning that she knew they weren't going to win," Allie told me.

I asked if I could talk to her, but Allie said Mom needed a little time to calm down and that she'd call me later when they got on the road. I understood, and told her that it was okay.

"Tell her I love her," I said.

I left the macaroni and cheese on the stove and took Em outside. Evening was coming, but the sun would still be up for a little while longer, so we sat in the shade of our strawberry tree, which now towered over the house. The leafy branches were blooming and laden with pink berries. Honeybees zinged in and out of the white blossoms, and Em spotted a bird's nest in the high branches.

My yard, which had once been an untamed jungle, was now filled with fruit trees and fragrant flowers. My parents were going to prison, but somehow, through all the drama, the vision Ben and I shared had still come true.

28

I couldn't remember the last time I'd been able to celebrate Easter, so that year I became a bit . . . obsessive. You've heard of Bridezillas? Well, I was an Easter Bunnyzilla, and I threw myself into creating an over-the-top holiday production the likes of which our family had never seen. Which was saying a lot, because our family had seen pretty much everything.

Coloring eggs; decorating in pastels, with lots of rabbits, chicks, and grosgrain ribbon; robin's eggs made out of malted chocolate; a dinner of macaroni with smoked gouda, fresh asparagus, honey ham; arranging pink tulips in mason jars—I did it all. I could blame Pinterest for my mania, but that would be like an alcoholic blaming Maker's Mark for his bender. It was as if I somehow believed that if I arranged the decorations and planned the dinner just so, I could create the illusion of normalcy, even if it was only for a day. But a candy bunny filled with Nutella never fixed anything, at least not permanently, especially when your mom's wearing an ankle monitor.

As soon as Mom got back from the trial, she was assigned a new probation officer who fitted her with a monitoring device that we lightheartedly called her "ankle bracelet," though it was anything but a piece of jewelry. She was under house arrest until her sentencing, which wasn't actually all that bad, especially since Mom never went anywhere now that Joel wasn't around to help her navigate the world outside the house. She didn't like to drive or go out much by herself, but if she wanted to, she could leave the house between ten A.M. and eight P.M. After that, she couldn't even go out in her yard without being surrounded by a SWAT team. If she bent the rules even a little, they'd haul her in just like they had Joel, who was in a New York City prison, awaiting his sentencing since he was still considered a flight risk. He seemed to be doing okay, though. He had an e-mail account and could make phone calls, and he wrote that he was in the same facility as several Al-Qaeda operatives, a bunch of old mafia dons, and even some dude known as the Cannibal Cop. He described everything with an air of cinematic glamour, but I pictured the jail scenes from *The Silence of the Lambs*.

Mom reminded me of myself in high school, whenever I was waiting for the boy I liked to call. She never set her cell phone down, and she checked her e-mail obsessively. Sometimes she was even reluctant to go to the grocery store, and I wondered what the big deal was. Joel could call later, right? But it was basically the same as telling a junkie that they could wait a few extra hours before they shot up again. Just ignore the projectile vomiting!

It was obvious that Mom missed Joel a lot, but I missed him too, much more than I wanted to (I still hadn't reconciled my feelings about his cheating). I missed his knocks on my door each morning and how he'd show up with treats for me and Em, and I missed his gleaming smile as he rode his bike down our street, Em strapped in her bike seat, wearing her Dora helmet and proudly dinging the bell he'd installed for her. Joel brought hope to our family. When we were sad, he'd find something to celebrate, cranking up the music, grabbing our hands, and twirling us around the kitchen like it was Studio 54 in its heyday. Before we had a chance to cry, Joel would whisk us away, and we'd find ourselves at the best restaurant in town, eating lobsters, or at the mall with Neiman Marcus bags in our hands. Sometimes his optimism might have been unrealistic, but we always gladly let ourselves believe his promises. He still had Mom convinced that they'd be free any day now. Something was going to happen—one big miracle would make everything go back to how it had been before the raid.

It was weird having Joel gone. The house was quiet without him, and I couldn't lose the sense that at any second he'd come through the front doors, singing and clapping like he always did, his cell phone buzzing on the waistband of his gym shorts. Even people who are still alive can become ghosts when they're absent. Sometimes when I was at my parents' house, I'd think I caught a glimpse of his red shoes in the corner of my eye or that I'd heard him whistling upstairs in the shower. His number was still listed under Favorites in my phone. So what now?

Easter baskets.

Celebrating Easter was going to be the silver lining of Joel's absence, because before he went to jail, we had to skip the holiday. For decades Easter had been our concession to make living in a mixed-religion family work. Passover was arguably the biggest, or at least the longest and most complicated, Jewish holiday, and it always coincided with Easter. Joel wasn't religious, per se—he had married a shiksa after all—but he did go to temple and was otherwise observant. Each year for Pesach, he followed the dietary laws and performed Seder with his parents, who lived forty minutes away in Delray Beach. Since Mom and I got to keep Christmas, Joel got Passover. Every year his two sisters and their families flew in to Florida and stayed with their parents for the eight days of unleavened bread, and once upon a time Mom and I had tagged along with Joel to every event at their house. I actually kind of liked Passover, but since Joel was in jail, his family hadn't invited us to the Seder, so I said fuck 'em. I'll take Reese's eggs over beet-flavored horseradish and crackers any day.

I'd planned to host Easter, but at the last minute Mom refused to let me have the dinner at my house. She wanted it to be at her house because her house was bigger, so Ashley and I packed up the food we'd already cooked and I hauled all of my decorations over and that was that. I was irritated, but I could either deal with it or throw a big fit, so I opted for peace.

The truth was that Mom didn't want to be away from her computer in case she got an e-mail from Joel. She hadn't heard from him in two days. As she helped me put the finishing touches on Easter dinner, her hands shook and she chewed constantly on the inside of her cheek, contorting her face sideways and twitching as she did it. She spent most of the holiday in the office, checking her CorrLinks e-mail account for any word from him. Later we'd find out that the prison had been on lockdown because some inmates had gotten into a fight.

I tried to forget about Joel as I admired the buffet table and loaded my plate with the delicious meal that Mom, Allie, Ashley, and I had cooked. We had a big honey ham studded with cherries and cloves; pineapple casserole; baked macaroni and cheese topped with sliced tomatoes and crispy bacon; and at least five kinds of salads. Allie had even made a flourless chocolate cake for dessert.

"This looks amazing!" Ben said. "You girls really outdid yourselves."

"I've been looking forward to this for weeks," I said, spooning an extra helping of fluffy ambrosia onto my plate.

"Don't forget these!" Mom called from the kitchen, where she was sliding a massive CorningWare pan of bubbling baked beans out of the oven. "I made them special!"

Everyone had finished making their plates, and we were just sitting down to eat when the doorbell rang, filling me with a familiar dread. I wondered if that feeling would ever go away, if I'd ever be able to hear a doorbell again without my heart skipping a beat. Mom left her dinner plate on the kitchen counter and went to answer it.

Liszka had arrived, with terrible timing, to pick up her last paycheck. Mom had had to fire her as soon as she got back from New York. She had to save what little money she had left, and with just her in the house, she "could scrub her own goddamned toilets." Mom let Liszka in, and invited her to stay for dinner, but she said she couldn't eat because she was too upset about the trial. Liszka hadn't lived at Casa dei Sogni for long, but the way she sobbed, you'd have thought she'd known us for years.

"I so sorry, Cecily. You so good to me. You no go to jail," Liszka cried.

Everyone at the dinner table tried to ignore the scene as Mom hugged her, assured her she'd be fine, and then tried to shoo her off as quickly as possible, but she was barely out the door before Barbara and Arlo came knocking. They hadn't seen Mom since the verdict, and as soon as Barbara walked in holding the puppy Mom had gotten her, she, too, burst into tears.

"I'm going to be fine," Mom comforted her. "I promise you. I've been through a lot. I can get through this, too."

"It's not fair, Cecily. You didn't deserve this," Barbara said, choking on her words.

Jeannie Lee was next, but at least she showed up with an Italian cream cake. Jeannie Lee was Mom's oldest friend from her drug-dealing days. We only saw her on holidays because she was always busy with church and her job as an addiction counselor. She and Mom had been close since they were kids, but Jeannie had bolted for Florida after high school and ended up dating a Colombian drug lord. When he was murdered, Jeannie, by then a junkie, started stripping to support her habit. She'd passed out one night, fatefully on the front lawn of a church, and was rescued by missionaries. They took her to a rehab facility in Appalachia, where she stayed for several years, finding the Holy Spirit while she took correspondence classes. Jeannie Lee had no memory of her pre-rehab life and neither did I. I'd only known her as she was now—a grandmotherly figure who occasionally spoke in tongues. With her holiday-themed outfits, her life of Pentecostal celibacy, and a "this car is prayer-conditioned" bumper sticker, it was utterly impossible for me to imagine Jeannie as a gun moll, but Mom swore it was true.

"People really can change sometimes," she always told me.

Jeannie helped herself to dinner, and we all scooted our chairs closer to make room for her at the table. She was about to say a quick grace, and I'd just raised a forkful of green beans to my mouth when the doorbell rang again.

"Who now?" I cried, setting my fork down.

"I might have invited a few people," Mom said, abandoning her meal once again to see who it was.

I'd never liked Nort, and I wasn't a bit pleased to see him crash our party. He had two claims to fame. Back in the early nineties, he'd led police on a high-speed chase that ended with him jumping out of the car and, as Joel told it, running on foot through a bad neighborhood pursued by helicopters and dogs. The whole mess had supposedly been aired on an episode of *COPS*. Fast-forward through several years of prison, and Nort had become a contestant on a reality series that was sort of like *The Bachelorette* except with more drugs and tattoos. Sadly, the show had to be canceled "out of respect" when Nort's fellow competitor decided to hack a swimsuit model to pieces, stuff her body in a suitcase, and throw it in a Dumpster.

Rumored to have actual mob ties, Nort called himself an "investor," but all that meant was he dabbled in penny stocks. He had porn connections of some sort too. Nort was the one who'd convinced my parents to rent out their house a few years back as the set for some online skin flicks, and he'd also tried to lasso them into sketchy deals. Mom had to throw him and some of his "partners" out of the house once because they wanted her to do something illegal, and now here he was, acting like his heart was broken because my mom was going to jail, when it was a miracle he wasn't headed there with her. I kept wishing he'd leave or at least be quiet, but all he did was stand in the kitchen, shaking his head and pinching the bridge of his nose while we tried to eat our candied sweet potatoes and string bean casserole in peace.

"I can't believe this is happening to you of all people, Cecily," he said with a sniff.

I leaned over and whispered to Ashley, "I swear to the baby Jesus, if one more person shows up in tears, I'm going to take the bunny-shaped coconut cake I slaved over all weekend and smash it right in their fucking face."

"Yeah," she said. "I'm done. I can't. It's a shit show. I'm about to give birth! I don't need this."

She was gone before the curtain went up on the biggest disaster of the day. It was evening. Em was getting fussy, and Jeannie Lee had left because most of the adults were well on their way to being sloshed. Ben had just grabbed a new bottle out of the wine refrigerator behind the bar when Mom spotted him from the kitchen, where she'd been polishing off a deviled egg. She made a beeline for him, shouting "No!" so loudly, Ben got startled and dropped the corkscrew. It landed with an echoing clatter on the marble countertop.

"What the hell do you think you're doing?" she yelled.

Ben raised his hands like he was in a stickup, his left hand still clutching the wine bottle.

"What are you talking about?" he asked. I could hear the defensiveness in his voice.

"Where did you get that bottle?" she demanded.

"Just there, in the fridge. What's the big deal?"

"That doesn't belong to you! That's Joel's special wine!"

"What do you mean? Joel's in jail, Cecily!"

"Not forever he's not! He's getting out. Maybe any day now!"

"Wouldn't he want us to enjoy his wine since he can't? You know, while we're still able to?" Ben argued.

Mom tore the bottle from Ben's hand and shoved it back into the fridge.

"Let's just go," I said to Ben. "It's late, and Mom's having a tough time. Come on."

I hastily packed up our belongings, and when we walked out, Mom was in a frenzy, taping signs all over the bar: *Do Not Touch!* and *JOEL's Wine! Not for Guests!*

I couldn't sleep that night, and as I lay in bed, I realized that all my cooking and decorating and trying to make new traditions had been in vain. Funny thing was, I thought celebrating Easter would make me happy, but all the bunnies and jelly beans only made me miss our Passover traditions more. Lord knows, it wasn't because I was craving gefilte fish; it was the memories and what those traditions had represented for us—how once we'd made it work as a blended family in our own crazy way.

The next morning I went to the grocery store and bought a box of matzo. At home, I slid one of the bland crackers from the box, spread it with softened butter, and sprinkled it with flaky, kosher salt, and spooned on dollops of tart cherry preserves.

"Try this," I said to Em, who was standing beside me at the kitchen counter, tugging on the hem of my shirt.

"This was my favorite when I was little," I told her.

She eagerly took the piece of matzo I handed her, gobbled it down, and asked for more. She said it was her favorite too, and gave me a thumbs-up.

29

Mom needed to find a way to get by until her sentencing. She was broke: now that her bank accounts had been seized, she had no access to cash, and she couldn't work anymore. She needed a new source of income.

"Short-term rental. That's your only solution," Allie convinced her.

Casa dei Sogni would eventually be turned over to the government and auctioned off, but that wouldn't happen until Mom and Joel were sentenced, so she was free to stay in her home and do whatever she wanted with it until then. As much as I didn't like the idea of strangers swimming in our pink pool, I had to admit that this was probably the best solution.

"You know how much foreigners'll pay for a mansion like this on the water? Big bucks!" Mom exclaimed. "I've been sitting on a gold mine this whole time! Heidi told me I should've rented this house out ages ago!"

Heidi was Mom's real estate agent and new "best friend." She was all of twenty-nine (pounds and years old), and to me she looked more like a South Florida party girl than a serious businesswoman. She was supermodel tall and dressed in loudly printed, flowy BCBG tops that hung off her bony shoulders. Heidi suffered from a severe case of bronzer abuse. Whenever I saw her, the motherly part of me wanted to take a wet wipe to her face and remove a couple of layers of the orange makeup she spackled on, but Mom said she used so much foundation because her on-again-off-again boyfriend was an NFL star who regularly gave her black eyes. Heidi got the job leasing Mom's house because Allie and Heidi were "best friends," and lately it seemed like without Joel around, Allie was running the show. Heidi had probably agreed to split the commission with her, I figured. I just couldn't shake the suspicion that Allie had an ulterior motive.

"She's always here," I whispered to Mom one afternoon as we sat on her back terrace. Allie was in the kitchen, whipping up a batch of chicken salad, and we were temporarily out of earshot.

"How does Allie not work, Mom? I mean, come on. She's hiding something," I said. "This is too weird. I get that she's a great friend to you and all, but don't you think it's a little odd that she's always here?"

"She's not *always* here anymore. She's working with Irving Birdy now," Mom said. I had to admit she was right. Instead of sleeping over seven nights a week, it was more like five now.

Irving Birdy was truly one of the most repugnant human beings I'd ever met. He was a doctor, but not a practicing doctor, though he kept his license up-to-date in order to call in prescriptions for his friends (which were few because no one liked him). I'd had the pleasure of knowing Irving Birdy for a long time, before my parents had become acquainted with him, because he lived in a community where I'd once worked, and he was a regular nuisance to me at the homeowner's association. He liked to call and rant and rave nonsensically about everything that was wrong with his property, and when he wasn't doing that, he was adding nineteen-year-old girls to his guest list. He was unattractive, but he had money (hence his ability to entice comely young women), and he had the money because he claimed he was disabled and couldn't work—though by all appearances, he was in perfect shape.

The way Mom explained it, Irving and Allie were running a major con.

"It's disgusting, really. Sickening. I can't believe it, and if this is what they're really doing, they are going to get into some serious trouble," Mom said.

Mom told me that, since Irving was "disabled," he and Allie were scoping out local businesses—mostly little mom-and-pop places—and threatening to sue them for discrimination if they didn't comply perfectly with the ADA design codes. Then they would offer to drop the lawsuits in exchange for a yearly payment made directly to them. Mom said they were getting under-the-table kickbacks from dirty lawyers and that, in the past year, they'd filed several hundred of these lawsuits and essentially blackmailed as many small-business owners. As far as Mom and I were concerned, it was a clear-cut case of extortion.

"So, Mom, if she's doing this and if you think it's disgusting, why are you letting her stay here?" I said. "I don't understand how you can get your life so wrapped up around someone you don't even like."

"It's not that I don't like her. . . ." Mom's voice trailed off as she lit another Vantage Ultra Light and stared off at the canal water splashing against the seawall.

A few days later Mom called me to say that Heidi had quickly found tenants—Swedish millionaires who wanted to spend the summer in South Florida and gladly signed a three-month lease, agreeing to pay more than ten thousand dollars a month to stay in Casa dei Sogni. Mom would be able to live off that just fine until her sentencing, as long as she controlled her spending. Em and I went over to her house that night for dinner. Ben was working late, and I wanted to spend as much time as possible with my mom, to help her figure out a budget.

"I'm not buying anybody anything anymore. Those days are over, let me tell you."

"I don't want anything," I insisted.

"And we're not going out to eat. I'm done with that, too," she said as she circled the kitchen island, fixing me a plate of baked chicken and coleslaw. I told Mom her home cooking was so much better than restaurant food anyway.

"You want gravy on your stuffing?" she asked. Her cell phone rang before I could tell her I'd take a little, and she took off through the house so fast, you'd have thought Leatherface was coming after her with a chainsaw. In her wake, the lid of the gravy pot clattered to the floor. She kept her phone by her side at all times, but once in a while she'd forget. Then, as it rang, she sprinted through the house to find it.

I finished making my plate, and Em and I ate alone. When Mom finally hung up and came back to the kitchen, she'd been gone so long, she had to reheat the chicken. She banged the serving spoon against the metal edge of the stuffing pan and used a steak knife to stab a baked sweet potato through its foil wrapping. She sighed and huffed and slurped her iced tea from a plastic to-go cup she'd saved and reused at least a hundred times.

"What the fuck am I going to do now?" she mumbled.

"What? Who was on the phone?" I asked.

"I have no place to stay once the renters move in," Mom said.

She'd planned to stay two doors down at the home of a neighbor. He was a wealthy surgeon from New Jersey who spent his summers at the shore. The house at the end of Mom's cul-de-sac was his vacation home, and it often sat empty until winter, so Mom had approached him about the possibility of staying there.

"What happened?" I asked.

"Dr. Bill changed his mind. Claims he's *not comfortable*. His lawyers don't advise it, or some bullshit. I don't have a place to go. I'm going to be homeless, and I need to get a landline installed before I move in anyplace so they can get my ankle monitor hooked up. I don't know what I'm going to do," she worried. "I have one week, do you understand? One week to find a place and get that landline installed."

"Start looking for apartments," I said.

Mom glared at me, but I wasn't going to offer her a place to stay.

When I told Ashley what had happened, she was adamant that Mom wouldn't be staying with her, either, but at least she had the perfect excuse. She was about to give birth, and her in-laws were already coming to help out.

"I can't deal with her drama while I'm trying to take care of a newborn and a two-year-old," Ashley said. "Fuck that."

"I don't think it would work out at my house either," I said. I was trying to be diplomatic, but I didn't want to deal with Mom's friends coming over. I wanted peace, and the last thing I needed was more tension between her and Ben.

"My house is like my safe space, and if I let her live here, which would be extremely crowded being that we only have two bedrooms, it would be like inviting all that turmoil in. Ashley, I can't deal with it mentally. It's like I've reached my limit. I'm over it. I want to live my own life," I tried to explain.

"Look, I understand completely. You don't have to defend yourself to me," she said.

"But I still feel really guilty—" I said.

Ashley cut me off. "Don't. Do *not* feel guilty. You're being healthy. You're setting boundaries. Our kids have to be our priorities now, not her."

"What about the times she took us in, though? As adults. What if she said she didn't want *our* drama, our friends coming over, or our pets living in *her* house? It was never an issue with her. She would never have said no to us," I countered.

"It's not the same. She had a lot more space, for one thing, and she didn't have babies to take care of. Plus, that was her choice, and she should be able to respect it if we make different ones. If she can't, that's her problem. She needs to take responsibility for the situation she's in. She rented the house impulsively and failed to plan accordingly, so she can't make everyone else feel guilty because she likes playing the victim."

There were times when I'd think of the things Mom had done for me—taking me in after a breakup, helping me find a job and never asking me to pay rent, pushing me to go back to college and better myself, assisting me with buying the condo I loved and lived in for years. I owed my mother a lot, and I'd never be able to pay her back for all the things she'd done for me, but I still couldn't offer her a place to stay. I'd given her all I had the past few years, and it was preventing me from living my own life and it was dragging me away from my daughter.

That was the last conversation Ashley and I would have before my nephew was born. The next morning Ashley went to yoga—she was so proud she'd practiced the whole nine months and could even do handstands with an enormous baby bump. After class, she had a doctor's appointment, but her water broke right there in the office. She dropped her daughter Amelia back at her house with her in-laws and headed straight to the hospital. We kept in touch by text for the next few hours, and after dinner Andrew's mom offered to babysit Em so I could visit my sister. I got to the maternity ward around seven that evening, and Ashley hadn't progressed much. We joked a little, watched some TV, and I held her hand when the pain got bad.

"Is Mom coming?" I asked.

Ashley shook her head and winced while she waited for her latest contraction to pass.

"It's almost past her curfew," I said, noticing the clock on the bedside stand.

"We talked on the phone. It's not a big deal to me that she isn't here," Ashley said.

Since Ben was in New York that week, and it could take hours for the baby to come, I had to pick up Em and get her to bed. I hugged Ashley, wished her luck, and went home. As I drove, I called Mom. She had a houseful of people over—I could hear them shouting and laughing in the background—and seemed almost uninterested in the impending birth of her grandson.

"I know you're probably sad you couldn't be there. I know how much you love your grandchildren," I said, trying to show some sympathy.

"I'm not sad at all," Mom snapped. "I was there for Amelia's birth. What do I need to see this one for? Vic, I'm barely going to know this child. He's not going to grow up with memories of me. I'll be locked up before we have a chance to bond, and I don't want to get attached, so I'm staying away."

"But that's got to be so hard. I'm sorry."

"It is what it is, you know? That's the reality now, and I don't want to waste time feeling sorry for myself. I'll see the baby when they get home from the hospital. Let's not make a big drama out of this."

But how could it not become a big drama? Mom was about to miss the birth of her first grandson because she was under house arrest, and while she and Ashley were clearly trying to downplay the situation, I knew they were each hurting inside, and neither one of them could convince me otherwise.

"Allie and Heidi are over with a big group of girls. We're making cosmos and watching *Stud Muffins*, so I need to get off the phone because I'm still waiting for Joel's call," Mom said. She hung up before I had a chance to say good-bye.

My nephew Jack made his grand entrance a couple of hours later. Ashley texted me a picture at about ten that night, and I choked up when I saw pictures of her healthy baby boy. But these weren't tears of joy. Jack's birth was bittersweet—the event seemed to magnify our family's loss. Mom and Joel should have been there, I thought, and of all the consequences they would have to face, missing their grandchildren had to be the worst. It broke my heart that Mom was pretending to be unconcerned while she downed cocktails with girls half her age, and she still needed to find a place to live by the end of the week. I didn't even know how Joel was doing. We hadn't e-mailed each other in a few weeks.

As I readied for bed that night, I tried to focus on the positive. Em and I were going back to Funland in a few weeks. We'd be spending the summer in Delaware. I knew my mother would find a place to live and people to help her move. I decided to ignore her livid how-could-yous, and committed myself to relearning how to have a good time. When your parents are going to prison and your sister is stuck in the house with a colicky newborn, dealing with the terrible twos doesn't seem so bad. I wanted to celebrate whatever freedom I had, so I declared that season my Summer of Fun: two months of orchards and water slides, hot dogs roasted over bonfires, family Cornhole tournaments, and buckets of boardwalk fries so hot, they burned my fingertips.

30

I stretched out in the cool grass, full of barbecued chicken and dishes that contained Jell-O and Cool Whip but were still somehow called "salads," and watched bouquets of fireworks blooming brightly across the night sky over Delaware's state capitol. I took a quick photo with my phone and texted it to Ben, who was back in Florida for work while Em and I were away. Em, up way past her bedtime, snuggled in her aunt Grace's lap, transfixed by the July Fourth pyrotechnics. We were surrounded by family members, who sat on blankets and folding lawn chairs, swigging Gatorade and passing tortilla chips and salsa, while they commented on the light show, which was apparently way better this year than last. I couldn't even remember what I'd done the previous Independence Day, but I knew I'd remember this celebration for the rest of my life. It was the first holiday I'd ever spent with my brothers and sisters.

"We're coming down from Philly for the Fourth of July, and there's nothing you can do to stop us," Sarah had told me over the phone as soon as she found out we were back at Mommom Alice's for the summer. "We're not taking no for an answer, plus it's my birthday, so you can't avoid me, because that would be mean," she added.

"I'm in a better place now than I was last winter," I explained. "Plus, I saw you guys once and survived!"

The week before Fourth of July, my aunt and uncle had thrown a little shindig at their house for Mommom Alice's birthday. It had been one of the main reasons for my trip—my grandmother was past eighty now and threatened with an aortic aneurysm. This time I wanted to be there to see Mommom Alice blow her candles out.

At the birthday party, I'd had an amazing time. All my siblings were there, and the second they arrived, Thaddeus scooped Em into his arms and carted her out into the yard to play tag. Grace found me and immediately asked if she could get me a lemonade, while Sarah peppered me with questions.

"I want to know all about your life," she said, and gave my arm an affectionate squeeze.

Lucas, the youngest, who I finally met in person, told me all about his artwork and showed me some photos on his phone (he was an incredible painter) until Grace came by and asked me to sign a book I was in.

"Where'd you get that?" I asked.

"I saw you were in it, and I ordered it from Amazon!" she said.

"That's awesome that you're a real writer," Lucas added.

"One day you can write my life story for me," Sarah said.

Thaddeus joked that it would be a comedy.

There'd been so many times since the raid when I felt cursed, and it had often felt like I was losing everything, but that summer in Delaware, I could finally see I had been wrong. I wasn't losing anything. My mother and Joel would still be part of my life, just in a different way (that involved jumpsuits, security pat downs, and really bad food, but whatever). In fact, in the midst of tragedy, I'd gained a lot—five brothers and sisters, and their families.

We filled each day with new adventures: shelling along the muddy shore of the Delaware Bay, lakeside rambles, chasing after hoptoads at dusk, and catching lightning bugs in mason jars. We fed mules, pulled the car over in a ditch, and gathered armfuls of tiger lilies beside a country road. At the state fair, we held baby chicks and let them peck at our freckles, and at the boardwalk, we soared high above the shoreline on the Ferris wheel. On a balmy July night, I introduced Em to the joy of digging into a cup of soft-serve vanilla while we sat on the hood of the car, watching the moths dance in the streetlights. Reliving my fondest child-hood memories with my daughter was the happiest thing I had ever done, but we made new memories together too.

Sarah's mother-in-law invited us over for a Sunday feast and instantly welcomed me into their big, hilarious band of rowdy South Philly Italians. My extended family grew instantly, over the most delicious chicken parmesan I have ever eaten in my entire life, and pretty soon I was sipping limoncello while the little ones splashed like ducklings out back in the kiddie pool. I felt like I'd known these people for years. They were warm and funny and hospitable—pretty much everything I wanted the people in my life to be like from then on out. I left their home not just full (I had to have one last almond biscotti) but ful-filled.

Because it felt so good, I started to reach out to more people. I called longtime family friends to say hi, and a day later ended up cracking crabs with them at a newspaper-covered table overlook-ing a landscape of marsh grasses and mirror-still waterways. I initiated barbecues and said yes to birthday parties, and found family members who were happy to babysit so I could play trivia at a local bar and eat burgers with people I'd grown up with. I won my first trophy, and it was one of the sweetest victories of my life.

That summer passed far too quickly, and soon it was mid-August and time for us to head home. The trip had revived my spirit and given me the strength I needed to say good-bye to my mother and start figuring out what my new normal would be as she prepared for a life behind bars.

Two days after we arrived back in Florida, we went to see Mom. I lifted Em out of her car seat and locked the doors. Then

I locked them again. Better safe than sorry in this neighborhood, so I locked them a third time.

On the corner, four lanky men, their faces hidden by the hoodies they wore, even though it was at least ninety-six degrees, rummaged through their pockets, quickly exchanged whatever they found in them, and scattered like startled pigeons. Sirens blared a few streets over. I heard Maury Povich declare, *You are not the father!* from the open window of an apartment at Mom's new digs.

I was nervous about seeing my mother for the first time since the end of June. I worried about her health and her mental state, and knew she felt depressed and bitter about her situation. While I was away, most of our phone calls had been pretty unpleasant. I wanted to hear: *Honey, I'm so glad you and Emmie are having such a wonderful summer! Can't wait to see you again.* Instead I got: "I can't believe I have to live in this fucking shit-hole apartment!" The way she said it made me feel like it was my fault.

Mom was living with Baron Von Bod's sister-in-law, Nadia, and her fifteen-year-old son, and neither of them spoke much English. Most nights, Nadia worked in a corset and five-inch stilettos as a cocktail waitress at Hot Pink, Fort Lauderdale's current "klassiest" gentlemen's club. Mom, Nadia, Nadia's son, and their two labradoodles, plus Mom's Doberman, were crammed into a tiny two-bedroom on the edge of a city park known more for crack deals and toothless hookers than its playground. It wasn't nice, and it made me sad to think of my mother being uncomfortable, but it was only temporary—and at least it wasn't prison.

"Hold Mommy's hand, Em," I said, and she clutched me tight.

"Where are we going?" she asked.

"This is Mommom's new house!" I said, trying to sound upbeat, but Em wasn't buying it for a second.

"Why's it so messy?" she asked, kicking an empty Diet Pepsi bottle off of the cracked walkway.

I ignored her question. "Look what a pretty peach color the building is!" I chirped.

But Em pressed on, "Mommy, why don't they cut the grass?"

I pushed an overgrown bougainvillea branch out of our way, and told her to watch out for the thorns.

Mom was so excited, she had come outside to meet us. Far more shocking than where my mother was living was how she looked, and my heart sank when I saw her gaunt face. My worries hadn't been unfounded.

"Look how skinny I am!" she said.

I lied and told her she looked great, but I was concerned. At least we were heading out to lunch, I thought. I hoped she was eating. After we arrived at the restaurant, I was relieved to see that at least her appetite seemed fine.

"It's incredible the way the weight is just falling off me," she said, shoving three fries into her mouth.

"Have you been dieting?" I asked.

"Does it look like I'm on a diet?" she said, and laughed.

She'd ordered a platter of beer-battered fish-and-chips with tartar sauce and was helping herself to generous bites of Em's pasta.

"I can eat whatever I want, and I'm still losing weight," Mom said.

"I wish I had that problem," I said. I'd gained seven pounds in Delaware that summer.

"You're in perimenopause," Mom diagnosed. "You won't be able to lose weight until you're fifty. It's hormones."

"You just love reminding me that I'm getting old," I said.

"Victoria, you have to face it. You're going to be forty in November. *Forty years old.* I know in your head you still feel like a kid—believe me, I feel like one too at times—but you've been a grown woman for a long time now, and things are going to change a lot—not just your body, but in your head."

"Yeah, look at this patch of gray hair I've got now. I look like the Bride of Frankenstein," I joked.

"You should look forward to aging. Women get strong in their forties. We've been through enough shit by that point that we can say enough is enough. You start getting serious about your life and making yourself happy. Look at my mom," she said.

Mommom Marie was in her forties when her twenty-seven-year marriage to my grandfather ended in divorce. He left her for Ashley's real mom, and my grandmother was suddenly left with nothing. Her husband was gone, her kids were grown and out on their own. She even lost her house, plus she was humiliated, because everyone in town knew the sordid ins and outs of my grandfather's scandalous affair. But if any of this got my grandmother down, no one knew it, because she picked herself right back up and made a new life. She'd never been anything but a housewife, but she got herself a job and a new apartment. For the first time, she did what *she* wanted to do, on her own terms. My circumstances might have been different from my grandmother's, but she inspired me. I wanted to show my life who was boss too.

Mom polished off her fish-and-chips and ordered a bowl of strawberry shortcake for dessert. She took forever to finish, scraping the bowl over and over to get every last crumb of cream-soaked cake. She must've asked the server for five more refills of iced tea, which she'd stir slowly and take tiny sips of while we made idle small talk, which was out of character for Mom—she even brought up the weather, talking about what a slow hurricane season it had been. Though our plates had long since been bused, she said we weren't ready for the check each time the server came back by. I sensed she had something important to say, but she stalled for another ten minutes, taking a smoke break, and then walking around the building with Em until she finally came back inside, sat back down at the table, and admitted it.

"I hate going back to that fucking apartment," she said.

I nodded in sympathy. I could imagine how she felt.

"I hate being without my husband and sleeping alone every night," she said.

"I know. I'm sorry," I said. The words came out automatically, like a conversational reflex, and she nabbed me on it.

"Really? What are you sorry for, Vic? You haven't talked to Joel all summer. You couldn't even find five minutes to send him an e-mail. After everything he did for you, how could you treat him that way?"

"I don't know. I just needed a break," I tried to explain, but Mom would never understand. I barely understood it myself. "I feel betrayed," I went on. "I feel like I didn't know the real Joel."

"That's a load of bullshit."

"Mom, language, please. Em's here," I warned.

"I don't care. She's playing with your damn phone anyway, and this is important. Yes, Joel did some stupid shit, okay. He made mistakes, and he had a serious problem. It kills me, being away from him, like you can't imagine, but I also accept that he was out of control and that he needs to be someplace where he can get himself right. I know this man's heart, though, and I know that no matter what he was doing with those whores, it had nothing to do with his love for you and for Emmie. That man loves you, Victoria, and more than that, Em is his world. Don't deprive him of the joy his family brings him."

I nodded, and Mom took a loud sip of her iced tea. It was watered down now and stuffed with bitter lemon rinds.

"It's not right what you're doing to him. Imagine if we did that to you, Vic. If we just cut you out of our lives because you made a bad choice. Look at all the dumb shit you did, but we stuck beside you anyway because you're our child, and we loved you regardless. Now that you're a mother, think about if Emmie grew up and got into trouble. Would you abandon her?" Mom asked.

"Of course not," I said.

"So offer your father some compassion and e-mail him."

I was supposed to be a writer, a person who was rarely at a loss for words, but figuring out what to say in Joel's e-mail was one of the hardest things I'd ever done. That night I typed and deleted, started and stopped, and finally settled on a simple apology. I was sorry I hadn't written, but I'd been upset about the things he'd done. I told him I felt confused by his actions, and I needed time to sort through my feelings.

The e-mail had drained me mentally, so when I finished, I took a walk to clear my head. Em was in bed and Ben was preoccupied with his phone, so I had a rare moment to myself. It wasn't like the time I'd tried to run away in the middle of the night, though, back when I'd been desperate and hysterical with fear that I'd fail as a mother. Those days when I'd staggered through midnight feedings and diaper changes, when I was ragged and delirious with sleep deprivation, were over. The first couple of years had been like running a marathon without any training—the kind of marathon where your feet have pounded the road so hard for so long, you forget your own name and address, where you lose control of your bodily functions and don't even care, and by the time you get to the end, you're barely crawling over the finish line.

I wandered down the street, and as I walked, I congratulated myself. Becoming a mom had worn me down for sure, but I was building myself back up again. I was doing so much better. Ben and I had even made the decision to enroll Em in preschool, so I'd have my mornings back. I was going to use that time to write.

Curiosity drew me toward Casa dei Sogni. A white Mercedes was parked in the driveway, and upstairs, the lights were on in the guest bedrooms. The breeze carried voices from the nearby backyard and a plume of delicious smoke rose high over the barrel-tiled roof: someone was grilling by the pool. Through the double glass doors I could make out a few figures sitting on the back patio. A shadow moved past the bar. A cork popped, champagne flutes clinked as the renters made some sort of toast, and strange laughter effervesced into the night. They'd closed the gates and I was on the outside, which was weird and unsettling. Sure, it was temporary—Mom would be home in a couple of weeks, but not for much longer, and when she went away for good, the government would come and shutter the house. They'd paste official notices on the doors, let the grass grow high and wild. There might be yellow caution tape. After that, the house would go to auction, new owners would come. They'd tidy things up, white out our pumpkin-pie walls with a thick coat of Kilz, and erase all the angel babies from the ceilings. Pretty soon the gates to the House of Dreams would close permanently, shutting all of us out forever.

31

I'd been back about a week when Ashley called to tell me that our yoga studio needed babysitters.

"It's the easiest job ever," she said. "You can bring Em, she can play with the other kids for a couple of hours, and in exchange you get unlimited free yoga! How can you beat that?"

I jumped at the chance, and immediately went to see Susan, the studio manager. She was the one who'd managed to convince me not to give up in the middle of my first class, and she'd helped me understand that yoga wasn't about how sexy you looked in your Lululemons while doing a perfect straddle split. Since I'd been practicing, yoga had taught me to make a commitment to my own well-being, and it had given me the set of tools I'd needed to start healing. I was grateful for this gift, and wanted to give back.

"We'd love to have you babysit," Susan said.

She winked, and then added, "Awesome Lord of the Dance in class the other day! I couldn't help but notice how much progress you've made since you started."

Spending so much time at the studio brought me into a new fold. I felt like I was now part of the local yoga community, and since I was around lots of new people, I decided to give making mom friends another shot. Babysitting had been a great way to meet other mothers, and although I'd prescreened them to make sure none of them were concerned about their children getting poisoned by conventional produce, I still kept them safely at arm's length. I just didn't have time for moms who were smug and serious. I needed friends who were as fucked up as I was and could have a sense of humor about it. One day after class, when another mom casually mentioned she was on her way to a twelve-step meeting, I invited her over for dinner, thinking a recovering drug addict–alcoholic would be cool with my mom wearing an ankle monitor and my stepdad being incarcerated. Not that I told her, but I figured that if it came up somehow, she wouldn't freak and hurry her little girl out the front door. Dinner went well, and at the end of the evening, as our daughters sat on the sofa mesmerized by *Mary Poppins*, I couldn't help but feel a little amazed at how simple it had been for me to make a new friend.

The moms at Emmeline's preschool were a different story though. They scared the shit out of me. You see, I was comfortable at yoga by then and had come to realize that most people go to yoga to heal and/or openly discuss their pain. The four thirty hot vinyasa flow was like a suffering convention. Your dad's in jail? Oh yeah? Big fucking deal, man. That girl has bulimia, this one over here was a foster child, that whole side of the room is filled with pill addicts: six people in here have survived cancer. Go into any yoga class, and you'll find that a good 75 percent of the people there are profoundly broken, but step into a Fort Lauderdale preschool, and you'll find that all the other parents are, in fact, perfect.

The moms at Em's new school wore expensive gym clothes and drove minivans, venti Starbucks cup in one hand, iPhone in the other. I'd see them in the drop-off and pickup lines, looking impossibly perky with fresh mani-pedis and recently highlighted ponytails, and I'd wonder when in the hell they found time to consistently keep up with their eyebrow waxing. I couldn't compete. My eyebrows looked like woolly bear caterpillars before a long hard winter, and I hid my Hobbit feet in scuffed Payless ballet flats. And it wasn't only that the other moms were so polished, but that they were chipper and happy and well rested. They were clearly in on some secret of motherhood I'd somehow missed. It was like they'd held a supermom orientation over the summer, where they'd all learned things like how to have flawless skin, glowing smiles, and spotless Range Rovers. The e-mail invite must have accidentally gone into my spam folder.

On the first day of school I rolled up in style in my now eight-year-old Saturn. It was dented in several places because I had run it into a concrete pole at the bank drive-through twice, and after that it had been repeatedly attacked by a flock of peacocks that roamed our old neighborhood, seeking revenge on their reflections. I wore faded Old Navy yoga pants because I wore them everywhere (except, incidentally, to actual yoga), and when I opened up the back door to let Em out of her car seat, an avalanche of empty fruit snack wrappers, Goldfish crumbs, and the sippy cup that had been missing for the past six months tumbled out onto the blacktop. I was a hot-assed mess. Turned out, I wasn't even in the right drop-off line. I was in the imago line when I was supposed to be in the larva line (I think), but I got confused because the larva line was next to the chrysalis class's drop-off but only for the day (and they were probably going to change it again), and oh my God, why couldn't they just name the classes based on the kids' ages instead of the freaking life cycles of a butterfly for fuck's sake? Everyone seemed to have their shit together and knew exactly where to go, except me.

Part of the reason I was freaking out was because this was the first time I'd ever been away from Emmeline for more than a couple of hours, and being separated from her scared me. I was afraid she'd cry for me or that she'd think I had abandoned her, but when we got to her new classroom, she trotted right in and made a beeline for a big plastic box randomly filled with dry rice, which I would eventually learn was called a sensory table. *Amazing,* I thought. Sometimes it was like she was not even my child. I hadn't gone to preschool, but on my first day of kindergarten I was the kid who sat all by herself and cried until she puked because I didn't want to be away from home.

I lingered outside the door, you know, just in case, but Em waved me away.

"Bye, Mommy!" she yelled, and I had to take that as my cue.

Some of the other moms were going to coffee at the bagel shop on the corner, but I made some lame excuse and turned them down. People like that wouldn't want to be friends with me. Instead, for the first time since Em was born, I went to Starbucks, completely alone. I took out my laptop and started writing, and when I was finished with the first freelance article I'd ever pitched to a real editor, I crossed my fingers and clicked send. Then I checked my jail mail account and saw there was a message from Joel. We'd been writing tentatively again, and I'd sent him a couple of books I'd read and enjoyed and that reminded me of him. In the letter he told me that the books were great, just what he needed, and I laughed to myself a little. I'd always wanted my stepdad to slow down and talk about books with me instead of wheeling and dealing all the time, and now I guess I'd gotten my wish—albeit in a twisted *Monkey's Paw* sort of way.

Mom moved back into Casa dei Sogni a few weeks later, and what should have been a simple half-day task turned into an official catastrophe when she realized that somehow the telephone lines had been cut, which meant she couldn't properly hook up her monitoring device. Her probation officer knew she was moving, and since she could go about freely during the day, the actual move wasn't much of an issue as long as she had her ankle bracelet running by early that evening. When Mom saw that the phone lines were down—as in literally down on the ground, dangling precariously off the pole—she panicked, thinking that if they weren't fixed immediately, she'd be spending the night in the county jail.

"Adolph's going to come arrest me!" she cried.

"Who's Adolph?" I asked, worried that my mom might be having some sort of disturbing Holocaust delusion.

"Adolph is her probation officer," Allie said in a stage whisper, covering the bottom of her phone with her hand. Allie was directing the move, all while wearing a Moschino maxi dress and Chanel platform wedges, and was trying to get someone from the telephone company on the line.

"Only you, Mom, would get a probation officer named Adolph," I said.

"Well, he's unfortunately named, but he's absolutely darling," Mom said.

"So maybe call him and explain what happened and see if he'll give you a pass?" I suggested.

"He's not *that* darling," Mom said.

We milled around in front of the gates for several minutes while Allie yelled at the phone company on her cell. Mom smoked and chewed the inside of her cheek until I finally suggested we start moving her clothes into the house again.

"Someone did this on purpose!" she said.

I was startled. "What are you talking about?" I said. "That's crazy. Who would purposely come over here and vandalize your telephone lines?"

"Someone who didn't want me moving back in. Someone who wanted me in jail!"

"Mom, that's nuts. Who would do that to you?"

But our answer was lingering at the corner by the street sign, walking her Pekinese in stiletto gladiators, spying on us.

"Oh my God, Ruffina?" I gasped.

Mom shrugged and then added, "Or somebody else."

Ruffina, unfortunately, hadn't disappeared from our lives. She'd stalked Ashley all summer and had even gone so far as to leave notes on her car, saying our family had wronged her and she just wanted a chance to tell her side of the story. The bitch knew better than to try that with me, I guess, and she gave up on e-mailing Mom, but several times a day she'd wobble down the street in her newest pair of designer heels, past our houses and past Casa dei Sogni, always glaring in our windows, looking for something she'd never find.

"Look," I said, "there's got to be a simpler explanation."

"There are no coincidences," Mom said.

"Calm down, Cecily," Allie interjected. "The phone company's on their way. Everything's going to be fixed before six."

We all breathed a sigh of relief as Ruffina glowered from the street corner and stomped off, practically strangling her dog in the process. Later one of the neighbors would tell us that a box truck making a delivery at the end of the cul-de-sac had accidentally snagged the wires and pulled them loose. It hadn't been sabotage after all, but Mom held on to her suspicions.

"After everything that's happened to me, I trust no one," she said.

Right then a taxi pulled up and dropped off a man I didn't recognize. He was tall, and I'd guess about fifty. By most standards, Lincoln Cruz was good-looking, if a little weathered and potbellied. He was sunburned and rugged and needed a haircut and someone to wash and iron the unbuttoned Hawaiian shirt he wore over his faded swim trunks, but he did have a bright smile.

"Who the hell is this?" I asked. "And what the hell is he carrying?"

"That's my new roommate," Mom said. She flipped her platinum hair extensions out of her face and smiled sweetly.

"Lincoln Cruz," the man said in a deep and charming Southern accent.

In one hand he carried a case of Budweiser and in the other he held a large birdcage, which he set down before he extended his hand for me to shake.

"Oh yeah," he added, "and this here's Tony."

He pointed to an enormous pale pink cockatoo in the cage he'd set on the grass. The bird bobbed its crested head and squawked so loudly, Em started to cry.

"Lincoln!" screamed the bird.

Then it beeped like a microwave and did a perfect imitation of the iPhone's marimba ring tone.

"Hello?" Em said, totally confused.

"So, which one's your new roommate? The bird or the dude?" I asked my mother.

"Both of them," she said.

"All right, enough small talk. Let's get this party started! Allegra, order some pizzas!" Lincoln Cruz said.

"Lincoln!" scolded the cockatoo.

Lincoln kicked the bars of the cage, told the bird to shut the fuck up, and cracked open a beer.

"Really?" I said.

"Sausage or pepperoni?" Mom asked me.

"I have to go. I'm volunteering at the school's bake sale in the morning. I have to make brownies," I explained.

"I've got something for your brownies!" Lincoln announced.

"I'm sure you do," I said.

"Lincoln!"

That damn bird was getting old fast.

Em's preschool was part of a church and required parents to volunteer a certain number of hours per school year; otherwise, I'd have never agreed to the brownies. I mean, seriously? What was I? My grandmother? I didn't know schools even had bake sales anymore, but once I'd committed, I realized I had accidentally stumbled onto my true calling. Turned out, I was pretty much born to spend my Sunday mornings handing homemade pastries to churchgoers. I liked being outside on a sunny fall day, doing something for a good cause. Being involved in a community, talking to people who knew nothing of the dark parts of my life, was refreshing.

Jess and Amy, two of the other moms, were talking about planning their kids' birthday parties when I suddenly realized that Em's third birthday was fast approaching and I'd better decide what to do. We laughed about some of the ridiculous spreads we'd seen on Pinterest and how crazy some people got, and I was enjoying the simple conversation so much that it just slipped out.

"This is going to be Em's first birthday without her grandfather," I said.

"Oh, sweetie, I'm so sorry. That must be so hard. What can we do to help?" Jess said.

"Yes, anything. When did you lose your father?" Amy wanted to know.

Their concern caught me completely off guard, and I didn't want to derail the conversation by admitting that my dad was in jail, so I stammered and finally blurted out that he'd been gone since last winter, which wasn't technically a lie except that these kind, caring women thought my father was dead and I did nothing to stop them from thinking that. They both hugged me.

"Seriously, let us know. Anything at all, okay?" Jess reiterated.

I nodded and excused myself from duty for the rest of the bake sale, wondering what kind of a fucking asshole would do what I just did. Now I could never tell them the truth.

I continued to go to all the school's events—I'd show up, paste on a smile, and maybe make a little small talk—but when the other moms invited me for playdates, I always told them I was busy.

And in a sense, I *was* busy. Mom's sentencing was scheduled for February, and I needed to spend every second I could with her before she went away for good. There were so many stories I wanted her to tell me one last time and so many recipes I needed to learn. I wanted her to show me how to make dumplings and matzo ball soup, and tell me the secret to her chicken salad that I could never seem to replicate.

It turned out to be a spoonful of sugar.

"If you want your food to taste good, just cook everything in butter," Mom told me. "Always add in a little more butter and salt than you think you need, maybe some pepper or a little pinch of sugar to balance out the flavors."

"How can you eat like this and still lose weight?" I asked, perplexed, as Mom dolloped another tablespoon of softened butter into the electric skillet. It skated over the Teflon and melted into a delicious sizzle.

We were standing in Mom's kitchen, making dinner, and she was teaching me how to sauté flounder. Lincoln's bird, Tony, sat perched atop her head—the only way she could get him to shut the hell up was to take him out of his cage and pay attention to him. Cooking with her reminded me of being Em's age, when I was living with my Mommom Alice. The first thing I'd do when I went to visit my mother was beg for her fried fish. Back then she lived in a little house by the marsh on the edge of the muddy Delaware Bay, and she was so poor, she wasn't about to buy the fish she made. She caught it, then scaled and gutted it herself.

"I was so ignorant back then," Mom said when I shared my memories with her.

"You were barely twenty," I told her.

"But I was a mess. I'd lost custody of you. I lost my waitressing job, and my boyfriend stole every last cent of cash I'd managed to save up. I kept my tips in this big can, and I was saving to pay for a lawyer so I could get you back, and he took that from me. I was in such a depressed and desperate state, you know what I'm saying? I had nothing. Can you even imagine, now that you have Emmie, if somebody took her away from you?"

"I can't even imagine. I'd want to die," I said truthfully.

Mom seasoned the fish and dredged the filets in peppered flour.

"I *did* want to die, Vic. I really did. But I knew I had to stay alive for you. I started making macrame plant hangers and selling them on the street corner down by the courthouse, hoping maybe somebody'd see me and take pity. I finally got a couple hundred bucks saved up, and I went to this lawyer and he told me to turn around, to get out of his office. That it was a waste of time and I would never get you back. That's when I started selling pot."

I dropped five ears of corn into a pot of boiling water, while Mom laid the strips of flounder in the sizzling skillet.

"Now let them sit there in the hot oil, and don't mess with them at all for a couple of minutes. And don't get the heat up so high that they burn before they cook," Mom said.

"So, you sold pot to pay for a lawyer to get me back?" I asked.

Mom nodded. "I wasn't a criminal. I didn't sell drugs because I was greedy or wanted furs and Cadillacs. I did it because it was the only way I could buy my freedom back. Imagine, I was a kid, with no education whatsoever. I had no skills, nobody would give me a job. My mother didn't know any different, and she raised me to get married and be a mother too. No one told me there was any other path I could possibly take. I sold pot because I needed to survive without depending on anyone else, and I needed to make enough money to fight in court to get you back from your father and grandmother who stole you from me."

"I understand," I whispered.

"But you see," Mom went on, "I was an entrepreneur at heart, and I was smart. I just didn't know it, so when I started selling drugs, I was fucking good at it. You know what I mean? I was brilliant, especially compared to all those dumb-ass rednecks up in Delaware, and I created an empire. But I was still ignorant about the world even though I was smart. Sometimes I think about all the things I could've been if only somebody had encouraged me when I was little."

She laughed as she flipped the fish.

"The first time I ever came down to Florida I was barefoot and wearing old ratty jeans. Thank God, I met Joel. You know, I'd barely even been out of Milford my whole life. I didn't know about anything. The first time I ever heard of people eating cheesecake was in Florida, and I was like, *Eww. Who would put cheese in a cake? Can you imagine? I didn't even know what cheesecake was!*"

We laughed. A gigantic cherry-topped cheesecake was, at the moment, waiting for us in the refrigerator.

"Joel showed me the world." She sighed. "Without him, I would've been nothing. He saved us, Vic. He got you and me out of Delaware and gave us a chance at a life. Look at all the places we've been and all the things we've seen because of him."

"But what about all the things we've seen and done because of . . . ourselves?" I replied.

"Do you ever think about what your life might have been like if we never removed you from rural Delaware?" Mom asked.

"Of course," I whispered. "It could've gone a lot of ways."

The fish was done. I pulled the coleslaw out of the fridge while Mom used tongs to take the corn on the cob out of the pot. Lincoln must've smelled the food because as soon as the spread was set out on the kitchen island, he showed up and piled his plate high. He rarely missed a meal, this guy. He was always around. When he first moved in, Mom claimed he was a pilot or a boat captain or God knows what, but I'd never seen him work a single day, and I don't even think he was paying rent. Mom kept saying she was going to ask him for grocery money, but I don't think she ever got around to it—it seemed to me that all Lincoln did was invite his friends over (more middle-aged single party animals in T-shirts printed with game fish) to drink on the back terrace and listen to Jimmy Buffett. Everything about the situation pissed me off, but I understood why my mother put up with it. She was lonely and scared without her husband around. Having a man in the house probably made her feel a little more secure, even if he was a useless jackass with a cockatoo.

"Peace out, y'all," Lincoln said to us as he sauntered back to his bedroom, dinner in hand, to watch reruns of *Everybody Loves Raymond*.

After dinner Mom showed me a strange rash she'd developed on her ankles and shins. She'd had it before but it kept coming back, and this time there were purple and red spots. She said the rash didn't itch, but that it was painful.

"I want you to see a doctor," I told her, but Mom refused.

"I think I have a seafood allergy," she decided.

"But you're losing so much weight," I said.

"You sound like Adolph. He's worried about me too. Started making random wellness checks on me. Can you believe that?"

The week before, Mom's probation officer had to switch her ankle monitor to her wrist because her legs had become so spindly, the hard plastic was making her black-and-blue. Then, she'd lost even more weight, and the monitor had slipped off her hand a few days later, causing a major panic as she desperately tried to get it back on before the cops figured out she wasn't wearing it.

"For real, Mom. I'm worried about your health. Please go to the doctor," I begged, but she wouldn't have it, and hastily changed the subject.

"I've got good news," she said.

My eyebrows raised involuntarily.

"Heidi may have found a huge opportunity for me," Mom said.

"To rent the house again? But you're leaving really soon."

"Just listen to me. I want to rent it while I can. Do you know who Patrick Brookshire is?"

"I know about his daughter Morgana. I think I saw her in *Us Weekly* a couple of weeks ago. Apparently, she's back in rehab or something. They had to have another intervention because someone saw her smoking meth at a party in the Hollywood Hills."

"Patrick said none of that stuff about her is true," Mom said breezily, as if she'd known the man for years instead of over the course of a single telephone conversation. He was the notorious father of an even more notorious starlet, and their tumultuous relationship was big-time tabloid fodder (not that I would, *ahem*, know what was in the tabloids or anything).

"Wait, you talked to Patrick Brookshire?"

"Of course. He's an angel. Very spiritual. Did you know he's a reverend? He's been sober for many years now, and he's doing incredible things. He wants me to help him," Mom gushed.

"Uh-huh. Like what?" I asked.

"He wants to turn this house into a high-end rehab facility for celebrities. How amazing would that be?"

"Sounds lovely," I said. "But I have to get going. I'm volunteering at Em's school again in the morning. There's a ladies' tea, and I'm making finger sandwiches in the shape of gingerbread men."

32

Em, my energetic extrovert, absolutely thrived in preschool, and the four hours I now had to myself each day were lifesaving. I could grocery shop alone again. I could even write at Starbucks! The first time I went to Target by myself, I wanted to burst into song and leap and twirl through the aisles like I was in a Broadway musical, joyously flinging Merona blouses and huge jugs of Alpine Breeze Tide into my shopping cart. I had my freedom back.

Before I sound like the worst mother in the world, it wasn't that I didn't like spending time with my daughter, because I did. But I'd come to realize that I needed a certain amount of solitude to stay healthy, room to reflect, and process and indulge my creativity without constantly being touched or fussed at because I put the toast on the owl plate instead of the piggy one. Having Em in a safe place where I knew she was happy gave me time to find the sense of self and the voice I thought I had lost when she was born. I'd rediscovered my passion, and was now publishing a few articles a week—I'd even had my first viral post on the Internet. Once again I was achieving goals that made me proud.

By Christmas I'd settled into a comfortable routine of dropping Em off at school, writing, picking her up, practicing yoga, babysitting, and volunteering. The rest of my spare time I tried to spend with my mother. Most nights Em and I had dinner with Mom while Ben worked, or went to yoga himself. Mom would cook the meals I loved, the ones I'd miss the most, and while we ate, she'd tell me my favorite stories or teach me how to get stains out of children's clothing, which was a particular talent of hers. I'm a little ashamed to admit this, but ever since Em was born, I'd been bringing my dirty laundry to Mom so she could work her magic, but now I'd finally learned that white vinegar works great on bloodstains, and that dish soap is a miracle for grease spots. Maybe before she went to jail, after I'd mastered her manicotti recipe and learned to whiten whites and brighten brights, Mom would even have time to teach me how to fold a fitted sheet.

For my entire adult life, I'd taken for granted that I'd have my parents around to rescue me from catastrophes big or small. If I had a flat tire, Joel would pick me up on the side of the road. If I was hungry and didn't feel like cooking, I could stop by Casa dei Sogni and grab a quick meal, plus get my clothes cleaned. More than that, I always knew I had my parents to fall back on, and that no matter what happened, I'd never end up alone on the street. But because they did so much for me, I hadn't learned to do enough on my own. I really was the spoiled brat that Baron Von Bod had accused me of being. Now life had given me the swift kick in the ass I needed to finally learn to rely on myself, instead of my parents, my grandmothers, Ben, or anyone else I hoped might save me from the responsibilities of adult life and scary grown-up emotions. Car maintenance, stains, managing my finances, keeping my child alive and happy—I had this covered, and I'd had these survival skills all along. I just hadn't realized how strong I actually was, but I still had one more fear to face—preschool moms.

"Come on, come to our meetings."

I was standing in the pickup line with Susannah, whose little girl was in Em's class. She had three kids, one of whom she homeschooled, and she was very active in the church that our preschool was part of. Susannah was the kind of mom who organized and volunteered and re-created elaborate projects she'd found online. She'd even started a support group for area moms, and she wanted me to join, but I'd put the brakes on that immediately. I never fancied myself as a joiner. I'd spent my entire life as an outsider, and while people might have thought I was a little weird, after forty years, I was fine with being a tad eccentric. The only place I'd ever truly fit in was grad school, where I spent three years bonding with a small, close-knit group of fellow misfits, who loved sharing stories as much as I did. It had been glorious, but once it was over, I suppose I just figured that was it for me, and I'd go back to being the zebra in the field of brown ponies. I certainly never saw myself in a mommy group—I'd already been burned once by the cloth-diapering, kale-chipping Earth Mothers, and I didn't want a repeat performance of feeling inadequate among a troop of superparents.

Yet, as introverted as I was, I also really, *really* longed for friendship and acceptance. Besides, I didn't want to hurt anyone's feelings, so I finally gave in and went to Susannah's meeting. At the very least, maybe she'd leave me alone if I went once, but the second I stepped into the meeting room, I panicked and wanted to back out before it was too late. Luckily, a big box of Starbucks coffee and a bag of powdered sugar Donettes beckoned, so I hesitated for only a second before I sat down at the end of the table. You can bribe me to do just about anything with good coffee and carbs.

"I'm so excited you came!" Susannah cried.

I nodded and smiled at her politely, then poured a paper cup of coffee, helped myself to a mini-doughnut, and tried to calm the fuck down. *Remember, you've survived a DEA raid. You can handle a pack of pretty women in stylish outfits, talking about how great their kids are.*

Next to me, another mom sat quietly, filling out an imposing stack of personalized Christmas cards printed on a glossy professional photo of her family posing on the beach in matching khakis and button-up shirts. I'd always envied those kinds of Christmas cards and the shiny lives they represented, but when I asked Ben if we could do something like that, he complained about the cost and bitched about having to endure a photo shoot in the sand, wearing silly clothes, so I gave up. Who was I trying to fool anyway? I'd never worn khakis with white linen in my life—those kinds of cards just weren't who we were.

"I love your cards," I told her.

"I hate them," she said. "I don't even know three-quarters of these people, and I'm only doing this because of my husband's business. Like I don't have enough stress around the holidays as it is."

"We all have holiday stress," Susannah sympathized.

Yeah, sure, I thought. I'd just made it through the first Thanksgiving that I hadn't spent with family in literally decades. Joel was choking down broccoli stems and bologna sandwiches in a maximum-security facility up in New York, while Mom was too depressed and broke to cook. Ashley and Andrew, as usual, did their own thing alone and didn't invite us, so Ben and Em and I went to a friend's house because we couldn't afford tickets to California to see my in-laws. That Thanksgiving was a glimpse of my new normal. From here on out, there'd be no family traditions to fall back on. I'd have to decide on my own where and how to celebrate, and it wouldn't always be with relatives. The pressure overwhelmed me. The other moms? I bet their biggest holiday stress was deciding if they should brine the turkey in regular sea salt or Himalayan pink.

"This time of year, my guess is we all need to vent." Susannah laughed. "Let's start with high/lows. That's where we go around and share the best parts of our week and the worst parts."

I almost had a full-on anxiety attack. This group sounded like a sorority, something I'd never wanted any part of. Ashley had wanted to pledge back when she'd first started college, but the girls who wanted in had to stand in their underwear and let themselves be judged by the senior members of the group. They'd circle the problem parts of the pledge's bodies with a Sharpie marker. Ashley had said, "Fuck these bitches," and walked out.

Whenever I found myself in a group of other moms, I was often reminded of Ashley's sorority hazing: I'd imagine I was the one standing naked, only instead of circling my cellulite, the moms would write words all over my body—*selfish; resentful; fights with her husband; disposable diapers; didn't get her prepregnancy body back; lets her kid eat gummies and watch TV; hates pushing the swing at the park; messes with her phone instead of reading Baby Einstein books.*

Susannah offered to go first.

"My high point was a much-needed date night with my husband, and my low was that, oh my goodness! My eighteen-month-old son will not stop peeing in the cat box!"

Everyone laughed, and we moved on to the mom who was filling out cards. Her high point was a spontaneous trip to Disney World, and her low point, predictably, was the cards. The next woman was excited that she had lost three pounds and bummed that she'd eaten some cake and gained it all back. *Well, at least I can relate to that,* I thought. The woman grimaced and added a packet of Splenda to her black coffee.

"All I want is a caramel Frappuccino," she said, and groaned.

Still skeptical, I was about to run screaming from the room, but it was my turn, and in a split second I had to make a choice: would I make something up, or would I tell the truth? I'd already sort of lied once when I let Jess and Amy believe my father died, and I still felt horrible. Instead of avoiding shame, I'd actually created more, and I didn't want to live that way. I wanted to be authentic. When I wrote articles, I tried to tell my truths as bravely and as often as I could, so when faced with a room filled with my daughter's classmates' mothers, why was I suddenly so petrified? It was like yoga and meeting my siblings. I had to do the things that made me uncomfortable, so I took a deep breath and tried to tell these women the truth.

"Well, my high was that my husband, my daughter, and I went swimming in a neighbor's heated pool the other night, and we had the best time, but my lows, well, I don't know if you all can handle them," I admitted.

Susannah stared at me with her bright blue eyes and blinked. I didn't know what she was going to do or say, and figured she was going to tell me to leave. Hell, she'd probably make me put my Donette back in the bag on my way out. Instead she brushed her strawberry-blond curls out of her face and laid her hands flat against the wood veneer tabletop.

"I promise you, Victoria, we can handle it," she said.

"Uh, this is pretty bad," I said.

Susannah stood up and closed the doors. Still standing, she explained that she had a story we all needed to hear.

"There is nothing any of you can say that will shock me or make me judge you, because when I was nineteen, I was a heroin addict," she began. "And my boyfriend was a drug dealer, and I got pregnant. I had no idea what I was going to do, and I was hooked on drugs and had a baby growing in my belly. I had no money, no college, and was with an asshole who spent all our money on drugs. It was Thanksgiving, so I told him I was going out to get some food, and I took the cat and left and never went back. I went to my parents' house and begged them to let me back in and help me so I could get sober and have this baby. And I did. And for the next several years, I struggled and went to school and took care of my baby, and then I went to grad school and became a teacher and finally, I kind of, sort of had my shit together enough to find a decent man to marry, but I'm telling you, it is still a struggle every single day. We all have our shit to deal with. And now I have three kids and they drive me fucking insane sometimes and I'm tired all the time and my husband thinks I drink too much and on the outside it might look like I am miraculously keeping it all together, but I can promise you all that I am falling apart on a daily basis. Just like all of us. And that is why I made this group, because we moms need a safe place that's free of judgment where we don't have to put on this perfect mom act all the time. Because we need one another. And, Victoria, I promise you that whatever your shit is that you're dealing with, we will support you!"

So I told them everything. All of it. The raid, my anxiety and depression and insecurity, about my stepfather being in jail, how my mom was under house arrest, how I was trying to forge a relationship with my five half siblings. I let it all out, and when I did, no one sniffed at me in disgust or declared that their children would never play with mine. Instead they embraced me and began to share their own stories. There were ten of us in the group, and more than half of us were dealing with some serious shit. I was not the only one with a struggle, and my struggle wasn't even anywhere near the hardest. Lucy was a double-amputee who'd lost both legs when she was hit by a train. For real. *Hit by a train.* I almost fainted when she stood up and walked out on her prosthetic legs—sitting at the table, she'd looked just like anyone else. She was gorgeous, well dressed, and elegant, and my first impression of her had been that she probably had an easy life, that she belonged to a country club and golfed on weekends. I'd been wrong about Dara, too. She had not one but *two* children with a rare genetic cancer, and both children would receive bone marrow transplants that spring. Nearly every woman in the room had had a miscarriage, and a few were currently dealing with the heartbreak of failed fertility treatments, while Claire had recently been diagnosed with rheumatoid arthritis. Sadie, the one with the perfect Christmas cards, told us that no matter how idyllic her life seemed from the outside (and it did, believe me), she constantly waged an internal battle with her emotions. She said she'd inherited a family tendency toward deep, unpredictable bouts of sadness.

I'd walked into the meeting that morning feeling nervous and isolated, but by the time I walked out, I'd become part of something bigger and better than myself and my problems: I'd instantly gained ten new friends. I'd listened to ten totally different, heartfelt stories about women who were more like me than they weren't, and I realized that—in the pickup line, at the class birthday parties, on Facebook—each one of us was totally faking it till we made it. We all felt insecure. We all had challenges to meet and hard choices to make, and we were all barely holding it together, smiling through our tears. I was not alone. I left the meeting knowing that these ladies had my back, but I was more excited about being given the opportunity to have theirs.

Like a character in a made-for-TV holiday movie, that December I learned the true meaning of Christmas. It wasn't tables laden with food or a twinkling tree that towered to the ceiling— Hell, Mom didn't put up a single decoration, because she was more concerned with getting everyone to write letters to the judge asking for leniency. Christmas wasn't about the spectacle— Rudolph noses on the grilles of SUVs, putting enough lights on your house to blow out a substation, beating the shit out of someone on Black Friday to get a five-dollar flat-screen. That stuff's all bull.

In the past, I'd approached the holidays as if I had been staging a show. There were costumes and lights, set pieces—practically even lines to memorize—and there was the constant underlying hope that when the curtain rose on the big day, everything would be perfect. All because I wanted a standing ovation from the audience—that reassurance I was doing it right.

My parents' sentencings were only two months away, and the doors to my metaphorical theater had been shuttered. Now that the show was actually over, I finally got it that "doing it right" during the holidays was doing it wrong.

Emmeline played a woolly lamb in her preschool Christmas pageant, and in the weeks before her performance she could barely contain her excitement. Mom couldn't go because the show started early in the morning and she wasn't allowed out of the house until ten. It reminded me of when my nephew Jack was born. The real punishment wasn't that Mom had to wear a monitoring device; it was that she had to miss her granddaughter crawling up the aisle of the sanctuary, bleating her little fleecy butt off. But as I craned my neck to see over the other parents who were clamoring to snap photos and videos with their cell phones, my heart grew three sizes that day, just like the Grinch's.

So this is what it is all about, I thought, a three-year-old on a stage, wearing a suit of cotton balls, standing in front of a cardboard manger, throwing her head back, and opening her mouth as wide as she could to belt out "Joy to the World." Every single miserable second of morning sickness I'd suffered was worth it for this moment. The true meaning of Christmas (or Chanukah or Kwanzaa or winter solstice) was being able to suddenly experience life through the eyes of my child.

After the Christmas play, we took Ben to the airport. He was flying to California to visit his family that year, and his decision to spend the holiday without us had gutted me.

"How could you leave your child on Christmas?" I yelled when he sprang the news on me.

"Victoria, I've spent every Christmas with you and your family for the past six years. We've never once spent a holiday with my family. I've put everything aside for you and your parents through all their drama and this is the last Christmas you're going to spend with your mom for a while, and that's really sad. This has nothing to do with how much I love you and Em. I just don't want to get in the way of the last memories you and your mom will have together," he said.

"But your daughter! And Santa Claus! You don't care about missing that?" I raged.

"Of course I do, but my parents are getting older, and I miss my cousins and aunts and uncles out there too. I never get to see them, and I spend every single day with you and Em. I want you to be able to be with your mother, alone, without the tension of having me in the same room. Victoria, do you understand, this is your last Christmas with your mother? Focus on her."

"Of course I do! Of course, and that's why I want my husband to be there to support me!"

I screamed for days and broke plates. I threatened to hurt myself, and I cried on the bathroom floor, begging Ben to please change his mind, to please stay home, but he'd already bought his plane ticket and, like so many decisions in life, it was nonrefundable. I had to let him go.

It was something I'd started to learn from yoga, this whole idea of letting go. I understood abstractly, but I didn't know how to do it. Hanging on to intangible things like expectations and disappointment and relationships is no different than physically clasping something with your hands. I felt like a character in a bad action movie, dangling over the edge of a bridge hundreds of feet above a bunch of white-water rapids, and I believed that if I let go of the steel beams, I would tumble to my death. I thought that grasping at my desired outcomes was the only way I could move forward, but I got tired of white-knuckling my way through life. I said fuck it, and made a conscious decision to loosen my fingers, one by one. When I released my expectations for the perfect Christmas and the perfect family and how I thought my husband and my mother and everyone around me should act and who they should be, when I said I would no longer hang on to my disappointment when things didn't go as planned, that was when I saw the bridge and the rapids for what they were. I certainly wasn't going to fall and die. Seconds before I hit the rapids, my remote-controlled, specially engineered, hot pink jet would swoop in to save me. I'd land on its roof, carefully maneuver my way over a wing, execute some sexy gymnastics moves, and crawl into the cockpit, where I'd wave at the audience before zooming off to safety (remember, this is a bad action movie). In other words, I was going to be fine.

So I threw a party on Christmas Eve, and I invited all my new friends and made a gigantic pot of meatballs, and you know, Ben was kind of right. Without him around, my mom got to have Em all to herself for her last Christmas, and it was lovely, although she did have to leave the festivities early to make it home in time for her curfew. The last thing any of us wanted to do was piss off Adolph on Christmas.

The guests had cleared out, but Em was antsy and overstimulated and wouldn't go to bed, so I decided to take her on a walk through the neighborhood to look at the Christmas lights. By the time we'd looped around the block and made it to the Catholic church, both of us were calmer, meditative even, so I took a moment to stop at the Virgin Mary statue. We hadn't paid her a visit in a long time.

"Mommy, what is this place?" Em asked.

"It's a quiet place for people to pray by the waterfall," I said.

"Who's that lady?" she wanted to know, pointing at the statue.

"That's Mary."

Her eyes lit up. "Baby Jesus' Mommy?" she asked.

I nodded, and we stood without speaking for a moment. The door to the choir room was open, and we could see inside as the choir members practiced a verse of "Silent Night" in preparation for midnight mass.

"Mama?"

"Yes, Em?"

"What's praying?"

"Well, it's where you say thank you for all the good things you have and all the dear people you love, and then you ask for everyone to be safe and healthy."

Em pondered this for a second, and then she turned her little gaze up to the statue at the top of the waterfall. She folded her hands solemnly and began.

"Thank you for Mommy and Daddy and Mommom and Papa J and Aunt Ashley and Uncle Andrew and Amelia and Baby Jack and Kitty and Brown Bear," she prayed. "And make sure nobody falls down and skins their knees or throws up on the floor and please let my mommy never be sad anymore."

I scooped her into my arms and covered her in kisses.

"I'm so happy, my love. I promise you. *Your mommy's all right.* Now let's go home and get in bed so Santa can come."

"Mama, can we leave him the cookies we decorated today?"

"Of course we can!"

As we walked toward home, something made me turn and glance over my shoulder. Mary's dress had been freshly painted in a new coat of fluorescent blue, and her skin was now as orange as if she'd gotten a bit overzealous with the self-tanner. The church groundskeeper had angled red and green spotlights at the grotto for the holidays, and the multicolored effect was a little psychedelic, but I swear my eyes weren't playing tricks on me when that statue smiled and winked.

"All is calm. All is bright," the choir sang.

33

I found the message by accident in my Other folder on Facebook one day when I was avoiding writing the letter to the judge that my mother believed would save her. The message had been written months earlier, and by the time I read it, I had no idea what might have prompted it. At first, I was shaken.

Your dad owes people a lot of money from the movies he "funded." He has devastated our bank accounts and nearly destroyed our marriage. It's disgusting how you can post these delightful comments while we are struggling to get by. Why don't you talk about your real life and the scum your mom and dad are? the note read.

I didn't know the woman who sent it. She was young and pretty, and her profile picture showed the smiling mom of a cute little boy. *How does she know my parents?* I wondered. What had happened between them that had made her angry enough to stalk me on social media, make a snap judgment based on a few mobile uploads, and then bang out this impulsive, angry missive? And while she may have had a legitimate beef with my parents, what did she hope to gain from lashing out at a total stranger?

I already knew the answer, though, because I had been in her exact position. She felt bad and believed I didn't, so she wanted to level the field a bit by being mean. I got it. I'd been desperate and pissed off before too and had scrolled through my newsfeed and felt bitter about the Hawaiian vacations and romantic scavenger hunts my acquaintances went on, carefully planned by creative lovers. A few times, I'd resisted the urge to snark on gushy up-dates. Like the woman who sent me the message, I'd also jumped to the conclusion that everyone else's life was better and more fun, more successful, more privileged than mine, and just like this woman, I'd judged people and publicly railed against what I felt to be the unfairness of my circumstances without realizing I'd become nearsighted and lacked perspective. And that was a really ugly place to live. I was glad I'd finally moved out of that banged-up, rusted mobile home state of mind.

In all honesty, my first reaction was to message this bitch back and cuss her out and ask her who the hell she thought she was, sending me something like that, but I chose to accept her nasty message as a gift in disguise. She allowed me to look at my life from a different vantage point and to see myself, at least superfi-cially, as outsiders might. I had a hot husband and a beautiful, vivacious child, and we lived in the best house ever, steps from the shoreline. We grew our own fruit and had a yard filled with sunflowers, and I had an enviable head of glossy chestnut hair. According to Facebook, I sure spent a lot of time at the beach and practicing yoga. Ben and I cooked delicious meals. I hung out at parks and took photos of magnificent sunsets. I even had the world's cutest cat. Shit, I had it made, and I didn't even real-ize it most of the time. Whoever she was, I wished her well, but I wasn't going to respond.

I had more important things to worry about—my parents' sentencings were looming. According to the papers, "Florida Couple," as they were now affectionately known, faced a com-bined 155 years in prison. There was a distinct possibility, espe-cially because Joel was already sixty and Mom was getting close, that I would never see my parents again without crossing through barbed wire and metal detectors first. That they could die in jail was a reality I had to accept. Joel had found out he was severely diabetic and had been on insulin shots since he'd first arrived at the jail in New York, and right after Christmas, he'd passed out—probably from hypoglycemia—and hit his head. His cell mate had found him bloody and unresponsive on the concrete floor. He had to get an MRI, and luckily, his brain checked out okay, but still.

I kept agonizing over the letter Mom wanted me to write. In the past couple of months, she'd amassed an enormous folder's worth of character references. Joel's family members had already written letters for him, but they'd conveniently left out any mention of his non-Jewish wife, and Mom's three siblings had gone AWOL the minute they were asked to pen a few lines in support of their sister. Ashley and Andrew were less than enthusiastic about writing something, and I figured the judge wouldn't place much value on anything someone named Baron Von Bod had to say, so I felt like the real heft of the burden rested on me. What magic words could I write that would change the judge's mind?

I didn't believe the letters were going to do a damn bit of good. A jury had found my parents guilty, and there were mandatory minimum sentences that the judge had no authority to override, so his job was to decide if he was going to give them the maximum, the minimum, or something in between. There was no get-out-of-jail-free card in this game. Mom insisted she and Joel were completely innocent, but that was irrelevant the moment the jury decided they weren't. She wanted to believe that her generosity to others could supersede her conviction, but justice doesn't work that way. Good deeds don't mean that someone isn't also capable of committing crimes—the law is only concerned with someone's actions, not their heart. Besides, for every letter Mom had saying how great she and Joel were, the prosecution had one that asked the judge to throw the book at them.

Still, I wrote my letter anyway. Sure, it probably wouldn't make a difference to His Honor, but I didn't really write the letter for the judge. I wrote it as a thank-you. It was a good-bye letter to my parents, and in it, I described their biggest success—that for more than thirty years, my parents had, in the face of enormous obstacles, created a quirky, larger-than-life family of stepchildren, love children, misfits, and pets, and that somehow we'd made it work in our own hilariously nontraditional way. I came out okay not in spite of my parents, but *because* of them. Joel and Cecily had never taught me to lie, cheat, and steal. They'd taught me to be generous, compassionate, and forgiving.

I'd spent a lot of my life being pissed off at my parents, even when they helped me probably more than I deserved. I'd always focused on how different we were, but going through a real crisis and becoming a parent myself made me focus on how much we also shared. I stopped feeling entitled to their generosity, and I finally realized how much they really *had* done for me, and how hard they'd tried even when, like all parents, they were aggravating as hell. More than anything, I now understood that my parents (and everyone else on earth along with them) were flawed, that they had broken parts too and that they made mistakes. The past few years had taught me to love them anyway.

In the end, Joel's attorney asked for five years, and the judge gave him nine. Right after that they bused him out of maximum, held him a few weeks at a jail in Oklahoma, and eventually resettled him into his new home, a federal correctional facility in central Florida. He'd be a lot more comfortable there, though in all fairness, he'd never once, in the year and a half he'd been locked up, complained about his situation. The way he talked about it, you'd think he had a suite at the Four Seasons.

"I paid a lot to be here, so I better enjoy my vacation," he said, laughing, over the phone one night.

Mom's sentencing was about a month after Joel's. She and Lincoln took the Amtrak up to Grand Central for her hearing, and this time Allie was noticeably absent. Mom said she was too busy with the side project she and Irving Birdy were working on. Same as the trial, I wasn't going either—Em in a courtroom would've been an absolute catastrophe. I could just picture the judge hammering his gavel and saying, *Young Lady! Snow White costumes are not appropriate courtroom attire, and any more outbursts from you regarding Cheddar Bunnies will put you in contempt of court!* Mom assured me that it didn't matter. She'd be gone for three days max, and wanted to be back home as quickly as possible.

Before they left, I asked Mom if she was okay.

"I'm fine," she reassured me. "I'm ready to get this over with because the second I'm sentenced, the lawyers can file my appeal and we can continue the fight."

A few nights later Mom called me while Em and I were at Whole Foods. We were with my friends Tom and Kate. I knew them from yoga, and they had a little girl close to Em's age. I'd been worrying about my mom nonstop—her rash had gotten worse, she was still losing weight, and she hadn't gotten any of her affairs in order—so Tom and Kate took us to dinner and, afterward, to the grocery store to distract me and keep Em occupied. I'd needed extra support that day, since Ben was on a mandatory business trip, and I couldn't have been more grateful when Tom plopped the kids in a shopping cart, plied them with vegan cupcakes, and raced them around the store. Kate and I browsed the health-and-beauty section, wondering if Argan oil could actually eliminate bad-hair days.

"Probably not, plus it smells like bad olives," I said, ever the skeptic, but Kate decided to try it anyway.

She was checking out when the phone rang.

"Hey, Mom. How did it go?" I asked.

"They gave me six years," Mom said. Her voice was flat.

Breathe, I told myself.

"Well," I said, "at least it wasn't ten, right? Six years isn't that long, is it? I mean, look how fast the time's gone by since Em was born. She's going to be four in a few months!"

I tried to smile and sound optimistic, because I knew my mom needed that, but I was lying through my teeth. Six years felt like forever. Six Thanksgivings, birthdays, first days of school, summer vacations—all missed. Em would be going through puberty by the time Mom got out.

"I won't do that long," Mom said. "I'll tell 'em I'm an alcoholic and I'll go to addiction treatment. You get eighteen months off for that. Besides, I'm old, and I just read a big article that says they're cutting the sentences of seniors in half."

"You're not old," I said.

"I'll gladly be old if it'll get me out of jail early," she said, and laughed.

"You sound surprisingly good, Mom." I was telling the truth that time.

"I'm all right, Vic. I've accepted it, and I can't change it. You know, when I was coming out of the courthouse, the paparazzi chased me down the street!"

"What? You're not even famous! What did you do? Run?"

"Hell no. I turned around, stopped, and smiled for the camera!" she said.

When I got home that night, I found the photo online. It was one of the most beautiful portraits of my mother I'd ever seen. She's standing on a New York sidewalk at twilight, bundled in a black coat, an enormous Chopard purse looped around her wrist. Her blond hair is pulled back, her makeup impeccable. Her eyebrows look a little raised, but that's probably from the Botox. Behind her, warm yellow lights glow from an old building. The winter trees are bare, and there is snow on the ground. The concrete is wet and slick, illuminated in the streetlights, and the courthouse steps fade into a shadowy blur behind her.

In the photo, the resemblance between Mom and Mommom Marie is obvious. They have the same elegant forehead and caramel-colored eyes. I also see Em a little in Mom's expression, but even more surprising, I can finally see how much my mother and I really do look alike. I must've stared at my laptop screen for fifteen minutes. I couldn't believe how beautiful Mom was, and this is how I wanted to remember her after she went to prison. In the picture, the darkness is behind her, and my mother's smile, with her slight overbite, outshines everything.

34

Mom was a self-surrender, meaning she was given a date in late spring to report to prison, and she just had to show up. The whole thing sounded sort of like checking into a hotel—a really shitty hotel, granted, where some three-hundred-pound, heavily tattooed Latin Kings bitch would cut your punk ass for the Pop-Tart you got from the commissary, but you get the idea. The murky and confusing arrangement with Patrick Brookshire had fallen through, so Mom could stay home until the end and get her affairs in order. Not that she did, but I probably would've procrastinated too.

Mom spent her last month doing everything she wouldn't get to do in jail. Mostly this meant that she ate a lot of really good food, and who could possibly blame her? If I knew I'd have to spend the next six years of my life gagging on canned peas and Grade D Beefaroni, you bet your ass I'd want a few last bites of Maine lobster. Besides that, she also started taking walks along the ocean every day. She'd lived in her house for almost a decade, but I could probably count on one hand the number of times she'd gone to the beach, even though it was barely a five-minute walk away.

Every day the house filled with friends and acquaintances, the few neighbors who still remained cordial and nonjudgmental. People we hadn't seen in years appeared out of nowhere. Tiffany, a distant cousin I barely knew, arrived on Mom's doorstep and proceeded to move in to one of the guest rooms with her toy poodle that wasn't housebroken. Mom said the poodle could shit everywhere for all she cared, because the government was just going to auction the house off anyway. The rest of the people who showed up, I didn't even know, because Mom had met them only recently, mainly through Lincoln Cruz. It frustrated me what Mom was willing to put up with in order for her to not be on her own, and she may have felt like these people were there to support her, but it was obvious to me that they were using her—for her house and her hospitality—and that once she left, they'd forget all about her, Lincoln included.

Lincoln had managed to drink and yell his way through a series of tumultuous relationships during his short stay at Casa dei Sogni. One of the women was an escort, while another was a mentally fragile addict who Lincoln had met while piloting one of Patrick Brookshire's rehab day cruises (which were, apparently, an actual thing, God help us). Mom had gotten him the job. She'd also, I noticed, gotten herself overly involved in Lincoln's love life. She spent hours trying to reason with him and reason with the women, trying to talk some sense into these people as they ranted and fought and relapsed and played out every imaginable scenario of romantic toxicity under the South Florida sun. Of course nothing worked, because most of the time Lincoln and whatever woman he was fighting with were drunk, but Mom tried anyway. Why couldn't Mom stay out of it and let them go at it and suffer their own consequences?

Growing up, I always felt like my mother was so controlling. She was always butting in, giving her opinions on everything. Usually, I fought against her attempts to govern me, whether she was trying to pick out my clothes or tell me who to date or where to live, but eventually I learned to just ignore her, or give in when that was easier. Sometimes her advice was sound, but other times I simply needed to make my own choices. What I couldn't understand, until I saw my mother inserting herself into Lincoln's fucked-up love life, was why Mom was like this, why she couldn't just leave well enough alone.

Mom wanted to fix everything for everyone. She didn't want the people she knew to suffer, even if their pain might lead to growth, and she couldn't let go of the people and things she loved because she had already lost so much throughout her life, including her ability to have children. Those losses scarred her and caused her to cling hard to whatever she had, even if it was just the illusion of control in a disordered and unpredictable world.

She and Joel wanted to be everyone's heroes, and maybe in the way that I had once idealized my parents, they had also idealized themselves. Mom and Joel hadn't given themselves permission to be flawed and vulnerable. That's why Joel had lived a double life and that's why Mom came off as overbearing. That same belief, that it wasn't okay to be imperfect, was what had led me to spend years running from whatever made me uncomfortable. Perfectionism had made me terrified of making new friends. It had conned me and then robbed me blind, but once I faced my fear and exposed my true messy self, I saw I was still lovable. Frumpy, anxious, socially awkward, and clumsy in yoga, maybe, but I was still okay. I accepted myself, and that acceptance allowed me to begin sharing a truer, better, and more open love with my family. What I mean is that I accepted them, too, and that was the most freeing thing I'd ever felt.

Observing my mother's behavior made me realize that going to jail might not be so bad for her after all. She would have women to mother and care for and give advice to, and she could probably genuinely help a lot of them. Maybe prison was where she was needed most right now, and maybe, forcefully stripped of her material wealth and addictive distractions, she'd have to confront her demons without the cushion of stuff; maybe, though it would be painful, that's where Mom would get to know the beautiful person she really was. Of course, I wished she could do that without being in the slammer, but sometimes you really do have to suffer to grow.

I was trying to be at peace with Mom leaving, and some days I was better at it than others. The hardest part was when she started packing—it was like someone had left a dead antelope in the middle of the savannah. The scavengers smelled fresh meat and appeared out of nowhere to fight for their share. Everyone wanted a piece of her house of dreams.

Allie Alonzo sashayed in one day with an entourage of smarmy old men in puffy shirts. Gold chains glittered in the wildernesses of their exposed chest hair, and they spoke in thick Middle Eastern accents. She led them through every room like she owned the place, while Mom and I looked on in bewilderment, and when she was done with the tour, they met in a huddle in the backyard. Whatever they were talking about involved a lot of arm waving and headshaking, and when it was over, Allie stamped back into the house, leaving the men in their blouses to continue gesturing wildly by the pool.

"Twenty grand. Final," Allie said.

"For what?" Mom asked.

"Everything in the house. That's their offer. They'll give you twenty grand on the spot to take everything."

"Have you lost your goddamned mind?" Mom asked. "Do you see that sofa? That's a Marge Carson. That one piece of furniture alone is worth at least thirty."

"It also played a starring role in the award-winning feature film *Hungarian Titty Explosion*, and that has surely increased its value," I added, but Allie and Mom both stared at me in complete disgust.

"Come on! It was funny," I said, but neither of them were in the mood for jokes.

"You're an idiot, Cecily, and you're almost broke, do you realize that? Take the deal. They have the cash right now!" Allie said.

"Tell them to get the hell out of my house," Mom replied.

Allie tried to convince her, but Mom wasn't negotiating, and in the end it was Baron Von Bod who got most of the furniture, because he was about to move in to a glitzy new home he could now afford as the star of *Stud Muffins*. The rest went into storage, and when Ashley even took a few items, Mom couldn't help but comment on the fact that she'd barely seen her in several months.

"Ashley's got her hands full with two kids. I don't see her much anymore either," I said. I wasn't trying to make excuses for my sister so much as I was trying to comfort my mother.

"I'm not fooled, Victoria. Don't be naïve. She doesn't care about me." Mom sighed.

It was true that I barely saw my sister anymore. Somewhere, in all the chaos, our paths had begun to diverge. As Ashley and I followed our separate interests, our schedules intersected less and less. Once in a while we ran into each other at yoga, but we always placed our mats at opposite ends of the room and spoke little when we shared the studio. The kids still enjoyed playdates at least once a week, but gone were the days when Ashley and I spent every afternoon together with our babies, and though I would always be thankful for those times, I was comfortable with the change. I didn't need that kind of support from her anymore.

"Once she's gone, we're going to sell the house," Ashley confessed to me one afternoon shortly before Mom left.

For a few moments I sat on the grass of our shared backyard in a silent internal panic. If Ashley moved, I'd be losing the last remaining member of my immediate family. First my father, then my mother, even the house, and now . . . my sister and her family. Gone. And what would be left for me?

The truth was, actually a lot.

I reminded myself I wasn't alone at all. I had five new siblings. I wrote to them and talked to them on the phone—our relationship was evolving more every day. Thaddeus called me regularly, and Sarah and I Skyped. Thaddeus had even come down for a visit that winter, and spending a few days with him had been a revelation. As we sat in a friend's hot tub in the dead of winter, belting out Disney tunes, I'd been amazed by how much I could love a brother who I'd known for only a short time.

I belonged to two new communities now—yoga and preschool—and the more I gave to those communities through volunteering and showing up and participating, by being there for other people, the more those communities nourished and fulfilled me. Besides, I was writing again, expressing myself and finally enjoying being a mother. With Em, I'd never be alone. We would always have each other, no matter what happened. In so many ways, my life was changing for the better.

"We just want a new life, away from all this, a fresh start," Ashley explained. "While the kids are still little, and we still have a chance to explore the world. We want to live in the mountains. I'm going to do my yoga teacher training, and after that we just want to live somewhere that's the opposite of South Florida—somewhere with seasons and without all the flashy people. We don't want to be tied down by owning property, and we want to enjoy some freedom," she went on.

I nodded. I got it, I guess. But Ashley and I were different. I thrived on creating ties and establishing roots, while she flourished when unrestrained. She had to make her own choices, and I needed to learn this one last lesson in letting go.

When I thought about it, Ashley had already checked out a long time ago. Back when she moved next door, I'd envisioned some kind of communal sisterly utopia in which our husbands were best friends and every weekend meant family barbecues. I imagined sleepovers and game nights and little hands unexpectedly knocking on my back door. But none of that had really happened, because Ashley and Andrew had a different vision. They needed more boundaries than I did, and they sought more privacy. They'd dealt with our family drama by retreating and distancing themselves, because that was what they required. I chose not to take their actions personally and to respect our differences even when they disappointed me, and believe me, I was disappointed, and I knew Mom would be even more upset, so when Mom brought up how disappointed she was in Ashley's behavior toward her, I didn't tell her that Ashley was also planning to move.

"I'm really hurt by how she's treated me," Mom said. "I've done so much for her. How many people would take in their father's kid by some other woman and raise that kid like their own? Nobody! But no matter how hard I tried for her, it was never good enough."

"You did the right thing for her in a really tough situation, Mom. A lot of times we don't get the glory or the recognition we feel we deserve. It's like the Jewish religion teaches. The reward for a good deed is that you got the chance to *do* a good deed, and that's going to have to be enough when it comes to Ashley," I said.

Mom sighed and said she knew, and asked me what I was taking from the house.

"I don't know," I admitted.

I'd been putting off taking much of anything. Ben and I had already moved a small dresser, mostly just because we needed it, but when it came to sentimental items or anything else for that matter, I got stuck.

For the past week I'd watched as boxes and boxes of my family's belongings were carried away. The government wasn't interested in the decorations, clothes, shoes, pictures, and kitchenware, so we had to figure out what to do with it ourselves, and Mom's storage was limited.

"I don't care about this shit anymore," she said. "None of it brought me happiness. It just caused more problems. Fuck it. Take it all."

I had to act fast, or everything would be gone. Lincoln's friends were looting the house like rioters. Allie claimed Mom's shoes since they wore the same size, and earlier that week there'd been mass confusion when a family of total strangers, who'd somehow spoken to someone who said they knew Baron Von Bod, invited themselves in and began lifting the pictures right off the walls and carrying them out the front door. Mom chased them down, and they dropped the paintings, but they took off with a box of knickknacks before she could stop them.

I stood in the middle of the living room, helpless. This was where it had all begun, almost four years earlier. Things had changed so much. It was like the moment I opened the door to those federal agents, the person I once was and the life I thought belonged to me saw their chance to escape and flew away. If there was anything left of my old self, the doctor had torn it out of me during my C-section.

The living room bar had been emptied of bottles. Who knows where Joel's fancy wine had finally ended up or if, after a decade in prison, he'd have a taste for it. The crystal knobs on the cabinetry had been taken, and the fixtures on the sinks were gone; Baron Von Bod, in a tight black T-shirt and his usual ripped jeans, was high atop a ladder, removing a chandelier. As I walked through the living room, I barely missed stepping in a pile of dog crap on the Persian rug. Empty beer bottles, Solo cups, and wineglasses sticky with the residue of purple wine, were strewn across the once elegant marble patio table. Mom smoked in the house now, so there were butts everywhere, and a haze of tobacco smoke hung in the hallways. All the toilet bowls had rings, and muddy footprints mapped the floors that had once shone like they belonged in a museum. Even the cherubs painted on the ceiling looked sad.

I made my way to the kitchen, where I grabbed an empty moving box off the floor and filled it with a few Tupperware containers, mostly because they seemed like a practical choice. After that, I slid a heavy, All-Clad frying pan from beneath a pile of pots balanced in one of the cabinets and put that in too. I snagged a few spices from the pantry and wandered upstairs. What could I take from this house though, when what I truly valued were the people?

I knew Allie wanted Mom's perfume, and hell, she could have most of it, but I was taking my favorite bottles before she could get her hands on them—the one Mom wore to my wedding, another scent from the day Emmeline was born, the fragrance that reminded me of summer afternoons on the patio, and the one she always wore on Christmas. I didn't take the bottles because I wanted to use them. I took them because so many memories of my mother had been distilled into those specific smells. It was the same with Joel. There'd been so many times since he'd been locked up when I'd been standing in line at the grocery store, or out to dinner, and a strange man in front of me would be wearing his favorite cologne, and the memories would wash over me—Joel singing "Do-Re-Mi" with Em, teaching her to play her pink drums. If I closed my eyes, I could pretend he was there again, and once Mom left, if I felt sad, I could spritz a little perfume from a heart-shaped bottle and try to convince myself she wasn't quite so far away.

When I was about fourteen, I bought my mother a glass vanity set at an antique market in Delaware, and she'd treasured it for years. It was nothing more than a clear oval platter with an empty perfume bottle. The bottle had a small squat round bottom, and the cap was a long-stemmed daisy with curling leaves, all fashioned out of molded glass. It was probably quite fancy back in its day, but by modern standards it was kind of plain. Still, I loved it, and it brought back a lot of memories. I wanted to keep it on my dresser and give it back to Mom when she got out in six years, so I put it in my box with the containers and the perfume and the frying pan.

Before I dragged the heavy box out to my car, I stopped in the kitchen again. Mom was taking everything out of the cabinets, and on the kitchen island she'd made a stack of her old Corning-Ware casserole dishes. We'd had those damn things forever, at least thirty-five years, and they must have held at least five hundred green bean casseroles, baked pastas, and sweet potato soufflés—probably more. I didn't even know how the dishes had survived that long intact. The CorningWare, with their blue cornflower and orange Spice of Life patterns—practically synonymous with the seventies—had been one of the only constants in our lives. No matter where we lived, or what my parents were doing to make money, no matter what dramas we'd gotten ourselves embroiled in, we could always count on a home-cooked meal served in those casseroles, and for some reason, Mom never got rid of the CorningWare. It would have seemed sacrilegious to serve our chicken and dumplings in anything else. Mom's friends could take the Le Creuset stuff, but the CorningWare was mine.

I managed to get the box into the car and then, when I got home, I managed to get it out. I managed to get it up my walkway to our front door even, but once I went to unlock the door, somehow the bottom fell out, literally, and all the CorningWare and the glass vanity set crashed hard onto the Mexican tile of my front step.

"No!" I yelled, but it was too late.

I cried as I picked through the shards of cracked ceramic and fractured glass. The vanity set was a lost cause, and I managed to save only one platter, plus the large baking dish Mom always served pasta in, so at least I had something. The rest, all the broken pieces, I had to throw in the trash. I couldn't bring myself to do it right away, so I left the mess on the front step and went into the house.

Ben was reading on the couch in the living room. The cat was on his lap, and Em was playing. Our house was clean and cozy and smelled like cinnamon. When I came in, Ben looked up and told me he had a batch of vegan oatmeal cookies baking.

"What's wrong?" he asked. "Is everything okay?"

"I broke everything," I said.

I collapsed in a heap on the floor of our entryway, my head between my knees, and I cried.

Ben opened the door and assessed the situation. He came

back in and rested his palm on the back of my head, tousling my hair a little.

"Come," he said softly.

He lifted me up and led me into our bedroom, where he sat down beside me on our bed. Em was still happily playing in her room, singing and acting out a conversation between her Sleeping Beauty doll and her teddy bear.

"I'm so sorry," he said. "I can't imagine how hard this is for you."

I nodded.

"You don't have to clean it up. I'm going to run you a bubble bath, and you can get in it and soak while I take care of the mess, and then you can eat cookies and watch TV, and I'll watch Em all night if I need to so you can just relax."

"Thank you," I said.

"I love you," Ben said. "And you're doing a good job."

"So are you," I said.

"Mommy! Daddy! Come see!" Em called excitedly. She was going through a new stage where she always wanted us to watch her do tricks and then applaud. She usually performed death-defying feats like jumping jacks and somersaults. Ben and I were always happy to oblige her, though.

Her room was a disaster. It looked like the episode of *Hoarders* had been filmed in there—the "Buried Alive Under Pink Toys" edition. She'd emptied her dress-up box and had decked herself out in her favorite Princess Aurora gown, which was tattered and graying at the hem because she'd worn it every single day since her birthday. Fairy wings were slung around her shoulders, and a plastic dollar-store tiara sat atop her head, but on her feet she wore Ben's canvas sneakers. She thought this was hilarious.

"Knock! Knock!" she shouted.

"Who's there?" Ben and I replied.

"Poop!" she yelled, and then she laughed so hard at her own

wit, she fell backward onto the floor into a pile of stuffed animals. Such was a three-year-old's sense of humor.

Ben and I exchanged a smile.

"She got this from you," Ben said, and laughed.

"Nope." I giggled. "This was definitely your genes!"

He tickled me in the ribs, and I squealed, turned around, and
pinched him in the butt.

"Let me run you that bubble bath," he said.

Mom and Em and I went to lunch the week before she went
away. We knew it was our last meal out, and we wanted to make
it special, so we went to our favorite teahouse.

The restaurant was a sentimental choice. We'd been there
many times over the years, just us girls, usually on birthdays or
around the holidays. It was only open for lunch and served fancy
salads and rich, creamy soups—the kind of place where a hat
wouldn't have been uncalled for, and where Boca Raton's frilliest
grandmas could feel elegant nibbling quiche. The restaurant spe-
cialized in decadent made-from-scratch desserts, and we ordered
three of them that day. When eating there, it was best to completely forget about fat grams and calories.

Em, of course, was oblivious. She seemed to think we were
celebrating something, and I figured it was best to keep it that
way. I'd struggled with how to explain this situation to her. We
told her Papa J had moved away, that he was working, and eventually she stopped asking about her grandfather, but his absence
had been so sudden and unexpected, we hadn't known what else
to do. With my mom, we were more prepared, and we told Em
that Mommom was moving away to go to school, and though
we definitely twisted the truth, we weren't totally lying.

"I researched the place. You wouldn't believe all the things
you can do there!" Mom said.

"I guess there's a reason people say it's a country club," I said,
attempting to joke about it.

"I want to use this time I'm going away as a break," Mom explained, putting on a brave face. "I've been running pedal to the metal my entire life, and it takes a toll. I forgot how to slow down. I forgot how to get calm and live in the moment. I was always trying to be a hundred steps ahead of everyone else. Always running, always feeling like I was being chased, feeling like I couldn't trust a soul, feeling like everyone wanted a piece of me. I look back and I see how many people just took advantage of me over the years. I'm glad I'm leaving, because now all those people will be out of my life."

I nodded and poked with my fork at the slab of wet black chocolate cake in the middle of the table. Mom went on.

"I never really lived, Vic. We had a shitload of fun, for sure. I saw amazing things, met stars, lived the life. I accomplished things nobody in Milford could ever dream of and for that, I have no regrets. None. But at the same time, I missed out. What's the one thing I always wanted for you, Vic?" she asked.

"For me to get an education," I said.

"Exactly, and I cannot tell you how proud I am of you. A master's degree! Aren't you glad you went to school? You can be anything now, whatever you want! But do you know why I pushed you so hard to go to school? Why I would do anything for you to get that education?" she asked.

I shook my head.

"Because I never got that chance. I thought it was too late for me, but now I'm going away, and I think maybe *this is my chance*. Right now. At almost sixty years old. This is my opportunity to finally get that education I always dreamed of, and they have so many classes there. A big library! I can go to culinary school or get a cosmetology license, take community college classes, art—whatever I want. And I told myself, I am going to think of this time away as a gift so I can truly focus on healing and making myself better."

"I think that's the perfect decision," I said. "But I still worry about you. It's still jail."

"I don't want you to worry about me. I thrive in the worst conditions, and so does Joel. We've been through it all. I'm tough, and I'm street-smart. You know that about me. You know I have what it takes to survive in there just fine, and trust me, I've dealt with worse in my life on the outside. Believe you me, *I am going to be fine.*"

"Mom, I'm worried about your health. That rash is worse. You look too thin."

"It's just stress. Look what I've been through. I've been putting tea-tree oil on the rash. That ought to clear it up."

But the rash on Mom's legs looked worse than ever.

"You've been complaining about your eyesight, too, and peeing all the time. Diabetes runs in our family, you know. Those are symptoms."

Mom said it was just age, and that these things would happen to me pretty soon too. There was no sense talking to her about her health. Mom wasn't going to budge. But then I realized there was an ironic silver lining to her prison sentence—mandatory medical care. If there was something seriously wrong with her, they'd find out pretty quickly and make her get treated. Going to jail might literally save my mother's life, and I let myself be comforted by this fact, but I had other concerns.

"I worry about myself too, though," I confessed. "Without you."

"This is my advice to you. Keep doing what you're doing. You are stronger than you think, and these next ten years of your life are going to define you. You're on an amazing path. Keep writing. Keep doing what you love. Focus on your life and your family and making it rich. I don't mean money. Be rich in love. Cherish what you have. When you can truly appreciate your blessings, that's the real windfall, but never forget the hard times because that's what gives you empathy, and empathy is what makes us kind to others. Nothing is more important."

Before we finished our raspberry tea and boxed up our leftover cake, Mom asked me one more question.

"Do you remember the song we used to sing when you were little?"

"Of course," I said. I couldn't help smiling.

The summer after I finished first grade, when I was six years old, the court had finally granted my mother a six-week summer visitation with me. It was the longest time I had ever spent with her since she'd lost custody of me when I was one. Going to be with my mother was a huge deal for me. Mom and I flew on a big blue Eastern Air Lines plane all the way to Florida. She'd made me my own bedroom in her house, and she had two Pomeranian puppies and a big swimming pool where she let me skinny-dip at night. Every moment of that summer was like a fairy tale, mostly just because I got to be with my mom.

Down the road from her house there was a French bakery, and in the mornings we'd drive there for breakfast. They had the best Linzer tortes and freshly squeezed orange juice, and on the way, we'd blast the radio—Blondie, Supertramp, Captain and Tennille. It was 1980. Our favorite song though, was Olivia Newton-John's "Magic" from the musical *Xanadu* (think Greek mythology with roller skates and leg warmers). We'd turn the car radio up so loud, it was a miracle we never blew the speakers, and then we'd roll down the windows and sing along at the tops of our lungs. When I heard the words to that song—a weird, shy little kid who just missed her mom and longed for a normal family—all my problems disappeared. When I heard that song, I knew my mom was always with me, no matter where she actually was. I felt strong and powerful, like I could do anything.

"Teach your daughter that song when I'm gone. Let that be your song with her, too," my mother said.

"I will," I promised.

You have to believe we are magic. Nothing can stand in our way.

EPILOGUE

Emmeline ran ahead of me. She couldn't contain her excitement, and in her Princess Aurora costume she looked practically edible, like one of the over-the-top confections they sold in the Jolly Holiday Bakery here at Disneyland. I understood her enthusiasm. The kid had waited months for this trip, and the day had finally arrived. We were at the happiest place on earth. Her dreams of real-life princesses and singing dolls, of mouse-shaped ice cream bars and pixie dust were finally coming true. When she saw the golden turrets of Sleeping Beauty's castle, she froze and just stood there in awe.

"Wow," she said, and gasped.

We stood on the bridge that leads through the castle and into Fantasyland. A couple of mallard ducks waddled past. The park was filled with roses, and the crepe myrtles were already in bloom. It was the perfect, warm, sunny Southern California afternoon—the first day of summer.

My mother had already been gone for a month. She was adjusting, and she was as fine as could be expected. We were all okay, at least as much as the situation allowed, and Em and I had come out to California to spend the summer with Ben's family.

"Come and relax and enjoy yourself," my mother-in-law had said, and I wasn't about to refuse.

Becoming a mom three weeks after a DEA raid hadn't been easy, and the past three and a half years had often been unpleasant. Let's not mince words here—most of the experience had fucking sucked. I didn't get what I'd wanted, and I didn't get the beautiful, perfect life I'd imagined, but like the Stones sang, I got what I needed: big lessons about love and loyalty, vulnerability, character, and independence, plus a whole lot of juicy writing material.

When both of your parents go to jail, there can't really be a happy ending, at least not in the traditional sense. But there could be happy moments, lots of them, in the middle of the sadness and confusion I was still sorting through. Taking Em to Disneyland was one of those happy times, and as I looked around the park, I thought it was fitting. It's tempting to write the Disney heroines off as spoiled, prissy, and helpless victims waiting for a man to save them, but those girls are tougher than people give them credit for. Fairy tales have a lot of dark and scary parts. Cinderella, Snow White, Mulan, Belle—those characters are survivors of some terrifying shit, and they got through it by being brave and kind. In the end, they were rewarded.

I didn't know what my reward would be. It sure as hell wasn't going to involve living in an enchanted castle with a talking wardrobe cabinet, as cool as that would be. With a calm resolve, I accepted that there'd inevitably be a lot more hard times ahead. More crazy, unpredictable things were bound to happen—we were still dealing with my parents, after all—but this time around, I realized my own strengths a little better. I'd be able to handle whatever happened, even if I didn't like it, and I realized I was in control of creating joy in my life in spite of the problems.

"What do you want to do first, Em?" I asked.

She twirled and spun on the bridge, and her smile was so wide, it just about split her face.

"Everything!" she shouted.

I grabbed her hand and led her through the castle. We were greeted by a magnificent carousel of white horses, and I asked Em if she wanted to go on it, but instead she pointed to the Dumbo ride in the distance.

After a short wait, we boarded our flying elephant, the one with the pink hat and pink ruffle around his neck (of course), and as we settled in and buckled our seat belts, I thought about how I never liked the movie, because the story was so sad. I saw it differently now, though. I got it. The baby elephant is born an outcast, and he's scared and unsure of everything, and his mother goes to such lengths to protect him, she gets locked up. Without her, he's lost. But being without her is the only way he can learn to make it on his own.

The ride started, and we began to circle the fountain.

"Higher, Mommy!" Em commanded.

I grabbed the black joystick that controlled the ride, and up we went. High as the sky.

ACKNOWLEDGMENTS

I owe endless gratitude to so many people who helped make this book a reality. The truth is, the writing is just the beginning. The creation of a book is a collaborative effort that involves a lot of work, dedication, and faith from a lot of individuals.

Thank you to my publisher, Stephen Morrison, for seeing the potential in my story and my writing, and for convincing me that I could definitely do this and that it would be worth it in the end.

I am thrilled to have had the opportunity to work with my editor, Elizabeth Bruce. Thank you for understanding what I wanted to say and showing me how to say it, for reining me in when I needed it (which was often), and for all the kind words of encouragement. Also, thanks for editing the old-fashioned way, with paper and pencil, and for sharing my love of the em-dash.

Without my agent, Terra Chalberg, none of this would have happened. She is where it all began, and there are not enough words to express my thanks to Terra for finding me, taking a risk on me, and truly believing in me. A good agent is invaluable, and I am so lucky to have her on my side that I often cannot believe my good fortune.

The ultimate thanks go to my parents. I am grateful for their unending support and for the many hard life lessons they've taught me. My parents have always been my biggest cheerleaders, especially in our toughest moments and, even from prison, they continue to shine hope and optimism into my life. Thanks to them for giving me a life worth writing about. My husband deserves so much gratitude for his loyalty, compassion, patience, and support. He inspires me to improve myself every day and has never once doubted my dreams. It hasn't been easy living through this, but he has remained steadfast. He's a wonderful father, a beloved companion, and an amazing gardener.

Thank you to my mentor, Ayse Papatya Bucak, to Courtney Watson and Gloria Panzera Fiedler for honest feedback, excitement, and texts at all hours, and to the MFA program at Florida Atlantic University for preparing me for this journey as a writer. Thanks to everyone at the Yoga Joint (you know who you are) for giving me the tools to start healing. To my girls at MOPS for being my second family, and to the staff at the Pompano Beach Starbucks for welcoming me every day and providing me with breakfast sandwiches and cold brew while I wrote this book. Much appreciation also goes to everyone who has ever helped me with childcare so I could write or just get some rest.

I must also extend bottomless thanks to my many extended family members on all sides who have been with me through the events depicted in this memoir. You guys got me through the darkest moments. I am so blessed to have such a big family of amazing people to love on both coasts. Because of you, I will never be alone.

I also want to thank everyone working tirelessly behind the scenes in every department at Picador to make this book the best it can be.

Over a decade ago, I discovered my voice as a writer by blogging. I owe everything to my readers, many of whom have been with me from the very beginning. My readers gave me the encouragement I needed to keep writing—to keep telling my stories—and that's the greatest gift I've ever been given. Thanks for all the comments, shares, likes, and e-mails. I hope I've made you all proud and that my words will continue to make you laugh and cry and inspire you to keep going when things are hard.

Finally, since she was born, my daughter has been the brightest star. She has brought laughter, levity, joy, and celebration to us in the most unexpected moments, and she has made me do better and be better even when it seemed impossible. Thank you to her beautiful little soul for coming into my life exactly when I most needed her.